D0336782

All Fired Up

All Fired Up

Tales of a Country Fireman

MALCOLM CASTLE

© Malcolm Castle 2012

The right of Malcolm Castle to be identified as the author of
this work has been asserted in accordance with the
Copyright, Designs and Patents Act 1988.

First published in Great Britain in 2012 by Orion Books
An imprint of the Orion Publishing Group Ltd
Orion House, 5 Upper St Martin's Lane,
London WC2H 9EA
An Hachette UK Company

1 3 5 7 9 10 8 6 4 2

All rights reserved. No part of this publication may be
reproduced, stored in a retrieval system, or transmitted, in
any form or by any means, electronic, mechanical,
photocopying, recording or otherwise, without the prior
permission of both the copyright owner and the above publisher

A CIP catalogue record for this book
is available from the British Library

ISBN-13 978 1 4091 3437 4

Typeset by Input Data Services Ltd, Bridgwater, Somerset

Printed and bound by CPI Group (UK) Ltd, Croydon, CR0 4YY

The Orion Publishing Group's policy is to use papers that are
natural, renewable and recyclable products and made from wood
grown in sustainable forests. The logging and manufacturing
processes are expected to conform to the environmental
regulations of the country of origin.

www.orionbooks.co.uk

For Karen and my girls, for life

1

Horse Whisperer

'Look, son, she's on her back, she can hardly move so she won't be kicking you in the head. All you have to do is crawl over there and lasso her front leg. It'll be easy. Get ready.'

It was the summer of 1980. I'd just turned eighteen. I was green as grass and this was my first day in the Fire Brigade. But this wasn't a fire. It certainly wasn't how I'd thought my first day would go. John, the gruff, greying fortysomething Station Officer and my new boss, handed me a rope – a line – and walked away to talk to the rest of the crew. He must have thought 'crawl over there and lasso her front leg' was all the instruction I needed. He must have thought I knew how to pull a racehorse out of a World War Two air raid shelter.

The call had come in at the station right at the start of my first shift. I'd been hopping up and down with excitement – especially when I heard the bit about the WW2 bunker. 'Is it an unexploded bomb?' I'd asked. 'Has it gone off? Is that why there's a fire?'

John had looked at me patiently.

'It's not a bomb, son, and there's no fire. It's a racehorse,' he'd said. The rest of the watch had all nodded sagely as if this made perfect sense. I tried to look as if I understood. But my mind was still working overtime. A racehorse? What's a racehorse got to do with us? We're the Fire Brigade, not the Grand National. Is this one of the jokes they play when you're new on the job?

Piling into the fire engine and speeding out across the Shropshire countryside proved it was no joke. So did the worried look of the farmer, the tear-stained faces of his kids – and the very short, very stern-looking vet who had greeted us in the farmyard. 'I've just given her another shot. I could only get it into her neck. But it should calm her down for a while,' the vet had said, packing a terrifyingly large syringe into his medical bag. As he spoke I couldn't help but notice that one of the little girls had her hand on her neck as she sobbed quietly at his side. Surely he couldn't mean . . . ?

'The horse, you damn fool. I've given the horse an injection,' the vet snapped, reading my mind. I swallowed loudly. I was desperate not to draw attention to myself and show I was new to all this. It wasn't really working. Less than five minutes since I'd stepped off the fire engine and I was already starting to feel like the biggest blinkin' idiot in Shropshire.

I walked across the field and tried to regroup. It wasn't easy, to be honest. I started out by testing the line in my hands. Then I tried to work out what the best knot for lassoing a horse's leg might be. Would something like a running bowline do the trick? Should I go for a hangman's noose? Or was there something else altogether? I thought back to the three months training I'd done up in a converted prisoner-of-war camp over in Chorley. They'd never really talked about cowboys and Indians games like this. They'd never really talked about rescuing horses, either. But they had said that being in the Fire Brigade was all about thinking on your feet. This was the proof. I went for the running bowline. If I hadn't been wearing big red fireman's gloves I'd have crossed my fingers.

The Fire Brigade didn't go in for girl's blouse things like introducing people to each other back then, so I didn't know many of my new colleagues' names. I just knew that most of them looked as if they'd been in the job longer than I'd been alive. That was certainly true of the man on my right. He was a big, barrel-chested bloke with a mop of jet-black hair and a tough, craggy face. He was chewing on what looked like a piece of grass and he looked utterly relaxed about the job in hand.

'Looks like rent-a-crowd has arrived,' he growled in a strong Geordie accent. He was looking beyond me and back towards the farmhouse. I turned and felt my jaw drop. Where the heck had they all come from? The farmer, the vet and the little girl had been joined by about six other men, four women and a whole swarm of little kids. Several of the children were pretending to throw imaginary ropes to lasso some imaginary horse's legs. They all looked a lot more confident than me. 'If you think this is bad, wait till we get called out to something in town. On a big job I reckon we could double our wages by selling tickets. Just ignore them all. Don't let them put you off,' the man said as some of the younger kids started to point at us and giggle.

Don't let them put you off? I flashed the fireman a quick glance to see if he might be joking. He wasn't. I felt my palms sweating inside my gloves as I re-tested the knot on my rope. And was that a trickle of sweat running down my back as well? I tried desperately to focus on the job ahead. But all I could think about were the eyes staring into my back. If I messed up I got the feeling I wouldn't just have to leave the field: I might have to leave the Shropshire Fire Brigade altogether. And there was nowhere else in the world I'd rather be.

I forgot about my own fears when the horse let out a horrible, agonised groan. Her name was Brandy and if my day was unusual hers was even worse. She was being trained by the farmer's grown-up daughter and had only been moved into this field while her usual one was being re-fenced. The farmer said she'd been wandering around quite happily when a bit of ground had given way beneath her. Apparently she'd been standing on top of the farm's old air raid shelter. When the roof of one of the main rooms had started to give in she'd stumbled sideways. She'd rolled on to the roof of the central corridor. That had given way as well and she'd fallen in, almost completely upside down. The poor thing had been wedged there since ten o'clock that morning. Her head was just below ground level and her four legs were kicking and waving and lashing around in midair. But her body was totally trapped against the shelter's metal walls and all the turf and earth that had fallen in with her. It had been raining heavily through most of May but this month the weather had finally started to turn. The sky was clear at last, a rich, comfortable blue. It was warm as well, the best early June day we'd had in ages. Bees and butterflies were darting around on the hedgerows beside us and the ground was drying out nicely. It looked to be the start of a perfect summer, the kind I used to love from school holidays as a kid. Not that Brandy would appreciate the heat. I looked across at her. As well as being terrified she must have been desperate for water. It was time to move.

'On your hands and knees, son. And keep your mouth shut. Don't let her know you're coming.' John had come back to pass on some extra instructions. The key detail was that I wasn't doing this job alone. While I tried to lasso Brandy's front leg my Geordie colleague would be aiming his line at her back one. Two other firemen were lining up to do the same on Brandy's other side. One was a fierce-looking man with dark, thinning hair. He was taking a final few drags on his cigarette before getting into position. The other looked to be a more cheerful soul. He was humming away to himself and looked utterly relaxed about the task ahead. I wished I had his confidence, especially as John had one final instruction for us. 'I want all four legs to be tied back simultaneously. I'll give the call when she's lying still. And I expect you to get it right first time,' he shouted out ominously. I swallowed again, so loud this time that he turned back to look at me as he walked away. 'Bit of a frog in my throat,' I said weakly. He didn't look convinced.

On John's signal the four of us got on our knees and crawled, commando-style, across the last bit of muddy grass towards Brandy. She had started to thrash her head around in panic and it was obvious why John wanted us to stay out of her sight for as long as possible. The last thing she needed was to see a group of uniformed men creeping up on her and swinging lines. Especially if the new boy at the front screwed up and missed.

John held up his hand to make sure we were ready for the off. The four of us were half kneeling, half standing in the middle of the field. The other firemen were silently swinging their lines and lining up their throws. I was thinking of all the cuddly toys I could never get hoops around at the fair. I'd played one of those arcade games a while ago and I had managed to get the metal claw on to a Smurf's head. I'd managed to transport it halfway to the prize slot as well, but it had fallen out at the last minute, the way they always do.

Come on, Malcolm, focus. This isn't a toy and it's not a game, I told myself.

'On the count of three,' John mouthed at us. As the count began all my training kicked in and I was ready. I had it. I was utterly calm, totally confident. No, this wasn't a fire, but it was my first call-out on the watch. I was going to show my colleagues that I had a future with them. I would help save this horse.

One. Two. Three. My line arced silently through the air. It felt as if it was in slow motion, though that might have been because I was too nervous to breathe. I was so terrified of messing this up. Somehow I seemed to have time to look at the other three lines as well. They seemed to be in slow motion, too. Were any of us breathing? Even Brandy seemed to be silent. It was as if she knew.

'Pull them tight!' We'd done it. All four lines had connected to all four legs and the whole world sped up again. John yelled out his instruction and I felt like cheering. Some of the kids in the background did just that. I felt my chest puff out, just a little, as a ripple of applause rang around the field.

'Watch it, son!' I threw myself to the floor as Brandy's left front leg lashed towards me. It seemed that I was the only one who hadn't pulled the line tight so I was the one Brandy tried to kick in the head. I spat some grass out of my mouth as I stood back up. And I had a horrible feeling that the ripple of applause had just been replaced by a wave of laughter. My face felt as red as a blinkin' beetroot. Of all the places to land, did it have to have been on the edge of what seemed to be the only puddle left in the field?

I caught up with the others and pulled my line close. I then threw the end to the fireman opposite and grabbed the line he swung over to me. To my right the other men were switching lines as well. Another big pull, a few turns of the lines and the two of us at the front had got our legs trussed up tight while they had done the same at the back. Now we could get close to Brandy without being caught by her hooves. John came forward with the two animal rescue slings. They're made out of toughened canvas and have two big hoops on each end. It was my job to dig away at the earth so that we could ease the slings underneath Brandy's body. 'It's OK, Brandy, it's OK. We're your friends, remember?' I muttered as I hacked away at the wet and heavy ground. The sweat was pouring off her flanks. It dripped on to my hands when I was close to her. She couldn't understand a single thing that was going on. It was hard to imagine how terrified she was.

The digging took a while and Brandy didn't stop making awful, terrified sounds for as much as a second. The little girl from the farmyard had come closer and her sobs were almost as loud. Ten minutes passed before we were able to push the first sling under Brandy's body from the back. It took almost as long again for us to work the other through from the front. I kept on digging to try and smooth their passage. 'Well done, lads. Now, she won't like this next bit,' John said when the two slings were lined up next to each other, roughly where a saddle would be.

It was the understatement of the year. Brandy must have thought it was bad enough to be upside down, dehydrated, overheated, ganged up upon and trussed up like a frozen chicken. Now she had to worry about being run over as well. The farmer had fired up a huge, yellow front-end loader tractor in the yard and was driving it right towards us. He was no slouch when it came to speed. Even I had to stop myself from flinching as he approached. And I knew what was going on. Poor Brandy, nostrils flaring and her moist, black eyes wider and more terrified than ever, must have thought this was the endgame of some awful nightmare.

The vast metal forks at the front of the tractor hovered just above poor Brandy. The machinery screamed out as it jerked its way down towards her body. One slip of the controls and it could have crushed her. But in the end the farmer had it in the perfect position. We looped the ends of the slings on the forks. Then the lifting began. If it was possible, that seemed worse than everything that had gone before.

The main problem was the noise. There, in the glorious Shropshire countryside we should have been listening to early summer birdsong and the gentle rustle of wind in the hill grasses and hedgerows. Instead we were deafened by the screeching, wrenching sound of a tractor, the desperate tears of a tiny little girl – and the desolate, anguished cries of a horse that had to be pulled out of a hole like a cork from a bottle.

'A bit more, a bit more!' John was directing operations and calling out to the farmer. He, in turn, was lifting up the loader as slowly as he could. The crowd from the farmhouse and neighbouring fields had got a lot closer and were willing us all on. I watched the slings pick up the strain and fell to my knees to try and dig out a little more earth to ease Brandy's passage. And then, finally, there was a squelching sound as she jerked free. A real cheer rose from the crowd this time. But we were getting ahead of ourselves. Brandy was twisting and turning as much of her body as she could. I had no idea how much a horse weighed but I guessed it was something like a small car. If she built up any more momentum I had a horrible feeling she might pull the loader over on top of her. My pulse shot back up – but fortunately the farmer moved the tractor fast. When Brandy was just above ground level he went into reverse and carried her away from the shelter and on to a safe, solid patch of the field. The screeching noise began again as the machine laid her down.

'You wanna get some oil on that, mon!' someone yelled out from the crowd as I joined the others and got ready for the next phase of the operation.

All four of us leaned against Brandy's flank to try and hold her still. It wasn't easy. If she'd been scared before, now she was angry. I'd read somewhere that horses sweat when they're scared. Brandy was sweating up a storm. I could feel the wetness soaking into my tunic. I almost slipped to the ground the first time I pushed my weight against her. It was impossible to find any purchase on her tight, wet, muscular body, but we needed to hold her down so that John and the farmer could untie the lines and free her legs.

'Get ready! On the count of three, lads!' John shouted as he prepared to pull the final line away.

When the call came we stumbled to our feet then ran like hell. Brandy was up on hers almost as fast. She twisted herself upright then bolted straight ahead – which turned out to be exactly where I was trying to get away. I closed my eyes for a split second, prayed I wouldn't trip up and tried not to hear the thundering hooves right behind. 'I was your friend, remember? I helped get you out of there,' I was saying under my breath. And maybe she heard me. She veered off, just as I felt her hot, moist breath on my neck. That's when I did trip up. I hit my second big puddle of the day, swallowed my second mouthful of grass and won my second round of applause from rent-a-crowd. But I was smiling when I got back up. I think I even did a little bit of a bow. We'd got Brandy out of her prison. This still wasn't how I'd expected life in the Fire Brigade to be. But it was one heck of a first day. I had a huge grin on my face as I ran across the field to join the rest of the men.

The vet hung around to watch over our charge while the rest of us trooped into the farmhouse for some cigarettes and big mugs of sugary tea. Most of the onlookers had gone back to work while the farmer and his wife were having a bit of a barney about the shelter itself and whether it should have been filled in years ago. I tried to wash the mud off my face at the toilet sink but I was quite happy about the bits I missed. I saw the dirt as a sort of battle scar. It was my first badge of honour. All of a sudden I was proud that I'd fallen down out there. I was thrilled that I'd got my hands so dirty.

'Remember the time the mare fell in the slurry pit?' the farmer asked when he and his missus declared a truce and rejoined the conversation. Everyone groaned.

'I had to throw my hat and boots away. Never could get the stench out of them. Next time it won't be me who has to jump in there and swim underwater,' said the Geordie bloke ominously, looking right at me.

'What about the two frisky cows that got stuck in the cattle grid?' Everyone laughed again. A whole series of memories were relived in great detail. I marvelled at how busy my colleagues seemed to have been over the years – and at how rarely their stories involved any actual fires. The vet came back in and triggered a new wave of reminiscences. A goat that appeared to know karate was one of his best stories. 'If you hadn't calmed him down with the tranquilliser then I wouldn't be a dad of two today,' Tim told the vet as the rest of us lads winced and crossed our legs.

'You'll soon have your own share of stories to tell, son,' John said at one point. I smiled back at him, glad I'd not been forgotten, pleased he knew why I'd kept my mouth shut. Once, at school, I'd seen my geography teacher get a bad paper cut opening up a map. But apart from that I couldn't think of a single dramatic incident to relay to the team.

All the farm kids had been drinking squash out in the yard and they rushed back in while their mum topped up our teas. John said I should show them the engine – but to make sure they didn't touch anything they shouldn't. So off I went into the yard, a uniformed-up pied piper to half a dozen wide-eyed children. 'What's it like when the bell's ringing?' one of them asked as we walked around the truck.

'It's brilliant,' I said, though in truth I'd never been on a real emergency call.

'How do you turn the blue lights on?' another one asked.

'The button's over there,' I said, pointing to the driver's seat and thinking I'd got a fair chance of being right.

'How do you get the ladder down?'

Fortunately this was the bit I did know about. I'd been one of the keenest new recruits on my three-month training course and I'd spent what felt like forever polishing every last inch of the engines we'd used for our drills. Out in the farmyard the kids and I spent a happy ten minutes admiring the kit. I let them all try on my helmet. 'What's it made of, mister?' one little kid asked, tapping the top of it and hearing the hollow sound.

'It's made of plastic and it's covered in cork,' I told him.

'Cork's a type of wood, innit?' he asked. 'Why doesn't that catch fire?'

'Because it's, um, because it's got special yellow paint on it,' I said vaguely. The kids were happy with that but I had a bit of a frown on my face as I took the helmet and put it on my seat at the back of the engine. The special yellow paint was actually your common or garden super-flammable gloss paint. The logic of painting that on a cork and plastic helmet before walking into a fire escaped me all of a sudden.

'Can I put these on, mister?' one of the kids was asking. He'd found a spare pair of red gloves and the driver's boots and leggings on the cab floor. I nodded at him and watched as he pulled them on and marched around the yard pretending to be a fireman. It suddenly hit me that both the gloves and the leggings were made of plastic. So we basically walk into a fire dressed up like a roman candle, I was thinking when John and the rest of the watch emerged from the farmhouse and distracted me. 'Scram, kids. Give me those gloves back. And hop on, jockey,' John instructed. As the jockey, the new boy, I was on the back, rear-facing row of seats. It was hot, cramped and airless inside the truck. I was in the middle, squeezed in by one fireman's bulk on my right and prodded by another's very sharp elbows on my left. As if that wasn't bad enough, I'd been massively travel sick all my life – and this position really wasn't going to help. I tried to look out to the distance across to the Welsh hills. I tried to breathe deeply. It would be a blinkin' disaster if I threw up now. I'd already spotted the fact that I worked with a bunch of prime mickey-takers. If I was sick in my helmet I knew I'd never get to forget it. If I was sick in someone else's I'd probably be booted out on the roadside and left to walk home on my own. But you know what? After a couple of minutes I managed to get my stomach under control. After a couple more I almost allowed myself to relax. Because however hot, squashed or sick I felt I couldn't think of anywhere else I'd rather be. I was a fireman. I'd done my first shout. I was on my way.

Things got even better as our driver steered the truck out of the farmyard. We swung to the left and a gust of warm summer air began to stream through the open windows. It tasted of school holidays and secret dens in the woods. We thundered over the cattle grid and lurched around the first of what felt like a hundred country corners. Most of the south Shropshire hills were behind us now, with the last of the rolling Stiperstones range stretched out far to our right. The road was getting a little less bumpy but it began to dip sharply as we headed towards the village of Minsterley. My stomach dipped with it – and the older man on my right seemed to notice.

'It's a whole lot better to sit the other way around, jockey,' he said. He put his helmet on the cab floor, covered it with his folded-up tunic then sat on it, facing forwards. The fireman next to the other window did the same – and I rushed to follow their lead. It wasn't the most comfortable position in the world, even with our knees pressed hard against the seats in front of us. It wasn't the most secure either. Every few minutes I thought I was going to fall off my pile of kit and end up on the cab floor. But there was a lot more shoulder room. The air from the windows was right on my face now, and as I had to focus so much on staying upright I soon managed to forget all about feeling sick.

I had something else to smile about as we passed through a few more little villages and hamlets and approached the outskirts of Shrewsbury. The schools must have just come out and dozens of little kids stood and waved at us as we passed. I mainly waved back at their mums, to be honest. I was eighteen. I was in uniform. I'd just got my hands dirty on my first real shout and I felt like the coolest cat in town.

John soon took the smile off my face when we got back to base and jumped off the engine.

'What the bleeding hell's happened to your uniform, Castle? What kind of state is that? You're a disgrace to the watch,' he barked, sergeant-major style. My heart sank. I'd hoped that being dirty would show him how hard I'd worked. I'd even been hoping for some praise on a job well done. Instead I just saw the back of John's head and the veins bulging in his neck as he turned on his heels and marched away. I'd not had time to say a single word. I rushed into the kit room to try and scrape the worst of the mud off my jacket and boots. John was back before I'd made much progress. 'We've missed lunch but there's some food in the hot box upstairs. Get yourself a plate when you're done here,' he said. I headed up to the mess room and ate in silence. John was back on my case the moment I finished. 'Get a move on, Castle, don't just sit around. The engine needs a good going over,' he said. Then I was left looking at the back of his head and the veins in his neck again as he strode away. I washed my plate and headed downstairs to the appliance room.

I spent the next two hours in there soaping, scraping and polishing every inch of the truck with the rest of the watch. I pulled leaves and twigs out of the bodywork. I dug a huge amount of cow dung out of the tyre treads then hosed them till they shone. We all washed down the windscreens, swept out all the cabs and lockers and buffed up all the paintwork. Every now and then one of the old hands would tell me I'd missed a bit and say the night shift would skin me alive if I didn't leave everything I touched spotless. Late afternoon sunshine was by now streaming through the appliance room windows, I was starving hungry and pretty soon I was sweating up a storm. But my job wasn't done yet. 'Mop the floor. Then get into your dress uniform. We're standing down in thirty minutes.' John had crept into the appliance room without me knowing. He was looking the engine up and down. His face gave no clues as to what he thought. I had no idea if I'd done a good job or if I'd be out on my ear at the end of the shift. He left without saying another word. And once again I'd not said a word either.

There was a lot of loud banter as the night shift, Green Watch, arrived for duty. Most of the men on it seemed to be my dad's age. One of them could even have been as old as my granddad, though he looked strong enough to take out almost anyone in a fight. They all had something to say to each other. They were all joking, taking the mickey, having a laugh. None of them spoke to me. I got a few terse nods. But none of them stopped to ask who I was or made any effort to say hello. At six o'clock precisely the joking stopped and we lined up in the muster bay while Green Watch did the same in the appliance room. Dress uniform was black trousers with fierce creases ironed in, a light blue shirt, a blue tie, navy epaulettes on our shoulders and a jacket that was a bit like a fancy blazer. We looked more like waiters on the *Titanic* than firemen. John called us to attention.

'Off-going watch, dismiss!' he barked. We filed out of the muster bay while Green Watch went to check their kit and put it on the engines. I walked fast. I wanted to be as far away as possible if they didn't like the way I'd cleaned the appliance room and all the vehicles in it. I also wanted to get changed and get home fast. Michael and Tommy, two old friends from school, were coming round to hear about my first day. They'd both got jobs tool-setting on the production line at Rolls-Royce out on the edge of town. My plan had been to impress them with a heroic story about a beautiful woman I'd thrown over my shoulder and carried out of a burning building just before it had exploded and collapsed to the ground. Digging a sweaty racehorse out of a muddy field wasn't the story I'd expected to tell, to be honest. But at least I was off and running. I was a fully fledged member of the county Fire Brigade. And all the burning buildings and the fair damsels in distress would come later. Wouldn't they?

2

Proper Charlie

At first I thought I must have misheard the emergency call. Because as far as I was concerned no one would call the Fire Brigade to say they'd lost their dog. If anyone did, then I was sure the 999 people would have given them pretty short shrift. We certainly wouldn't be speeding across Shrewsbury in a fire engine to help out.

But there we were. Less than an hour into my second shift five of us were loaded up on the engine and speeding across town to help do just that. I was so busy trying to get my head around it all that I managed to forget about being travel sick. I just checked all my kit was in place, put my yellow helmet on the floor, balanced my tunic on top of it and turned around fast to face the direction of travel.

We'd been called to an address in the quaint little village of Cardeston on the outskirts of Shrewsbury. The village is one of dozens scattered across the Shropshire countryside like half-hidden secrets in dark green dells. If you don't know the area you might just stumble across them at the last moment. One minute you're in the middle of open countryside, driving along unusually straight lanes without a building in sight. The next minute the road starts to drop down into a shallow, perfectly shaped little dip. Suddenly a whole world opens up. You'll find centuries-old stone houses lost behind rich green ivy. You'll see post office stores and country pubs, little grocery shops and newsagents, corner garages and beautifully tended village schools. Most times a ribbon of a river will be flowing to your left or right as you pass through. The greens of the moss will be even darker on the slick, wet stones. There'll be a church with a steeple – and you'll wonder how you never saw it from afar. These are the tiny treasures of my county – the places that get overlooked by the guidebooks and remain beautifully untroubled by too many visitors.

The house we pulled up outside was neatness itself. It was the last one at the end of a row of small, low country cottages with tiny windows and what looked like thick, ancient stone walls. It had a well-cut front lawn, a row of well-tended flowerbeds running up the edge of the front path and a colourful and healthy-looking hanging basket on each side of the front door. A very worried-looking elderly lady was standing on her polished doorstep as we all piled out of the truck. She was wearing a flowery summer frock and a smart, dark navy blazer. Every few moments she would run her hand through her thick white hair. Then she would hold both hands together in front of her. Her face was etched with worry and she suddenly leaned back on her door frame for support. All of a sudden I was glad we were there. The lady looked desperate. However crazy this seemed, I wanted to find her dog.

'Oh my goodness, what a terrible fuss, thank you so much for coming, we didn't know what to do and we've been at our wits' ends since first thing this morning,' the lady said, her words coming out in a terrible rush as we walked through the front gate. 'I'm Mrs Knight. My husband is in the back with Charlie. Charlie is our dog. He's such a treasure. We're so worried. Do please go through,' she said, stepping back and giving a quick involuntary look at our boots.

'Is there a side gate, Mrs Knight? There's no need for us to trample all over your carpets,' said John, who'd obviously spotted the look and had dealt with situations like this before. She clutched her hands together in thanks. Two people had just come out of one of the cottages opposite to see what was going on. Mrs Knight gave them a quick, apologetic wave. She looked pale, I noticed. She was certainly mortified at all the fuss.

'I thought the dog was lost,' I whispered at our own Charlie as we drew up the rear.

'It is. Lost under the garden shed. Weren't you listening?'

The back garden was even neater than the front – and halfway down it we met Mr Knight. He looked the same height as his wife, around five foot five, and a good ten years older than her, maybe in his early seventies. He was leaning on a stick and looked a little shaky on his feet. But he was smartly dressed in brown trousers, a white and brown checked cotton shirt and matching tie. Mrs Knight rushed up to him. He reached out his hand. She held it and helped support him. The pair of them looked close to tears.

'We're terribly sorry about this but we didn't know who else to call. Charlie has never done this before. He's a Jack Russell terrier, he's a terribly good dog. He's never run away or been in any trouble. He's seven years old and he means everything to us,' Mr Knight said, talking just as fast as his wife had done. I gave him what I hoped was a reassuring smile. He seemed to latch on to me after that, perhaps thinking that, as the youngest person there, I would be the most sympathetic. 'Charlie is round the side,' he said. He took a few slow and what looked like painful steps around the shed. I followed him – but there was no dog to be seen. 'He was trapped just here all morning. But a few minutes after we called you he got in even deeper. He's completely underground now and he's been there for several hours,' Mr Knight explained. As if on cue there was the sound of distant digging and scratching. Then there was silence. Then there was a bit more scratching. Then a few confused sounding growls and some soft, lost barks. Mrs Knight was at her husband's side again. She clutched his arm even tighter and this time it seemed to be him supporting her.

'We have to help him. He hates to be on his own and he must be terrified down there in the dark. It's breaking my heart,' she said. It was almost breaking mine – and I swear that's why I said what I did a couple of moments later.

John had pushed me forward. 'Well, Mrs Knight, we've got a brand new recruit fresh out of training school here today. Let's see what kind of newfangled ideas he's bringing to the Shropshire Fire Brigade.' He turned to me. 'We've got a dog trapped underneath that shed. He's clearly in distress. What do you suggest we do?'

'I suggest we do whatever we can to put him out of his misery straight away,' I began.

Mrs Knight let out a little wail and her husband visibly flinched. Even John looked a touch surprised. 'No, I didn't mean it like that,' I said, suddenly realising what I'd said. 'I meant that we need to put him out of his misery by getting him free. By digging a hole. Or by lifting up the shed. Or by moving it. Or by digging through the floor. Or by doing whatever we need to do, just as quickly as we can.'

John was shaking his head and smiling ruefully at the Knights. 'Typical beginner. Open mouth, insert foot,' he told them. 'I think all his fancy training has gone to his head. Either that or it's the heat. Let's see what some older, wiser heads can come up with instead.' He pushed me back a little and began to assess the situation the way I should have done. 'Now, Mr Knight, tell me a little bit more about this shed of yours. Can we take a look inside? Has it been here for long? Has it got a concrete base or any form of foundation?' He was business-like, organised and professional. He got the information we needed quickly and efficiently. It was obvious how much I had to learn.

Mrs Knight disappeared into the kitchen to get a bowl of water for when Charlie was finally free and the rest of us looked around and into the shed. It was about twenty foot long and twelve feet wide. It had a pitched roof, and inside it had shelves and bookcases on all four walls and was full to bursting with, well, junk. Charlie started to whimper as John's heavy boots creaked on the doorway of the shed above him. All of a sudden I forgot about my stupid comment. I just started to worry about the poor dog trapped underground. The little fellow must have been terrified. I was as keen as his owners to get him free.

Four of us tested out different corners of the shed to see if we could get some purchase on it and lift it. We couldn't, but Charlie upped the volume on the whimpers, whines and little barks as we tried. 'We can't crank up the shed when it's full of all this, erm –' John glanced at Mr Knight and decided to choose an alternative word '– all this stuff. Is it OK if we empty it?'

It was, so we did. Very little of the 'stuff' was in boxes and the Knights didn't seem to have many spare bags. So we spent the next twenty or thirty minutes passing individual items down the line where I laid it all out on the lawn as if it was a Cub Scout jumble sale. The garden equipment came first – a whole series of ancient tools that included possibly the world's heaviest lawn-mower. Next came dozens of empty jam jars, seed trays and flowerpots – all of which had unaccountably been stacked on the top shelves along one wall. Then there were all the old treasures that the couple must have moved out of their house. We carried entire sets of faded china, dozens of old wine glasses, pots, pans, teapots, toasters – you name it. Then there were all the old table lamps, dinner trays, rolled-up carpets and stacks of books and magazines. Mr and Mrs Knight spent half their time round the side of the shed, talking to little Charlie, and the other half talking to me about all the hidden treasures that were coming out of their shed. 'Blow me if that's not from when we were first married!' Mr Knight said when I was passed a hefty wooden carriage clock. His wife picked it up the moment I laid it on the grass.

'We bought this on our honeymoon in Lytham St Anne's,' she said. 'It was always fast, it never did keep proper time. We replaced it when the kids were born, I think. I don't think I've seen it for nearly thirty years.'

'More like forty, my dear,' her husband told her.

She dismissed the comment with a wave of her hand. She'd already put the clock down and was looking at a very dusty kid's tricycle. 'Oh Charles, do you remember the fun the boys had with this?' she asked. There were tears in her eyes. We stepped aside and carried on with the removal job. John called a halt when most of the shed's floor space was clear and all the breakable objects had been taken from the shelves. We got some planks of wood to use as levers and I was told to dig some holes on one side of the shed that so we could get them underneath and gain extra purchase. Then John positioned us one on each side of the structure. 'OK, gentlemen, we're going to lift this up on the count of three,' he said. Mr and Mrs Knight were clutching each other tightly.

'It won't collapse on him, will it?' Mrs Knight asked suddenly. 'I'm sure you know what you're doing but he's such a tiny little dog.'

'We're going to take it very slowly. If there's any danger at all we'll stop straight away.'

The early summer sun was almost directly overhead as John began the count. It wasn't that warm, but a couple of minutes later I think we were all sweating as we lifted the shed up inch by painful inch. 'Right, lads, just hold it there,' John instructed as one of the others pivoted it on the planks and let it rest there. I was on my knees fast to look underneath. Straight away I could see what I was looking for: the white tip of a little Jack Russell's tail. 'He's there, I can see him!' I shouted out. The tail began to wag furiously. We got the floor of the shed a few inches higher, giving the dog plenty of room to run free. I think that was when it began to dawn on us that things weren't quite as they seemed.

Little Charlie didn't run anywhere. Mr and Mrs Knight both called for him excitedly. Charlie started to bark back at them.

He sounded just as excited, but he didn't move. Apart from a still furiously wagging tail it was as if he was set in stone. We pivoted the shed again so that we could all crouch down and see what was going on.

'One of his paws must be stuck somehow. Oh, my goodness. It might be caught in a mole trap. He could be bleeding to death!' Mrs Knight said, clearly panicking. Three torches shone light into the gloom. We could see it all now and there was no mole trap and no blood. Charlie himself turned round. He looked quizzically at all the strangers in his garden. His little eyes were blinking in the torch light. He was a lovely little dog, a hotchpotch of soft browns and blacks splotched all over his tight white fur. He was wagging his whole behind now, not just his tail. But he certainly wasn't trapped. Mr Knight, a look of utter embarrassment on his face, was the first to admit the truth.

'Blow me if he's not been chasing a rabbit all along,' he said, horrified. At which point Charlie dismissed all of us strangers and diverted his attention back to what he saw as the job in hand. His little snout went right back into the hole he'd burrowed in front of him. He began his series of little growls, barks and scratches. He was about as happy as a dog could get.

'He wasn't whimpering because he was stuck. He was whimpering because he was frustrated. He's been having the time of his life. He's been rabbiting,' Charlie said with a laugh.

'I can't believe we called the Fire Brigade!' said Mrs Knight, her face a picture of embarrassment.

'Well, I can't believe we emptied your entire garden shed!' added John.

If possible, Mrs Knight looked even more embarrassed at that. She clutched her hand to her face. 'I'm so very, very sorry,' she said.

John put up his hand. 'I was only joking, Mrs Knight. This is our job. Let's just get the little fellow out from under there and block up the rabbit hole so he doesn't go back. Then we can start moving all your,' he paused again and tried to remember the word he'd used last time, 'all your stuff back to where it was.'

Mr Knight made his stand when a suitably chastised Charlie had been dragged away from his little lair and shut up in the kitchen. 'We can't possibly expect you to put all this back,' he said when the shed had been lowered back into position.

'Well, we're going to put it back, and that's the end of it,' John said, snapping his fingers and getting the human conveyor belt up and running again.

Mugs of tea were brought out as we secured the shed. A bit of a party atmosphere developed as we started to carry all the couple's possessions back into it. Two of their neighbours popped round with a jug of iced squash and we downed it fast. Charlie drank about a pint of water himself and turned out to be a real character. As soon as he was let out of the kitchen he leaped around like a puppy. He was overcome with joy at having so many new people to play with – especially people who were carrying things. He tried to grab each and every item we picked up. He had a huge amount of fun fighting us for possession of rugs, old sacks and anything else he could chew, chase or destroy. I think the Knights would have let him work his way through every one of their treasured possessions, they were so glad he was free. They'd been transformed. Both suddenly looked years younger. They were so delighted their little friend was back. Mr Knight regaled us with stories about the scrapes Charlie got into when their grandchildren came to visit. His wife smiled indulgently and said she was convinced the postman would one day forgive him for all the trouble he caused whenever he tried to deliver a parcel.

About half an hour went by, the sun was even stronger and we'd got the shed shipshape again when Mrs Knight headed back into the kitchen to put the kettle back on. 'My goodness, we've run out of biscuits. Give me two minutes and I'll pop down to the shop to buy some more,' she called out of the kitchen window.

John looked at his watch then put up his hand to stop her. 'There's no need for that, Mrs Knight. Lunch will be waiting for us back at the station so we'd better get going. Our meal went cold while we were out on a job yesterday and we all got into a great deal of trouble with the ladies who cook it for us. I don't want to risk that happening two days in a row.'

Mrs Knight gave him a quizzical, slightly mischievous look. 'A big group of strapping firemen like you. You don't strike me as the kind of men to be afraid of the daily help,' she ventured.

John gave her a rueful smile. 'You haven't met our cooks, ma'am,' he said drily as we said our goodbyes and climbed back into the vehicle.

3

'A fine old mess'

Betty and Mabel had run the kitchen and cooked the lunches at our Shrewsbury fire station for more than thirty years. They'd joined shortly after the end of the war. They'd seen station officers, sub-officers, leading firemen and new recruits like me come and go. They'd seen their favourites grow up and grow old. They'd built their empire. And they very clearly ruled the roost.

'They're waiting for us. That's not good, not good at all,' John said, pointing up at the mess room window when we climbed out of the truck at the station. Looking up I could see the outline of two short, stout ladies. Both had their hands on their hips. Even through glass and from a distance it was still pretty clear that they weren't happy.

Both figures disappeared sharply as we strode across the driveway. 'I'll bet you a pound to a pinch of salt that Mabel asks if we've washed our hands,' the man next to me said as we thumped up the concrete stairs to the mess room.

A tiny grey-haired woman in her late sixties was standing at the far end of the room when we got to the door. She was wearing stout, sensible black shoes and her long, dark blue skirt and a matching, high-collared blouse were almost fully covered by a green and white striped apron. She had a pair of faded tartan oven gloves in her hands, and something in the way she was twisting them seemed to flash out a warning as we began to walk towards her. The whole watch stood still and shut up. We must have looked like a rugby squad in front of her. But this tiny woman was very clearly in charge. 'I trust that you gentlemen have all washed your hands,' she said sharply.

'Yes, Mabel,' the crowd of grown men lied in unison.

Mabel did not look convinced. She pursed her lips, shook her head disapprovingly and gave the oven gloves one final twist. Then she turned away. We'd been dismissed so we spread out in the far corner of the room. But no one sat down, no one put their hands in their pockets and no one really spoke. Mabel clearly had very well defined standards of good behaviour. We were very clearly expected to comply with them in full.

John, representing all of us as Station Officer, walked towards the kitchen to try and make peace in our time. Mabel, who clearly had eyes in the back of her head, turned sharply to face him.

'It's nice of you to find the time to join us today, I'm sure,' she pronounced with heavy sarcasm. The oven gloves were taking a beating again. She had raised her right eyebrow and she was tapping her foot on the polished parquet floor in a threatening manner. The tension, from my vantage point several feet away, was extraordinary.

'We were unavoidably detained yesterday as I'm sure you understand,' John said, exuding reasonableness from his every pore. 'A farmer needed our urgent assistance with a horse. The job took far longer than we had anticipated and we weren't back here until very late.'

'A likely story' came another voice from inside the kitchen. I took a sharp intake of breath. John was our Station Officer. He was the boss. Surely no one was allowed to speak to him like that?

'It's the truth, my dear Betty, and you know we'd not vol-untarily miss one of your lunches for all the world,' John called out to the second lady who had stepped up towards the kitchen hatch. She looked to be in her late fifties. She had a big, pale, moon-like face with crinkly eyes half hidden by strands of dark, wispy hair. Her mouth was lined with thick red lipstick and, just like Mabel, her lips were pursed in a distinctly disapproving fashion. She, too, was twisting something in her hands, this time a blue checked tea towel. She, too, managed to make the action look mildly threatening. A stand-off appeared to have been reached. John decided that something had to be done to break the impasse. He grabbed me by the arm and thrust me forward into the danger zone.

'Betty and Mabel, I'd like you both to meet our new recruit,' he said.

I regained my balance, nodded and said hello. I noticed that John hadn't gone as far as telling the ladies my name, nor did they ask for it. Did any of us ever learn each other's names, I wondered, as I stood there like a lemon. Would I ever feel as if I was here to stay?

'Hello,' I repeated weakly, because I had no idea what else to do or say.

The ladies barely seemed to hear me. They were too busy putting me through the kind of examination they might give the last, sorry lamb chop on the counter of the local butcher's shop. Betty's examination was relatively quick and utterly dismissive. She gazed at me from top to toe and back, pursed her red lips even tighter, then looked away. Mabel took a little longer. She, too, looked me up and down. Then she looked at the other firemen. Then she looked back at me. A frown appeared on her already well-lined forehead. I wondered, suddenly, if I was supposed to have stood to attention. All the others were behind me now. Were they saluting or something? Whatever was going on I had a horrible feeling I didn't entirely measure up to Mabel's usual high standards.

'I suppose he's tall enough for the job,' she concluded, grudgingly. 'But he's a bit of a string bean, if you ask me. Could use a bit of fattening up. Does your mam not feed you properly at home then, lad?'

I felt myself start to blush. How did she know I still lived at home? I glanced around to see if anyone else on Red Watch was listening in. They all were. 'I eat well enough at home' was all I could think to say.

'Got yourself a girlfriend, then?' Mabel asked. 'Does she cook for you as well?'

An unexpected cackle of laughter from Betty on the other side of the hatch saved my embarrassment and stopped me from answering. 'Leave the poor lamb alone. We'll have plenty of time to find out about him later. Right now, I need you to reheat these sausages and get started on the gravy.' Mabel scurried out of the mess room and into the kitchen. I stood there for a moment trying to work out who reported to whom. John was our Station Officer so he was supposed to be at the top of the tree. But he'd been like a naughty schoolboy in front of Mabel. And Mabel had come running the moment Betty had called. It was all very confusing. But I loved it.

Pots banged, saucepans boiled, frying pans sizzled. Plates chinked as they were lined up on the hatch and there was a low crashing sound as a dozen and a half sets of cutlery were laid out. Then lunch was served. I stood back thinking I might have gone to heaven. This was fantastic. Betty and Mabel had made a real Desperate Dan mixed grill. There were rich, bloody steaks, piles of sausages, lamb chops, black pudding, big red fried tomatoes as well as piles of fried onions and peas. The white plates were stacked full. Every inch was covered with food, right up to the edges. You couldn't carry it without getting your thumb covered in gravy. I was so happy I was almost frozen on the spot.

'Good old-fashioned firemen's dinners. You can't beat them,' said the man next to me, pushing me aside as he selected the largest, fullest plate from the hatch.

'You spill any of that food on the floor and you'll be answering to me, young man,' Mabel shouted from the other side. The fireman she'd yelled at was at least six foot two. Mabel could barely have been five foot three. 'Sorry, Mabel,' he said, immediately slowing down to make sure he got to his table without any accidents.

I hesitated at the hatch as I chose a plate, stuck my thumb in the mashed potato to get a proper grip on it, and then tried to work out what to do next. Where was I supposed to sit? It was clear that everyone had a specific place. They'd probably had it since before I was born. Our Station Officer, John, our Sub-Officer, or Sub-O, whose name I didn't know and two of the leading firemen were sitting at a table for four in the middle of the room. That was clearly the officers' table. Three other tables for four were lined up near the mess room windows. Over to my left I watched as two of the men who'd helped with Brandy the previous day headed to the far table, almost on autopilot. There was one spare seat over there, no spares on the next table where a smaller, wiry man was already holding court, fork in one hand, cigarette in the other, telling a story about a massive Friday night fight in his local pub. 'That's when I got my comb out to finish them off,' he concluded, pulling a shiny metal comb out of his trouser pocket and tapping it threateningly on the table top. The man had barely a hair on his head, but his comb looked as if it saw a lot of action. I made a mental note to find out where he drank – and to try and avoid it. So where should I sit? The two other tables each had one spare seat – and there were two more people still to collect their food and find their places. The mash was piping hot. I could feel my thumb start to sting. I moved from foot to foot uncomfortably.

'Got a problem with your dinner, son? If you've got any complaints then we want to hear them straight away. If you're one of them new-found vegetarians then you'll have to make do with the mash. If you're not I won't be serving seconds till you've eaten every last bit. Is all of that clear, young man?' Mabel asked sharply.

'Yes, thank you, miss,' I mumbled. I felt closer to eight than eighteen. I felt as if it was my first day at school, not at work. And once again I felt as if all the eyes in the watch were on me.

'Jockey. You drew the short straw. You have to sit on that table. You're with Arfer and his merry men. Prepare to have your ears bent. And don't believe a word Arfer tells you. He lives in a dream world.' One of the old hands had come to my rescue. He was about my dad's age, he had strong looking arms, a mop of messy, greying hair, a soft, south Shropshire accent and I think I heard the watch call him Mike Cadwallader, Caddie for short. It's funny but I swear he had his back to me when he called out. But he'd still managed to spot my dilemma and help me out. I made a mental note to somehow try and thank him. In the meantime I carried my plate over to the table he'd indicated and sat down in the spare seat. It was finally time to meet my colleagues.

4

Lunchtime Stories

A rfer was probably in his early forties. He was a lean, spare-looking and slightly hunched man with a wolf-like look in his eyes. Ever since I'd seen him on my first day I'd been trying to think who he put me in mind of. As I sat opposite him at the dinner table it finally hit me: in a bad light he could have been mistaken for Fagin. His dark hair was greased back on top and at the sides of his head. He had a tough smoker's face. Thick six o'clock shadow was already clouding his chin and big bushy sideburns crept down towards a fierce, uncompromising-looking mouth.

The merry men, as Caddie had described them, were the next youngest members of Red Watch. When I met them I was still convinced that they were pretty ancient and at least a few decades older than me. I later found out that they were only just approaching thirty.

'This is Charlie. And this is Woody,' Arfer said, nodding at them both but looking intently and not particularly welcomingly at me.

'All right,' I said. 'Hello.'

Charlie held out his hand. He was short, only about five foot seven, and he seemed one of the friendliest people I'd seen at the station so far. To be honest, he looked a bit like Father Christmas's younger brother, which I quite liked. I'd noticed him on the shout at the farm the previous day because he'd told a lot of jokes when we'd gone into the farmhouse for tea. He had an infectious giggle – which I'd heard a lot of as he'd laughed louder than anyone else at all his punchlines.

Woody looked even more of a character. His dark hair was receding a bit but it was still much longer than anyone else's on the watch. I wondered how he got away with it. He had a bushy, unkempt moustache and sharp, quick eyes. He was a tall, gangly man, who'd already demolished a fair bit of his mixed grill by the time I'd sat down. This was obviously a man who liked his grub.

'So, jockey, any regrets?' Arfer asked as I cut into a perfect, tender pork chop. He was a Londoner, I realised. I wondered what had brought him all the way to Shropshire.

'About the job? Not so far. I'm loving it.'

'So what made you sign up? Was your old man a fireman? Is the job in your blood?'

I told them my story as I bolted down my meal. That I'd liked school but had been in a hurry to get out and earn a wage. I said I'd had this dream of being a helicopter pilot so when I was seventeen I'd gone over to Biggin Hill in Kent for some big recruitment event. The RAF had assessed eighty-three people that day but only chosen three men to go on to the next stage of the selection process. I wasn't one of the lucky ones so I'd come back to Shropshire with my tail between my legs. Then, I said, I'd seen something in the local paper about steeplejacks so I'd applied to do that instead. 'I got taken on a head-for-heights test. They took me to the bottom of a three-hundred-foot chimney.' It had sixteen vertical ladders running up the outside of it attached by four three-foot stays. They gave me a big leather weightlifter's belt and a couple of rusty old karabiners. 'Use them to attach yourself to the ladder if you get out of breath and want to stop for a ciggie,' the man in charge had said. 'The test was to get a hundred and sixty-five feet up but I wanted to do it all. I made it. On the top the guys were showing off, pretending to be monkeys and hanging off the edge with one arm. The whole chimney was swaying in the wind and one of them offered me an unfiltered Woodbine which I finished in about four drags – and back then I didn't even smoke. I came down on the inside of the ladder and the gaffer offered me a job on the spot.'

'How much were they paying?' Arfer asked.

'It was £27 a week for the first two years. Even after that it only went up to £58 a week. I could make more than that on a farm.'

'I make more than that on my backin' spivin,' Arfer said.

I tried to work out what a 'backin' spiv' might be. Was it cockney rhyming slang? I couldn't work it out, but decided to stick to my new 'keep your eyes and ears open and your mouth shut' rule. If I needed to know, I was sure I'd find out eventually. In the meantime I tried to keep the conversation going, regardless.

'I said no because of the money, and a little bit later a pal of mine got a leaflet about the Fire Brigade. It was paying over £100 a week and I decided to go for that instead. Now I'm here,' I finished, feeling it wasn't perhaps the most exciting story in the world.

Charlie asked about my training. I said I'd done it up in Chorley.

'Is O'Connor still there? He was a right hard barstard as I remember,' Arfer said, pushing a piece of lamb chop round his plate and mopping up the last of his gravy.

I smiled: Sub-Officer O'Connor was hard to forget. 'He was still there and he was terrifying,' I said. 'On our first morning we had this nice little welcome speech from the boss who made it all sound dead friendly and nice. Then O'Connor came up on the stage and shot us all to pieces.'

'Did he use the line about the dictionary?'

It all came flooding back. 'Has anyone in this room got a dictionary with them?' O'Connor had barked. No one had, of course. 'Well, I've got a dictionary,' he had continued from the stage. 'And in my dictionary sympathy comes between shit and syphilis. So don't expect any molly-coddling from me. I'm here to turn you into firemen, God help me. I'll push you harder than anyone's ever pushed you before. I'll make you do things you've only done in your worst nightmares. I'll make you run and carry ladders and lay out hoses when your body is screaming at you to rest. Then I'll make you run, carry ladders and lay out hoses all over again. Dismiss.'

The others laughed at the description. O'Connor must have been instructing at Chorley for a very, very long time if all these guys remembered him.

'How many recruits did you lose on your first day?' Arfer asked.

'Three.'

'Then they're making it easier. Five people quit on the first day when I started training and two more got booted out by the end of the first week.'

'Half the people I trained with were too soft to make it. They had to quit and join the army instead,' Woody said, leaning back in his chair and aiming his words at some of the old-timers two tables away.

'Lay off the army or you'll end up with a dead bird in your bed next time we do nights,' the man with the metal comb yelled over.

'You'd be too scared to touch a dead bird. You squaddies are just a bunch of backin' girls,' said Arfer.

'Language, gentlemen!' shouted Mabel. They all apologised immediately.

'Did you still have the smoke test?' Charlie asked while Arfer and the others tried to evade Mabel's eye and make rude gestures at each other across the room. It's just like primary school. It's brilliant, I was thinking, till Charlie interrupted me.

'The smoke test? In the smoke chambers? Did you still do it?' he repeated. I told him we had. They were yet another way O'Connor and his crew separated the stayers from the walkers at the start of training. If you couldn't cope with the smoke then you wouldn't be back the next day. The chambers were built out of a massive old Nissen hut on the edge of the training complex. The hut was made of brick and concrete with an iron roof. Rooms opened out on each side of a central corridor. O'Connor and his henchmen set all the rooms on fire then made us walk from one end of the corridor to the other. The smoke hit after less than ten yards. It was about then that your walk became a crouch. Then it became a crawl. Getting through that building and out the other side was our first big test. The point was to show us what it was going to be like for people trapped in fires – the people we were expected to rescue. And the shock wasn't just how hard it was to breathe. You can't see, you find out how little you can hear in heavy smoke and how little you can feel through your gloves. As well as the smoke and the heat you have to fight the claustrophobia, the panic and the disorientation. We all came out of that chamber with black snot, black tears and black sweat streaking our faces. We came out coughing so much it was as if we were going to lose our guts. And the first thing the instructors did was to tell us to walk through it again. Then they told us that in real life it would have been so much tougher.

'That was just wood smoke. It can't poison you like real smoke in a factory fire when you've no idea what kind of chemicals have caught alight,' O'Connor had barked at us.

'I read that in America or somewhere they've even stopped using wood smoke for training,' Charlie said as we relived it all at the lunch table. 'They're using fake smoke, instead. The kind of stuff you get in discos.'

'That's a bad backin' move. That's never going to prepare you for the real thing,' declared Arfer contemptuously.

'You know what else they can't prepare you for?' Woody added. 'The shock you get when someone jumps out and grabs you in a house fire.' I was torn between sitting back like the other two and trying to pretend I knew exactly what he meant, and leaning forward and asking for the full story. I did the latter – and Woody was more than happy to tell it.

'It's human nature,' he began in a rather overdramatic tone. 'If a member of the public's trapped in a burning building they lie low. When they realise there's no way out then they shut down for a while. Self-preservation takes over. People crouch under tables, behind doors, even in cupboards. They're deafened and blinded by the fire. So they don't see us until we're right next to them. That's when they leap out. They grab us. They cling to our legs, our arms, our backs like limpets. They scream like their lives depend on it.'

'Which they do, to be fair,' added Charlie.

'Exactly. But they nearly give us a heart attack in the process. We've got breathing apparatus on. We can barely see or hear ourselves. And suddenly it's like the bogey man has just taken a running jump at us. It's like the exorcist is on our backs. You can't know how bad that is till it happens, jockey.'

I nodded, storing all the information away for later. Part of me was being spooked by it, just as the others were intending. But another part of me was thrilled. All I wanted to do was test myself. I wanted to know if I'd be ready for that kind of fear. More importantly, I wanted to know just when we might get our first major fire. I was like a coiled spring, I was so ready for it. In my mind's eye I could see myself setting off on a feel through of a smoke-filled room. I was working in pairs with a colleague. We'd started a systematic search. He was walking down the left-hand wall, I was walking down the right. We both turned at our respective corners – ready to meet in the middle and give the official 'Room searched!' call before moving on. That was when I imagined myself finding her. I saw myself scoop up the member of the public who had run at me without scaring me for a moment. I pictured myself dragging the beautiful blonde woman – it was a beautiful blonde woman, of course – to safety. A little later I could see her again. This time she was wearing a sexy evening dress, clapping her hands together in pride and applauding loudly. I was stepping forward, in my full-dress uniform, ready to be commended by the Chief Fire Officer for a job well done.

Mabel's voice, louder than any fire bell, snapped me out of my daydream. 'It's first come first served for seconds, gentlemen!' she yelled from the kitchen. There was a thunder roll as sixteen chairs all pushed back against the parquet floor at the same time. There was an aftershock as sixteen pairs of shoes took their wearers to the serving hatch at speed.

I polished off my second plateful and was fit to burst. I sat back and smiled. 'I've not eaten that much since last Christmas. We're not going to go hungry with grub like this every day,' I said.

'You haven't seen anything yet, laddo,' said Charlie. 'We'll be having afters in a sec. It's sponge pudding with custard today. And Betty makes the best custard this side of Welshpool.'

She also made the most custard this side of Welshpool. I watched the way our ladies served the food as I lined up for my portion. Mabel almost disappeared behind a cloud of steam as she began carving out brick-sized slices of sponge for the first set of bowls. She then scooped up several huge spoonfuls of syrup and poured it on top. Then she passed the bowl to Betty who poured on the rich, yellow custard. She clearly took the view that bowls didn't count as full if a single inch of china was visible on the insides. Less was never going to be more when Betty was in charge of the custard bowl. I was on the point of saying 'That's enough for me, thanks' when she'd put about a pint of custard in my bowl. Fortunately I stopped myself. It was pretty clear that 'that's enough for me, thanks' weren't words anyone ever used in the Fire Brigade. We were doing a man's job so we ate men's food. I let Betty defy the laws of physics and get what looked like a second pint's worth in the bowl then took it from her. I got my thumb burned again as I carried it back to the table.

The meal was washed down with a couple of mugs of strong, sugary tea followed by a cigarette. A bit of a breeze was coming in through the mess room windows and it looked set fair to be a perfect afternoon at last. I drained my second mug of tea and sat back in my chair. If this was a fireman's life then I wasn't going to give it up without a fight.

We carried our dirty dishes to the hatch where Betty and Mabel collected them for washing up. 'Do we help?' I whispered at Charlie as we lined up behind the others.

'You want to get in the way of those two?' he asked with a sudden laugh. 'They'll chew you up and spit you out soon as look at you.' I took this as a no and joined the rest of the watch as they all moved down to the other end of the mess room. A mass of shiny, metal-framed armchairs were lined up in front of a television set with a big box and a small screen. The set was encased in plastic designed to look like wood, and it had two doors to cover the screen when it wasn't on. All the usual buttons ran down the right-hand side of the screen and there was an antenna on top that looked powerful enough to reach the moon.

One of the old hands opened the doors, clicked the TV on and turned up the volume on the local news. There were all the usual stories about the binmen's strike, the empty shopfronts in the town centre and a load of job losses in Telford. The whole world seemed a bit grim, to be honest. I had to pinch myself to believe that I'd not only managed to get a job in the middle of the slump, but I'd got one that offered me all this.

The last spare chair was on the edge of the room, a long way from the telly. I threw myself into it and grimaced. It was probably the most uncomfortable chair I'd ever sat in. There were shiny metal ashtrays on the arms of every chair and by the time I sat down most of them had at least one smouldering butt in them. Funny that in my first two full days in the Fire Brigade the only smoky room I'd been in was here at the station. I took a closer look around. Behind the sofas, back where we'd been eating, we had a pool table and a couple of card tables. There was a dartboard on the wall near the service hatch. It looked like a working men's club and it was better than a youth club, I thought as I wondered if I dared cadge another ciggie from Charlie or if I was allowed to go back down to the locker room to get my own. I'd pretty much decided that neither option was worth pursing when Woody came over. He threw himself down into the seat next to me. He must have felt that the gang hadn't spooked me enough at the lunch table so he gave it another shot. 'Did you use high-expansion foam up at Chorley?' he began.

We had done. It was the stuff we used to smother a fire by taking the oxygen out of the air. It was the most disorientating thing in the world. They called it 'panic testing' when we used it in training. It was a spot-on description – when you walked into a room that's got Hi-Ex Foam in it you panicked like a baby. The bubbles were like sound insulation so you didn't know what was going on around you. You couldn't see much either. And then there was the worst thing – the bubbles themselves burst in your mouth and nose and the water they were made of went into your lungs. No surprise that your body thought you were drowning. Especially as the longer you stayed in the room the more water got to your lungs. The instructors said that if you waved your hand in front of your face the bubbles would burst there and you'd be able to breathe normally. It wasn't true. 'You can't see, you can't hear and you still think you're drowning. Still want to do this job, jockey?' Woody asked.

'Yes I do,' I said, trying to sound defiant.

I can't have been a very good actor. 'You don't look it, jockey. You look like a scared rabbit,' he laughed. Then he softened. 'You want a tip from me on how to deal with it if you're ever in a building with high-expansion foam?'

Of course I did. 'Put your helmet in front of your face. The bubbles will burst when they hit it and the water will drip down the sides and down your arms. You'll be able to breathe better. You won't feel like you're drowning that way.'

I nodded, genuinely pleased with the tip, genuinely thankful that he'd bothered to give it to me. I was about to ask for more when Joe, our Sub-O, interrupted us. He stood by the mess room door. 'Volleyball!' he yelled.

'Volleyball!' everyone echoed, stubbing out their cigarettes, swinging off their sofas and heading towards the door. Half the group took the stairs and the other half launched themselves towards the pole drop. I went with that lot – because I was still so excited that firemen's poles actually existed and that I could swing down one whenever I wanted.

Down on the ground floor everyone was piling out of the station. I followed as quickly as I could. When I'd arrived I'd noticed some sort of sports court marked out towards the back of the yard but we'd hardly be playing so soon after a mixed grill and eating our body weight in custard. I decided that 'volleyball' had to be code for some other activity. But what?

5

If it moves, paint it

I couldn't quite believe it, but five minutes later I was on the court playing volleyball like mad. We all were. Young, old, junior, senior and everyone in between. We played like maniacs. Everyone mixed in and just went for it. We didn't waste time selecting proper teams or working out positions. We just piled on to any spare square inch of the court and fought our way to the ball. It was just like a happy brawl. Sixteen men displaying wildly different levels of skill and violence. All of us having the time of our lives.

The net was strung up across a patch of concrete behind the training tower. A court had been marked out properly with white paint. This was clearly one of the most important and well-used parts of our station. 'If we hadn't been on an early shout yesterday and today we'd have played in the mornings as well,' Charlie said with one of his usual infectious laughs as he elbowed past me to get closer to the net. 'Two of these games every day and you'll never struggle to roll out a hose or carry a ladder again.'

I must admit the idea of playing in the morning appealed a lot more than playing so soon after eating a record-breaker of a Betty and Mabel lunch. I was convinced I was going to be sick as I leaped up to spike my first ball. But I could barely contain my excitement as I got a clean, unreachable hit. I was six foot four. I was young, stringy and full of energy. Volleyball was a game I could play. I was well on my way to working out that everyone in the station needed to have some sort of edge to set them apart from the crowd. This could be mine.

About ten minutes into the game the ball was smashed out towards the flat roof of the breathing apparatus, or BA, chamber next door to the appliance room. The building was one storey high and had metal railings all the way around the roof. A huge groan went up as the ball flew over the railings and disappeared out of sight. In a split second I decided to act. It might end badly. I could be horribly embarrassed. Or I could run at that wall, use every inch of my height and reach, grab the railings, pull myself up and over and return the ball to the court as the hero of the moment.

I went for it. 'The jockey's going to kill himself!' someone yelled out as I ran at the wall. Someone else seemed to be laughing. So I knew I couldn't fail. I took a deep breath, planted my foot against the wall and grabbed the railings. Fortunately they held firm. I swung my legs around in the air. I wrenched my body up and over them and on to the roof. It didn't give way under my fifteen-stone weight either. I got the ball, spiked it back to the court and jumped back down to the ground. I'd not fought a fire. But I got a cheer. I don't think I'd ever been so pleased in all my life.

We carried on playing for another half-hour or so. The game didn't get any more structured or any less violent. We were all dripping with sweat as we headed back to the locker room to change out of our trainers and back into our shoes. I was tying up my laces when one of the old-timers came up to me. He had a south Shropshire accent, just like Caddie, but I couldn't remember his name. 'You could turn into a useful player, jockey,' he said, without introducing himself. 'We're in a league with all the other watches and all the other stations in Shropshire. We've got some handy players, as you'll have seen. We're doing well this year. But if someone's away we might need you to help out one match. You'd better be ready,' he said, walking away.

I was ready. I'd have played that afternoon if they'd needed me. I'd play every afternoon. I stood up, hardly able to believe how great all this was. All of a sudden I pictured all my school-mates hunched over the production line over at Rolls-Royce. There was no way that they got to stop work twice a day to have a laugh on a sports pitch. I bet they didn't spend their afternoons convinced they had the best job in the world.

'It's not a bad life, is it?' Charlie said, reading my mind as he walked past me and headed upstairs for a cup of tea. 'And we get to play ice hockey on Saturday morning as well.' I nodded and smiled as he passed. I'd thought volleyball was code for some-thing else when the Sub-O had announced the game earlier on. I'd been wrong about that. But ice hockey? Surely we couldn't play that in a fire station. Could we?

I was whistling along to something from the charts and getting ready to go upstairs for a cup of tea when John came into the locker room. I was about to give him a cheery hello when I saw his face. There was none of his usual good humour on it. This wasn't the man who'd shared the fun when we'd rescued the dog, or the one who'd played along with Mabel and Betty upstairs at lunch. This was the man who was in charge of the station. It was the man I had to impress. I knew, the moment I looked up at him, that whistling on duty was off-limits – especially for the new boy and especially when it was something as annoying as 'Davy's on the road again'. I could have kicked myself. I knew I'd crossed a line and that he thought I'd got too cocky, too soon.

'This is not a holiday camp,' he barked as I stood to attention in front of him. 'Nor is it a discotheque. I want you properly dressed and in the appliance room PDQ. I want the water ladder and the rescue pump cleaned and this time I want the job done right. When you've finished that, I'm sending Leading Fireman Stanton in to show you what needs to be painted. I want this station shipshape and I don't want the likes of you treating it any other way.'

I almost saluted I was so determined to show John how serious I was. But he was already walking away. As usual all I could see was the back of his head as he strode into the distance.

The rescue pump and the water ladder are pretty much two versions of the same thing – they're both what most people see as a fire engine, though to us they have slightly different equipment on board and are useful in slightly different circumstances. That day the RP looked spotless. It hadn't got remotely dirty on the way to Mr and Mrs Knight's house as the roads had all been dry and fully paved. The WL was even cleaner – hadn't been out since its last clean less than twenty-four hours earlier. But after John's bollocking I wasn't going to let this hold me back. If he wanted clean I would give him sparkling. I examined both vehicles with the intensity that Mabel had examined me up in the mess room. I looked for every dead fly on the windscreens, every piece of dirt on the bumpers, every drop of grease on the wheel arches. Then I blitzed them. I put in twice the effort I'd used yesterday – and I thought I'd done a pretty good job then.

One hour into the job I had company. It was Leading Fireman Stanton, one of the old hands from the top table. I'd not been properly introduced to him yet, and that didn't look as if it was going to change any time soon. He walked slowly around the appliances. His richly lined, walnut-coloured face was impassive. For a couple of minutes he didn't say a single word. Then he nodded towards the station store next door.

'The Station Officer wants you to start doing the painting,' he said gruffly.

'What does he want me to paint?'

I got one word in reply: 'Everything.'

Over time I would learn that on quiet afternoons my job was indeed to paint everything in sight. Shovel heads, crowbars, spades, tool boxes, door breakers, the feet of all the ladders – if it didn't move I had to cover it in light blue Hammerite paint. If it did move – well, I'd be expected to paint or polish that, too. We had some vintage fire bells from yesteryear hanging up above the notice board near the Station Officer's room. My job was to keep them shining. My job was also to make sure the step outside the main door to the station was smooth as silk and pillar-box red. My job was to polish the door knocker so hard you could see your face in it from fifty yards away. And so the tasks went on.

'Happy in your work?' one of the others yelled down at me from the mess room one afternoon when everyone else was drinking tea and I was out in the yard with the cleaning kit.

Funnily enough, I was. Two things in particular made it all worthwhile. The first was that the work somehow gave me the pride that everyone else felt about our station. It began to matter to me that the wrenches and the spade heads and the tool kits all looked as good as new. My mum would have fallen over in shock if she'd known. I'd hardly ever done any cleaning at home. But all of a sudden it would have bothered me if someone had come into our station and seen cobwebs, dust or dirt.

The other thing I liked about my afternoons in the appliance room was quite simple. I would end up pleasantly high on all the paint fumes. No wonder I spent so much of my first few months in the job smiling like a blinkin' idiot.

Most afternoons Stanton or one of the other leading firemen would come down to check up on me every half-hour or so. None of them ever looked wildly impressed. On one occasion Stanton spent a couple of minutes staring hard at one of the wheel arches I'd just polished. It had been streaked with mud so I'd spent a while on it. I was convinced it was as clean as the day it had left the production line. 'You're going to want to do that one again before the SO comes down,' Stanton said. He didn't say what was wrong with my first attempt and I didn't ask. This was the Fire Brigade. I just did what I was told and gave it a second go.

Back on my first day with the paint and polish I spent ages making sure I didn't drip or spill anything anywhere. I tried to spruce up everything Leading Fireman Stanton had glared at on his earlier visits. And I wondered if I'd ever be allowed out. I looked at my watch. A quarter to four. I was gasping for a drink but I didn't want John to see me sneaking into the gents to drink out of the tap, let alone going upstairs to see if there was any tea on the go. I was also a little bit intrigued about what everyone else was doing. Every now and then I saw someone walk by outside the appliance room doors. Occasionally I might hear someone zip down the pole or thump up the staircase. But most of the time all I could hear was the muffled hum of cars from the main road and the sound of birds in the trees alongside our station. It was peaceful, relaxing and ever so slightly strange. I was lulled into a sort of dream by the fug of the paint fumes and the richness of all the Brasso and the polish. Every now and then I stood up and gazed through the appliance room doors. It was a glorious early June afternoon. It was dry, warm, clear and utterly relaxing.

Or it was until the alarm went off.

The single word 'Attention' cut across the station's Tannoy system followed by the standard three-tone alert. It nearly gave me a heart attack. That word, and those tones, are cut into the soul of every fireman. They're designed to interrupt anything you are doing. They rise above anything else that is happening. Stop it, drop it, shut it. That's what you do when the tones sound. Because the moment they stop you'll find out where you're going and why. I stood, frozen with anticipation and awash with adrenaline, while a voice I didn't recognise spelt it out. 'Rescue pump and water tender ladder to the White Horse Public House, Abbey Foregate, Shrewsbury. Property fire.' The whole world changed the instant the announcement finished. The appliance room was swallowed in a storm of noise. One after another bodies slammed down the pole while equal numbers swung down the staircase. I saw Arfer grab the door chain and begin rolling up the appliance room doors. I couldn't quite believe how quickly the whole world had changed. The empty room was full. The birdsong and the summer's breeze were drowned out by the noise of a dozen burly, uniformed men. Tension and excitement were in the air – and all of a sudden the older officer who'd told me where to sit at lunch was at my side. 'The name's Caddie,' he said calmly. 'Get back on the engine, jockey. You're gonna to see your first fire.'

6

First Fire

So this was it. A fire. The horse, the dog, the volleyball and the firemen's dinners had all been a bit of a laugh but this was what I'd spent three months training for. This was why I'd joined the Fire Brigade in the first place. I was fizzing with a mix of excitement and nerves as my team of five pulled open the fire engine doors and threw ourselves into our allotted positions. Caddie was on one side of me on the rear-facing back seat, Arfer was on the other, John was up front and Charlie was driving. On the far side of the room four other firemen were jumping aboard the water tender ladder. The rules said that on a day shift everyone had to be on the road within thirty-three seconds of getting an emergency call. We were big men and we all had a lot of kit to manoeuvre around and change into. But it was almost like ballet, the way we got into place so fast. Everyone had a focus. Everyone had experience. Everyone except me.

'You all right, jockey? Hold on tight,' Caddie said sharply. He was still looking out for me but his warning came just a split second too late. We didn't have any seat belts and I was thrown back towards the storage compartments, the breathing apparatus and all the other equipment as we lurched out of the appliance room and on to the main road.

'I'm fine,' I said, pulling myself upright and grabbing my plastic leggings. I got them on then leaned down towards the cab floor to reach for the rest of my kit. That was when the first wave of travel sickness hit me. I gulped and swallowed and tried desperately to think of something else. 'Not now, not on an emergency call, not when you've got a job to do,' I told myself. 'And not when someone like Caddie is watching.' I pulled on my tunic, helmet and gloves to try and distract myself. It didn't really help. I felt more hemmed in now, especially as he and Arfer on the back seat were pulling on their tunics on either side of me. Elbows were everywhere. Then knees and feet were everywhere, too, when we all started to pull our boots on. I wasn't quite done when the engine braked sharply. We were all slammed back into the seat rests. Then the engine lurched forwards. This time we were propelled backwards against the storage compartments. Everything was disorientating. It all seemed the wrong way round. My head was reeling. My stomach was everywhere. In one sudden, awful moment I felt as if I wasn't going to make it.

The water tender ladder was tight on our tail as we passed under the ornate, cast-iron railway bridges and headed past the railway station into the town itself. To our right was the town library, the original Shrewsbury School with its bronze statue of former pupil Charles Darwin outside. Out in front of us was, well, what looked like every car in the county. Suddenly the streets seemed to be full of late afternoon traffic. Kids were being picked up from school. Early starters were heading home after a full day's work. Shoppers were expecting a leisurely drive as they headed out of the town centre. It was my first rush-hour experience on the fire engine and I couldn't imagine how we could get through it. There seemed to be a wall of cars ahead of us – with just as many trying to come the other way. My eyes were darting from left to right, trying to spot a gap that we could take. There didn't seem to be one. I'd never felt such urgency in my life. I'd never felt so powerless.

'Time to get the rest of your kit on, jockey,' Caddie instructed. That took my mind off the traffic. He and Arfer had been getting ready as we edged forward in the jam. I watched as they did their final preparations for the shout. The big thing was to get their breathing apparatus ready. Those are the face masks and cylinders of compressed air that could save their lives and help them save others'. The two men twisted around, tied up the shoulder and waist straps, and hung a torch from the former and a fireman's axe from the latter. When their masks and helmets were secure they pulled on their red plastic gloves. They settled back when they were finished. Then it was my turn. I was number five, on the middle seat at the back of engine. I had a different role to play at a fire. As the new boy I was the BACO, the breathing apparatus control officer. I pulled on a yellow and black checked tabard to mark me out in the job. Then I got the breathing apparatus board out from the storage cupboard beneath me. When we got to the fire I'd use it to record everything that the firemen with breathing apparatus on did. That way I would be the early warning system if anything looked set to go wrong.

'You're happy with what you're gonna be doing?' Caddie asked sharply when I was ready.

'I'm collecting the tallies. I'm marking up what time everyone goes into the building. Then I'm going to work out how long they can stay in the fire if they're using the breathing equipment.'

'You're the one who knows where everyone is and when they need to come out,' Caddie confirmed. 'We'll be relying on you.'

'So you're going in?'

'Me and my man Arfer here,' Caddie said.

I was about to ask what they were expecting to find when Caddie silenced me with a look. A message was coming in on the radio up front. John, the Officer in Charge of the shout, picked it up from the passenger seat. He wrote something down and reported our position back to base. Then he turned around. 'Get ready for a bit of earache. I'm going to get us moving,' he yelled. Then he fired up the two-tone siren. I was glad of the warning. The sound was shocking, deafening, truly ear-splitting.

It echoed around the cab, bursting eardrums and raising the tension sky high. It also seemed so modern, so incongruous amidst the serene, timeless beauty of old Shrewsbury. It did the trick, though. We were just alongside Shrewsbury Castle when it first went off. Twisting around in my seat and looking ahead I could see cars inching forward and mounting the kerbs to let us through straight away. I felt the engine swing to the right as Charlie took us on to the other side of the road – and the momentum then swung the other way as we headed down the steep Wyle Cop and through the heart of the gloriously beautiful Tudor town. We went through the red lights and were hardly ever stopped again. We powered on, thundering across the Severn on the English Bridge that had been left almost entirely clear for us. I'll never forget the rush of that first blue-light ride. It was like nothing else. This, I was thinking, this is what every kid dreams of. All my nerves disappeared as we came out on the far side of the bridge. I'd not felt sick since we'd first pulled out of the traffic jam. As we got towards the end of the drive all I was left with was excitement. In my mind's eye I could see all the disasters we'd trained for, all the blazes we'd seen on video up in Chorley. I wanted a big fire, a huge crisis, a massive challenge. I wanted to prove myself to my team – and to my town. My heart was pumping like a piston and I was ready for anything.

My mistake was to let all this show.

I turned to Caddie and shouted above the sound of the siren. 'This is brilliant. It's the best day I've ever had. I can't wait till we get there. It's going to be a big one, isn't it?'

Caddie didn't answer straight away. When he did I knew that I'd said the wrong thing. 'My friend's daughter works at the White Horse,' he said, finally. That one short sentence was like a kick to the stomach. His dark, older eyes stared into mine for what felt like forever. They were rich with meaning and experience. Then he looked away.

I stared at my boots, suddenly short of breath and cursing

what I'd just said. 'Why did you say that? Why didn't you think how it would sound?' I was asking myself. For in that one short comment Caddie had reminded me of something I should never have forgotten. Fire was real. It affected real people and destroyed real lives. In a small community like Shrewsbury it could also affect people you knew. People you loved.

I tried to think of some way to apologise or explain myself for the rest of the journey. I couldn't. My mind was racing but no words came. No one else spoke either. Traffic was lighter now we were over the Severn and John clicked off the siren. The moment the sound died the silence seemed almost tangible, even though the engine still made more than enough noise on its own.

'We're nearly there. Get ready,' John yelled from the front.

'Caddie, I —' I began suddenly.

'Don't worry about it, jockey. Next time just engage brain before you speak and everything will be fine,' he said, talking loud enough for me to hear, but not too loud for John to listen along. That was another kindness I'd one day want to thank him for. 'Anyway, this is not going to be a big fire. Didn't you hear the message on the radio? It's a kitchen fire. There are no persons reported and it's probably been extinguished already. Arfer and I might not need our sets after all. I doubt that anyone's going to be running through any flames. But you still need to be on the ball, jockey. You need to do your job well. Remember your training. Be ready for the unexpected. And don't let any of us down.'

'I won't. I'd never do that.'

He nodded, gave a curt smile and then looked round and out of the window. I twisted around as well to try and see past him. All my senses were heightened again after the pep talk. All my muscles were tense.

'There's Lord Hill's Column,' said Arfer, testing the torch on his shoulder one more time. The column was one of Shrewsbury's many useful landmarks. Built to commemorate a general from the Napoleonic Wars it was the tallest Doric column in the country – taller and fatter than Nelson's Column in London. I couldn't see it from my position in the middle of the engine, but I knew that just ahead of the column was the Shire Hall, the ill-named and utterly monstrous glass and concrete council building in Abbey Foregate. I felt the fire engine slow down. We must have arrived.

The five of us jumped to the ground. The White Horse pub was on the bend just ahead of us. With the council offices just opposite and plenty of other shops, offices and houses all around it was no surprise that a big crowd had already gathered outside. A police car was parked up on the other side of the street and an ambulance was pulling in alongside us as well.

'It was at the back. In the kitchen,' a man yelled from the front of the crowd. John moved towards him fast to get as much information from him as possible.

'Who are you?'

'I'm the owner. It's my pub.'

'Is there anyone inside?'

'No, there's no one.'

'How about someone who shouldn't be there? Someone who's snuck in somehow? Someone you've forgotten about or don't know about?'

The man said he was sure that everyone inside had got out safely, but there was a note of doubt in his voice this time. Fortunately we wouldn't take his word for it even if he was convinced he was right. Up in training in Chorley we had been told too many horror stories about the forgotten victims of fire. Parents who'd sworn blind that their homes were empty – not realising that one of their kids had bunked off school and was hiding in a bedroom. Workers who'd tried to check every room as they evacuated an office – but hadn't realised that one of the early morning cleaners had been taking a nap in a store room no one else ever used. Our job was to use as much local intelligence as we could – but then to double-check it all ourselves. The first thing the officers would do when they got inside the building was to sweep it for trapped or terrified occupants.

'Jockey, are you ready with the breathing apparatus board?' John yelled out to me.

'Ready, sir!' I replied. I'd moved as fast as I could since getting off the engine. I'd wanted to get everything right. The board was set up at the front of the engine and I was already keenly aware that John wasn't the only one checking up on me. I was the closest to the crowd and dozens of people on the pavement were watching my every move. This did feel real now. It felt serious.

John called us together when he'd finished talking to the public and the police. He quickly briefed us on what to expect. He ensured we all knew what we had to do. Caddie and Arfer were ready for their tasks. They stood there, the late afternoon sun glinting off their gloves and leggings and their shiny painted helmets. They handed me their tallies, the plastic identification badges that they'd detached from their BA sets. Every BA set had a tally attached. They had loads of vital information including spaces for the fireman's name and brigade, the BA set number, the cylinder pressure, the time the fireman starts breathing the air and all sorts of other things.

'Got them?' John asked.

'Got them,' I replied and slid them into the clear Perspex slots on the board. Then I overwrote Caddie's and Arfer's names on top, just in case the tallies somehow fell out. After that I wrote in where they were both going – and when. The board and its tallies were a vital safety tool on a fire. They would show exactly who was where. The system recorded when firemen went into a building and when they needed to come out. I marked the times as Caddie and Arfer headed towards the pub door with the hose reel and walked into the building. There was a small chart printed on to the top of the control board. I used it to help calculate how long the men could last on the compressed air they were carrying. This was the vital figure and I calculated it and recalculated it endlessly in my head amidst the organised chaos of that first real shout. I had to get it right because I was the canary in the mine. We didn't have any radios to use on jobs like these. There was no easy communication from inside to out – the men couldn't ask for help. If they were in the building for too long it was up to me to raise the alarm and send in reinforcements.

I looked up from the control board. This might just be a kitchen fire that's already gone out, I told myself, but as Caddie had said we had to be ready for the unexpected. Two of the other firemen had pulled off a second hose reel so we could supply more water if needed. Just behind me Charlie was working the pump, supplying high pressure water to the hose reel. If we needed water then one of his jobs would be to monitor the gauges for the rest of the shout to check that the flow stayed strong. Everyone else was as busy just in case. The four firemen from the other appliance were ready to step in and help with any other jobs. If required, they would put a ladder up to a window, break down a door, locate the nearest hydrants and supply our pump with more water, or get their own breathing apparatus on and head inside to fight the fire with their colleagues.

'What's going on in there? What are they doing?' a woman from the crowd shouted out at me.

I felt my mouth open and shut like a goldfish. I wanted to know why she was asking me, of all people. Then it hit me. I was wearing the uniform. She didn't know it was my first week. She didn't see a green-as-grass eighteen-year-old. All she could see was a fireman. I tried to stand a bit taller and work out what to say. Then, fortunately, John took over. He had been striding around the engines, his eyes on everything and everyone.

'They've gone in to assess the situation and see what's happening. If there's a fire there then they've got the hoses so they'll extinguish it straight away. If it's bigger than expected they'll be back out here and we'll tackle it another way. But we're not expecting any problems. Everything is under control. You just need to stay back where you are and wait.'

We all had to wait.

'Why aren't we using Dictron?' I asked Charlie a few minutes later.

'Because it's crap.'

Dictron was the only communication device we did have for use in fires. We'd tried it out back in training. You attached a microphone to your face mask and slung an amplifier over your shoulder. You then let out a wire behind you as you walked into a fire and the wire carried your words back to the BACO outside. Charlie was right in many ways, it was a notoriously unreliable system. In all the years I had ahead of me I'd never once use the system on a real fire. But outside the White Horse on my first real shout I'd have given anything to be connected up and to know what Caddie and Arfer were seeing inside.

The pub doors were flung open from the inside as I did the sums on the board one more time. Caddie strode out towards John. The crowd surged forward and one of our other officers, a quiet man called Howard, stepped over to keep everyone back. A couple of people didn't want to move and a bit of an argument began but Howard eventually got the crowd where he wanted it. The noise meant I couldn't begin to hear what Caddie was saying, though. But after a brief conversation he turned round and headed back inside the pub. The waiting game began again.

'Did you hear any of that, Charlie?' I asked. It was probably wrong to ask questions at a time like this but I was desperate to know.

'The pub's empty. There's been a bit of a blaze in the kitchen and there's been a hell of a lot of smoke but not much burn damage. The electrics and the gas are off now. The big thing is to ventilate the place. That's what they've gone back for. We'll be reeling the hose back in soon. Get ready.'

I stood back, digesting it all. Was I relieved or disappointed? I didn't know. Until Caddie had brought me up short on the journey I'd wanted the excitement of a big fire. Now I'd realised that lives could be at stake I'd wanted it to be over as quickly and safely as possible. So I suppose I was relieved.

Five minutes later Caddie and Arfer were back. They headed off for another huddled conversation with John. Then they walked over to me. 'We'll be wanting these back now, son,' Caddie said, as they took their tallies out of the board and reattached them to their sets. As he did so Caddie examined everything I'd written on the board. I could sense him checking my figures in his head. I was convinced they were right but my heart was still pounding. 'Good job, jockey,' Caddie said as he walked away. They were only three words. But I felt on top of the world..

Caddie and Arfer cleaned up their breathing apparatus sets and attached new air cylinders to them, just in case, while John briefed the rest of us on the salvage operation. After an incident like this we had to clear out all the dangerous burnt materials and check there were no dormant pockets of fire that might reignite once we'd left.

'I do not want a call-back. I do not want anything to be missed. This fire must be out, full stop. Get to it,' John told us. We got to it. There was still a heck of a lot of smoke in the pub, so we probably breathed in all sorts of bad stuff. But we carried on all the same. It took a good half-hour for everything inside the pub to be made safe, checked and double-checked. Only then did we make up all the hoses and other equipment and stow it back on the various appliances. I'd put the control board away just after Caddie and Arfer had taken back their tallies but I checked it was safely in place just in case I needed it again any time soon. Ending one job is no guarantee that you won't immediately be starting another. If we had a call on the way back to base it was vital that everything was as ready now as it had been at the station.

'So you really reckon it was a pan of boiled potatoes that set it off? I don't believe you. I'd have put money on it being a deep-fat fryer or a proper chip pan,' Charlie yelled back from the driver's seat as he turned the engine around.

'It was a pan of spuds on an electric cooker, nothing more, nothing less. Some dozy mare put the wrong ring on or just forgot about the pan altogether. It boiled dry then we all know how much smoke you get from potatoes. That's all it was, Charlie.'

'Well, I had chips at one of the pubs near Lord Hill's Column one time and they were rank,' Charlie said, refusing to let his chip-pan theory go.

'So rank chips mean the only fire you're going to have is a chip-pan fire? And you're probably talking about a completely different pub because you can't quite remember where you were?' Arfer asked him, trying to divine his logic.

'You know what I mean,' Charlie said, though we didn't.

I joined in the jokes on the way back. Shrewsbury's version of the rush hour had passed so we made steady progress. Our only delay came on the far side of the English Bridge when a driver was so keen to pull to the side and let us past that he stalled. He was an old guy and he blocked us in while he repeatedly flooded his engine and spent about five minutes kangaroo hopping ever further into our way. We were still hooting with laughter about it when we pulled into the station. The engine got parked in its usual slot in the appliance room and we all jumped down.

'Tea. Upstairs,' John shouted when the appliance room doors had been closed and everyone had checked their kit. Then he turned to me. 'Not you. It's an hour till Green Watch arrives. I want the vehicles cleaned inside and out. I don't want those buggers to have anything to complain about. Get to it.'

I did as I was told. I connected up both machines to charge

up their batteries. Then, for the next forty-five minutes, I washed then polished the outside of both appliances. I brushed out the inside of both the cabs. I cleaned all the lights and I was working on the windscreens when the appliance room door swung open. John was back. 'That was good experience this afternoon,' he said, walking round the room examining everything the way he always did. I'd already noticed that his eyes were never still. Even when we were all up in the mess room having a laugh he never stopped noticing or checking things.

'I enjoyed it,' I said. Then I backtracked a bit in case I'd given the wrong impression yet again. 'Not the fire. I didn't enjoy that there was a fire or that people could have got hurt. But I enjoyed the shout. I enjoyed that bit of it.'

John held up his hand to shut me up. 'Caddie told me that you're keen,' he said.

I winced. I bet that wasn't exactly how he had described it. At best he might have said I was too keen. At worst he might have said I was like a bull in a blinkin' china shop.

'Sorry,' I said.

John's hand was up again. 'It's OK to be keen. It's not OK to be stupid. It's our job to show you the difference. But you handled yourself all right today. I didn't have any worries about you on the board. It was an OK start.'

He walked away – and it was all I could do not to punch the air and cheer. I had a feeling this was the kind of job where praise was thin on the ground. Back then the Fire Brigade's career development and professional support basically boiled down to the fact that if you couldn't hack it you were booted out. You'd only know you were doing OK if you still had a job at the end of the month. But John had just said I'd made an OK start. He'd said it out loud. So what the hell – when I was certain he'd gone I really did punch the air. I might even have given a very quiet cheer.

I was finishing off the windscreens and I had a huge grin on my face when the first few cars began to arrive outside. Green Watch, the night shift, was here. Everyone made a lot more noise tonight. The new arrivals wanted to hear what had happened at the pub. They wanted to explain how much better it would have been handled if they'd been on the shout. I barely had time to run back to the locker room to get out of my overalls and into my dress uniform for the shift change. I checked my tie and epaulettes in the mirror and joined the others in the muster bay. We all lined up opposite each other, as usual. John brought us to attention. He looked us up and down. His face was impassive. Then he said it: 'Off-going watch, dismiss!'

Green Watch practically forced us out of the building the moment we stood down. They had ownership of the station for the next fifteen hours and they didn't want us hanging around their patch for a moment longer than necessary. Most of us were happy to oblige. If I'd thought Charlie, Woody and all the others could move fast on the volleyball court it was nothing to their performance in the car park at knocking-off time. Everyone was in their motors, hooting their horns, yelling obscenities and getting in each other's way at the exit within seconds. Everyone except me. I took ages walking to my car – a racing green HB Viva that had flared wheel arches and Rostyle wheels but just a 1159cc engine. It was a sheep in wolf's clothing but I'd bought it with the money I'd earned on the farm and in all my other odd jobs so I loved it. That day I didn't want to turn the ignition on, though. I didn't want to leave the car park. If someone from Green Watch had yelled out of the window and said they needed an extra body for the next fifteen hours I'd have volunteered in a shot. I reckoned I had more energy now than I'd had at the start of the shift. And a lot of my energy was about to go to waste. A quirk of the rotas meant I'd been given the next two nights off. After that the whole of Red Watch was off for four days before our next tour of duty began at the end of next week.

'You lucky sod. Six days off! Have you any idea how much

blinkin' money I could make if I had six days off in a row?' Woody had grumbled when he'd seen the duty list.

'I'll swap with you,' I'd replied.

Woody had laughed and slapped me round the back of my head the way he always did. But I was serious. Six days off? When I'd just had my first taste of facing a fire? When I'd had a few words of praise from the boss? Why would anyone want that?

7

Under My Skin

O n the first of my days off I tried to pass the time by fishing. It didn't really do the trick. I got up early and drove up to the carp pool near Picklescott, a village of beautiful stone cottages about a thousand feet up in the Shropshire hills and slap bang in the middle of nowhere. The sky was already a rich blue when I left home and the sun was gloriously strong by the time I found a pitch beside the pool. I should have enjoyed every moment of it. I should have got some serious fishing in for the first few hours. Then I should have eaten my mum's sandwiches and had a bit of a doze amidst some of the least known but most beautiful scenery in Britain. When I reopened my eyes I should have seen the dragonflies dancing on the surface of the water. I should have watched the carp lifting their backs out of the pool, spreading ripples that shook up all the colours of the water and making the whole scene come alive. Last but not least, I should have revelled in the silent companionship of the few other fishermen up at Picklescott pool. All of us should have tasted the warm summer air, daydreamed a little and forgot about real life all the way below us in the valleys.

Unfortunately I couldn't quite pull all of this off. The Fire Brigade wouldn't let me go.

I knew the rhythm of the shifts now, so every time I looked at my watch up at Picklescott I could guess what would be happening back at the station. If they weren't on a shout I reckoned I knew exactly when the others would be playing volleyball, doing drills, drinking tea or laughing about some crazy story in the *Daily Mirror*. In my imagination I could hear Mabel telling the men to stop swearing. In my mind's eye I could see Betty slamming a frying pan down on to the gas or pouring a pint of custard into some other lucky man's pudding bowl. I kept thinking of Woody, telling me I was so lucky to have six days off. But all I really wanted was to be back at work.

One day down, five to go.

I tried not to look at my watch on my second day at the Picklescott pool. It didn't make any difference. I still spent the day trying to guess what the others might be doing. I tried to put myself on the fire engine for a really dramatic shout. I made up incidents and acted out dozens of improbably heroic scenarios. In my head I saved loads of beautiful women from fates worse than death. It was another glorious summer's day up by the carp pool but, oh boy, did it drag.

Two days down, four to go.

I tried to cheer up by reminding myself that I was being paid to fish. In all my other jobs I'd earned by the hour. If I'd not been working I'd not been earning. Now I had a proper wage so days off should be wonderful, valuable things. But these ones weren't. I was missing out and I hated it. But the day finally passed. I headed back home to get some fish and chips, watch *The Dukes of Hazzard* on telly and pretend I was happy where I was.

Halfway there at last.

I decided to see if time passed faster if I loafed around at home the way I'd done as a kid. It didn't – not least because the Fire Brigade had found another way to get under my skin. My mum and dad's house was on the edge of a fifties housing estate near a main road and a big school. We didn't have fire engines going past every day. But there'd often be the sound of some kind of siren in the distance. It could have been a police car or an ambulance. It didn't matter. My adrenaline kicked in the moment I heard it. If I closed my eyes I was there: unknown adventure ahead, perched precariously on my helmet and tunic while our driver guided all fourteen tonnes of us through traffic and across the wrong side of a major junction to get to our destination.

Four days down. Two to go.

I got up late, killed time all day then headed to the pub with a group of old school friends. We all talked about our jobs and exaggerated our new, grown-up lives. One of my mates was a store detective in town. I was a bit impressed with the stories about how he'd recently held someone down on the ground till the police came and made an arrest. I was pleased for one of the girls at a building society who'd already got promoted. I knew that Michael and Tommy were genuinely happy over at Rolls-Royce. But it was all as nothing compared to my job. At one point someone said I was a bit quiet. 'You've only done two days. It's probably too early to know if you're going to like it,' one of the girls said, sympathetically. I didn't want to tell her I'd liked it after two hours. Or that if I started telling them why I'd never stop.

Five days down. One to go.

I don't think my mum had ever seen me iron a shirt before. I don't think my dad thought I knew how to. But I did it that night. I set up the ironing board in the living room and got to work while *Nationwide* was on the telly. I spent forever on the cuffs and the collar. I aimed to get the creases as straight and as true as a die. I used all my weight to make sure the front and back were as flat as the surface of a pond. The whole family took a look when I was done. 'Not bad, not bad at all,' said my mum, whipping it away. 'But you forgot to do the arms. Maybe I'll do it one more time for you in the morning.'

Six days gone. Thirty-five minutes to go. My Viva was the first Red Watch car at the station. I was the first to uniform up in the locker room. I was ready to parade before half the guys had made it out of their front drives. I wasn't just keen, that day. I was blinkin' mustard.

When the night shift stood down and ran for the exits we listened as John read out the notices for the day. We were told about the shouts that Green Watch and the others had done on our time off. There had been an arson attack at the back of a shop on the high street, some fire alarms had gone off at the hospital and a couple of sheep had needed to be rescued from a disused mine shaft up towards the Stiperstones. I listened intently, desperately jealous. To think I'd been wasting time fishing when I could have been helping out on one of those.

We changed out of our dress uniform and into our usual overalls when John dismissed us from parade. Then we started our checks. First task was to look at the board. That told us all where we were positioned on each of the appliances. As the jockey I was almost always in number five slot on the back seat of the main engine. When we knew where we were sat we checked our kit, testing our torches, breathing apparatus and radios. These radios were a bit of a joke. They weren't classed as intrinsically safe and therefore could potentially cause sparks inside when operated – so there was a rule that said you couldn't use them when you had your breathing apparatus on. And when did we have our breathing apparatus on? In big, dark, smoky fires when radio contact would have been pretty nice. It was years before the powers that be sorted that one out. More's the pity.

'OK, bags and boots in position on the appliances then upstairs for a cup of tea,' John announced, interrupting my thoughts. Then he added the three little words that I'd soon start to hear in my sleep. 'Not you, jockey.'

I tried to ignore Woody's smirks as he turned around and stamped off up to the mess room. 'Right, jockey, I want you to watch while the drivers do the A routines. They'll check over all the appliances. They'll check they're fully charged. They'll check the lights and the fuel levels. They'll do a visual check of the tyre conditions and check the fuel levels on the light portable pumps and the electric generator. Then they'll make sure there are no gaps in the lockers or any missing equipment. Then what will they do?'

I did my goldfish impression again – I'd not expected a question so I wasn't ready with an answer.

'They'll sign the logbooks for all the checks that have been done. Then they'll join everyone else upstairs and see if there's any tea left in the pot. You'll be staying down here. Leading Fireman Stanton will tell you about the B routines. Off you go.'

I followed the drivers around the machines and tried to remember everything that they did. 'Now, what are the B routines?' Stanton asked when they'd rushed off upstairs.

'They're the bigger checks?' I ventured.

'Correct. They're done weekly, on a Saturday. Anyone can do them, not just the drivers. The boss will expect you to volunteer. He won't expect you to wait to be asked. You'll start off by checking the oil levels, tyre pressures and washer fluids. Happen you should do that now then I'll show you the rest,' he said. The checks took us about ten minutes, including all the criticism and corrections Stanton threw at me. But in the end he did seem satisfied with my work. He dismissed me and said I could join the rest of the watch upstairs. If I moved fast I could catch the tail end of the tea break, he said. Apparently that day we had biscuits.

'They're courtesy of Mr and Mrs Thom at the frozen food shop on the corner by the main road,' said Arfer, grabbing three before grudgingly passing the near-empty box across to me.

'They give us a lot of stuff. You'll soon get to know them,' Charlie said. And I did. It was mainly Mr Thom who turned up – we never found out his first name. He and his wife were both in their mid-sixties and had been running their pie and frozen food shop for more than forty years. Mr Thom was a short, busy little man with tiny round glasses and slightly wild, mad-professor hair. He always wore a brown checked suit and tie under a red and white apron. And he was always smiling. 'I've got some lovely frozen fish for you today, gentlemen,' he'd say, handing over some out-of-date cod. His wife, who in the interests of equality would only ever be referred to as Mrs Thom, tended to bring the frozen cakes, puddings or, as she had done that day, the broken biscuits. 'Better you gentlemen eat it up than we put it all out to waste,' she would say, before telling us we didn't eat enough and should pop by the shop on the way home for some of their latest special offers.

'It's just a cheap insurance policy. They want to make sure we get off our backin' arses if their shop ever catches fire,' Arfer said cynically that first morning. He didn't mean it and none of us believed it. The Thoms were great. They liked feeling part of station life, even if it was just for a few minutes at a time. They knew most of our names, they stopped for a mug of tea some mornings when things were quiet, and whenever we did buy anything in their shop they'd add something else to the bag for free. 'For luck, love,' Mrs Thom would say.

I tried to dunk one of the biscuits and it had just broken off and splashed into my tea when Charlie came across to my chair. 'Guess what the boss wants you to do before we hit the volleyball court?' he said.

'Does it begin with P?' I asked.

'Got it in one.'

I poled it downstairs and got the paint brushes out. One of the night shifts had done some digging on a shout at a farm out near Church Stretton so a couple of shovels were looking a tad less than perfect. I knew that if I'd spotted the scratches then John was never going to miss them. It took me about fifteen minutes to get them sorted and I was ready, brand new Slazenger tennis shoes on and a fired-up bad attitude in place, when we had the volleyball call at ten.

The game was as vicious and brilliant as ever. I made a mental note of all the most psychotic and effective players. One of them in particular, a man who was probably a foot shorter than me and twenty years older, looked to be the one I had to impress the most if I was to make it on to the Red Watch team. He played like a man possessed. I'd never seen someone so short jump so high. His reach was amazing; his spikes were deadly. We came off the court for our second tea break of the day at eleven o'clock on the nose. Everyone was pumped up and sweating.

'Go see if Mrs Thom's got any more stale biscuits,' Woody instructed me when we thundered into the mess room.

'Ignore him. I want you to take a cup down to Pete James in the watch room,' John said more seriously.

I did what my Station Officer had told me. And I sobered up as I tried to get down the stairs without spilling the tea. In the madness of our volleyball game I'd somehow forgotten why we were all there. It had slipped my mind that one of us was sitting by the phone every minute of every shift, ready to put the call out if we were needed.

The watch room was at the front of the station on the ground floor. I'd been secretly hoping it might look like mission control or at least like something out of *Thunderbirds*. It didn't. It was a small, square room containing a metal desk and chair, a wall of filing cabinets, a couple of steel lockers and a roll-up bed for the night shift. The only high-tech items, if you could call them that, were the phone and the microphone for the Tannoy system.

I knocked on the glazed door and brought in the tea. 'All quiet?' I asked as I put the mug on the desk where the man indicated.

'So far, son,' he said, not looking up from the blank notepad in front of him. He was a tall, sharp-faced man with thin, fair hair and sharp eyes. I stood there looking around me for quite some time. I was drinking in all the details of the room. And I realised I had loads of questions for the man in it. I wanted to know how often we got a call, how many of our mornings were uninterrupted, how often a shout would come in when we were already out on a job. I wanted to ask how he judged the urgency of every call, or if he treated them all alike. I wanted to know so much – but Pete had already struck me as being a man of very few words. A few more minutes passed as I tried to decide whether to speak and why I was still standing there.

'I'll leave you to it,' I said in the end, feeling foolish.

He nodded. Then, in a low, soft, south Shropshire drawl, he put the fear of God in me. 'Did you not know it's 11.15, son?' he asked, pointing towards the wall clock ahead of him. 'You should be outside already. Reckon you're going to be late for drills.'

8

Drills and More Drills

The rest of the watch was already outside when I barrelled down the white, breeze-block corridor from the watch room to the rear of the station. I threw myself against the back door, sped up when I was outside and practically skidded to a halt alongside Charlie and Woody. John's deputy, our Sub-O, Joe Morgan, was in the process of taking control. He stood in the middle of the drill yard and looked at us as if we were the least attractive objects he'd ever seen in his life.

'Fall in on the squad line,' he bellowed with a voice you could have heard in Telford. It was exactly like being in the Forces – and was a clear reminder of how many of the older firemen had come from the army in the post-war years. We all lined up, standing to attention, soldier-style. I couldn't have been more tense if I'd been plugged into the mains. We'd done drills every day I'd been training up in Chorley. The worst of them had nearly killed us all, but I'd still loved the challenge of them. Would the ones we did on the proper watch be even tougher? All the other men looked serious. Even the jokers like Charlie and Woody were standing to attention. I had butterflies the size of budgies in my stomach as I waited to hear Joe's instructions. I also had a bit of a dream in my heart. I was the youngest and I had to be among the fittest here. This, surely, could be my chance to shine. I could show everyone I was up to the job.

'Squad, from the right in fives number!' Joe commanded, with what seemed like bad grammar but made perfect sense to us. 'The first drill today will be to supply water from a pressure-fed supply using two lines of hose consisting of two lengths each. The pump will supply two lines of delivery hose consisting of three lengths each. Any questions?'

I guessed, rightly, that the correct and final answer to this was 'no, sir'. In plain English we'd been told to connect one end of the hoses to a hydrant in the ground and the other to the pump on the fire engine. From there we had to connect further lines of hose, ending up with what we called the branch at the end that turned the water into a smooth stream when it began to flow. All we needed was the instruction to move. And in typical Forces fashion we knew we couldn't do a thing till it came.

'Number one crew, three paces to the rear of and facing the appliance. Fall in!' Joe yelled. Then we moved. We turned to the right and jogged smartly to the allotted position at the back of the fire truck. 'Crew mount!' Joe demanded. We got in the engine and slammed all the doors shut behind us. Joe walked to the front of the engine, checked we were all in place and paused. Then he nodded. 'Crew as detailed. Get to work!' he yelled. The drill had begun.

Everyone flung the doors open and burst out of the engine like shaken beer from a bottle. Four pairs of boots hit the ground almost simultaneously. I'd pushed myself along from my middle seat and was out of the engine only seconds later. The lines of hose were stowed in the lockers at the side of the engine. We rolled up the doors and began to drag the hose out. We got it laid out, in position and connected to the hydrant and pump ready for the water to flow.

It wasn't the most complex drill but throughout it all I was painfully aware that, while Joe was checking up on the whole squad, his main focus was on me. 'Rest!' he yelled at one point, when he decided he wanted to make a comment or a criticism of something I was doing. Everyone froze and listened. On his command the drill then continued, always a little faster and more furious than before, and always with all the attention on me.

'Don't drop that coupling!' he yelled at me a little later when I knew that was the very last thing I was going to do. 'Don't drag that hose!' he bellowed when I could swear I wasn't.

For all the interruptions, we got the job done fast. When we'd got all the right lines of hose in place and connected, Charlie opened the delivery on the pump and the water began to flow. I felt like cheering. Doing this kind of task alongside all the other new recruits in Chorley had been one thing. Doing it here, as the one youngster amidst a full squad of experienced firemen, was quite another. Though, of course, it wasn't finished just yet.

'Knock off, make up!' Joe yelled when he'd seen enough. That was our instruction to get the kit back into its original positions almost as fast as we'd rolled it all out. It takes effort, as the hoses need to be emptied of water before they can be re-stowed. We moved fast to under-run, roll up and stow them. When that was all done we shut the engine's lockers and lined up behind the truck. 'Drill completed, sir! All gear stowed!' Woody shouted.

Joe barked out a rare sound of approval. 'Carry on, number one!' he yelled, so we headed back to the original squad line for a debrief – most of which was based on what I'd done and what I needed to do better next time.

The second squad was given its drill when the Sub-O had finished with us. We watched them do it, listened to their debrief then stepped up to be given our next task. And so it went on. On all our drills we'd practise anything and everything the officers could think of. Over the next few weeks and months I'd learn the real names and the nicknames for all the drills. The thread running through all of them was an emphasis on old-fashioned rote learning. The aim was to hammer everything home. Things had to become second nature, so your body did things automatically while your mind focused on the true situation in hand. You had to be able to roll out and connect lines with 5 per cent of your brain while the remainder was looking for hazards and coming up with a variety of ways of dealing with them. The other purpose, of course, was to keep you fit. You couldn't do the job if you couldn't get our heaviest ladders up to the highest floors. And out in the Shropshire countryside ladders would sometimes be the least of our worries. We had a 'light portable pump' that was anything but. Carrying this 1200cc engine and its metal cradle over fields and fences to a new water source when you're fighting a barn or a grass fire would floor you if your body wasn't ready. That's why we lugged that cradle round the drill ground so often. That's why Joe and the others put so many obstacles in our way when we practised with it.

That first morning I lost all sense of time as the heavy-duty drills went on – and I couldn't have cared less. If the session normally lasted two hours I'd happily have done three. If Joe wanted me to lay out ten lines I'd willingly have done twelve. I wanted to keep on pushing myself to the limit. I loved exercise, so as far as I was concerned the day couldn't get any better. Except that it could.

'Fall in on the squad line!' Joe shouted again. 'We're going to finish off with two situation drills. Listen up!'

Situation drills were the best. I'd got a real buzz out of doing them at training in Chorley. They were detailed, serious and designed to test our minds as well as our bodies. We'd be given a scenario and told to deal with it using whatever equipment we required. The drills could be as simple or as complex as our instructor chose. They could also change or get more complicated halfway through the exercise – just like real life. Any mistakes and we got a massive bollocking. Any major screw-ups and we'd be bawled out for the rest of the day.

'Attention!' Joe began. 'The first drill will involve squads one and two. You have turned up at a property fire with persons reported. You are told that two children were seen at a rear window five minutes ago. You need to locate them and bring them out. Get to work!'

Both squads moved fast. We were being timed. Just like in a real shout, we had to be on the fire trucks fast. My squad boarded the rescue pump, the other stormed on to the water ladder. We got kitted up while the drivers took us to the foot of the training tower – the site of our imaginary incident. Numbers three and four, on the back of the rescue pump with me, jumped off in full breathing apparatus. I set up the BACO board, just as I'd done at the pub fire. I got their tallies while our Officer in Charge sent his number one around the property to check for windows and other openings.

'Pump in gear!' yelled our number two, a newly serious Charlie. 'Drop the tank!' he yelled, the signal to open the tank valve and let the 1800 litres of water on board come into the pump. The driver increased the revs on the engine to create enough pressure for the hose reel jet to work properly. Water shot out like a weapon. We were doing this for real.

While the water smashed against the walls of the training tower, and with two men in the building aiming to rescue the kids from upstairs, two more firemen, also in full breathing apparatus, gave me their tallies then headed in to search the ground floor. Just because we've only been told about the children upstairs didn't mean there was no one else around somewhere else.

'Times, jockey!' Joe yelled at me. I called out the figures I'd calculated and written on the BACO board. He gave a curt nod and walked away to check up on the others – and a hell of a lot was going on.

The second crew gave the all-clear for the ground floor, just as the first crew requested a crowbar and a door breaker to get to the kids. The officers from the water ladder carried them over then put a short extension ladder up to a window in case we needed another way in – or out. The training tower was still being doused in water, instructions were being shouted across the yard and extra equipment was being lined up in case it was needed. Then our numbers three and four ran out carrying the two dummy bodies. We had a minute-man resuscitation machine at the ready and two officers ran through the first aid exercises as I passed the others their tallies and updated the board. We dealt with an imaginary ambulance and then Arfer called the end of our task.

'Fire extinguished. Salvage to begin, sir!' he shouted.

The Sub-O put up his hand. He'd seen enough. 'We'll stop it there. I have things to say but I want the equipment re-stowed first,' he yelled. We jumped to it. There was always an inbuilt risk with drills, especially complicated ones like these – we might get a real shout when all the engines, hoses and ladders were being used on the drill yard. So the sooner everything was back in place the safer the world would be.

We lined up for a debrief that occasionally veered more into a bollocking.

When we'd taken our criticism the final squad was given its situation drill. Joe pointed to two lines drawn on the drill ground. 'Between those two lines is a river. There is a casualty on the other side who needs to be recovered to this side. The only equipment you have is what's on these two appliances. Get to work!'

Looking back, I can't believe how keen I was on all of this. I can't believe that I was itching to take part in the other squad's drills as well as my own. As I watched them lay out a 10.5-metre ladder, tie a line to its head and then foot it securely on the virtual riverbank. I was desperate to help. Maybe it was because I was new, but the situation drills felt totally real to me. I had a healthy imagination and I could almost see the victims the way Joe had described them. On that first morning I could see the river as well. I could almost feel the water as the ladder was raised to the vertical, extended to two-thirds its maximum length and lowered, using the line on its head, towards the far bank.

Our two situational drills turned into three, which suited me just fine, especially as my squad was given the extra task. We had a couple of battered-up old cars in the far corner of the ground, donations from local garages keen to curry favour. Joe led us over to them. 'Someone was under that car when the jack failed. They have been under there for half an hour and may have serious crush injuries. Deal with the car and their condition. Go.'

We used a heck of a lot of equipment and even more imagination on that one. I loved it and, while I could have gone on forever, I could hear my stomach start to rumble when the squads lined up at the end for another aggressive debrief from Joe. Bang on cue, though, we had the world's best interruption. It was Mabel with the lunch call. I could sense my eyes lighting up, but fortunately I didn't move a muscle. We all stood there, desperate for our grub, but knowing full well that the Sub-O had to get to the end of his rant and dismiss us before we got it. No surprise that a whole lifetime seemed to go by before we got the one-word bark we were waiting for: 'Dismiss!'

Within seconds we'd got inside the appliance room. Fire kit was never allowed upstairs so we took it off next to the machines and stowed it ready for a shout. Then we thundered up the stairs to the mess room like a herd of cattle. I swear that if anyone had stumbled that day they'd have been trampled alive. When food was on the hatch it really was survival of the fittest – and being able to take the stairs three at a time meant I managed to get close to the head of the pack. 'That's the kind of customer we like,' Betty said, seeing me cross the mess room floor at a cracking pace. She was holding a frying pan the size of a dustbin lid. After the massive mixed grill last week they'd got gammon steaks for us today. 'This is one of my favourite meals, Betty,' I said.

'Well, if that's the case then you'll be wanting to take this plate. It's got the most on it,' she said, pointing to a particularly fat steak on the second row. I was about to pick it up when Mabel moved forward and added another shovelful of chips on to it. Both ladies smiled indulgently as I plunged my thumb underneath the chips and carried the plate across to what had become my seat, at my table, beside my window. I was smiling just as widely when I sat down. Mabel and Betty were brilliant. I was starting to feel as if I belonged.

'I'm sweating like a backin' pig and those tunics scratch like a bear's arse' was Arfer's opening gambit once we'd shovelled most of our first helpings of food down our necks.

'I'm sweating so much it's like I've wet myself,' agreed Charlie cheerfully.

He wasn't the only one. The tunics were like donkey jackets. They were crazy things to have been wearing on a hot mid-June morning. There had been as much steam rising from them when we flung them off in the appliance room as there was coming off our dinners. We had silk scarves to wear round our necks so as to stop the chaffing from the sweat. I'd rung mine out and seen a little puddle form on the floor beside all my kit.

'Seconds, gentlemen!' Mabel announced.

I was first in line again. 'You won't be a string bean for much longer if you keep this up. That's good,' Betty said approvingly as she piled up my plate once more. She was wearing thick red lipstick, as usual, but while she'd been cooking she must have been rubbing her face with her hand. I let myself smile, just a touch, as I realised I'd seen through one of the many riddles of the station. Until now I'd thought Betty had the biggest, fattest lips I'd ever seen. Now I realised she had the thinnest. The bright red lipstick was her camouflage. She must paint it on every morning. She mustn't realise how quickly it got wiped away in the heat of the kitchen.

Back at our table we'd finished our seconds and were waiting for pudding. 'Do we ever do the scenario drills for real and cut up any cars?' I asked Arfer. We'd done a bit of that in training and I defy any eighteen-year-old lad not to ache to do it again.

'We do when we go down to the scrap yard over in Astley. They put some bombed-out cars aside for us. We use all the kit on them, the Cengar saws, the zip guns, all of it. It's brilliant.'

'When are we going to be doing it next?'

Arfer shrugged. 'We don't do it all that often. Maybe every month or so. It's a good day out. It's worth it.'

He didn't need to sell the idea to me. I could hardly wait.

I was one of the first in line for dessert when Mabel gave the call. And I got the fullest bowl of them all when Betty tipped me the wink and told me which one to choose. All was well in the world as I sat down with my mug of tea ten minutes later. At least that's what I thought.

'So, you enjoyed those drills, jockey?' a voice asked me. Not a particularly friendly voice, I thought, as I turned around. One of the old-timers was standing by my chair. He had a cigarette in his mouth, an angry expression on his face and I wasn't sure of his name. Arfer, Woody and Charlie were all heading over to the armchairs. I was on my own.

'I loved them. I like drills,' I said warily.

'Well, the first ones were bullshit. They were bullshit drills for bullshit mornings.'

I was still trying to remember who this man was. Maybe I didn't know. All my introductions had been pretty informal. I'd seen him before. He'd not been at the pub fire but he had been on my first shout up at the farm. He'd been in the second squad this morning. He sat two tables down at lunch. Was he a Mark or a Martin? And what the hell was he so pissed off about?

'We're only going to be doing those bullshit drills because of you,' he continued. His voice was low but direct. 'We can do them in our sleep. We don't need to be shown how to lay out a line or carry a light portable pump. We don't need to practise them every bleeding day or to work for three hours when we could normally do it in two. It's you the Sub-O is watching. He's reporting back to the Station Officer. They need to know that you're good enough. Everyone needs to find out if they can rely on you in an emergency.'

He drew on his cigarette and exhaled very slowly. All I had to breathe was his smoke. I forced myself not to cough.

'You can rely on me in an emergency,' I said firmly.

'Well, you'd better prove it. The SO will be running the drills himself one day soon. If you screw up then we'll all be doing punishment drills for the rest of the effing summer. None of us wants to do bullshit drills every morning. Just remember that and don't screw up,' he said. He didn't blink once as he took another long drag on his cigarette. Then he walked away.

I was more than ready for the drills the next day. I'd found out that my new heavy-smoking friend was called Martin. I wanted to prove to him that I could handle anything the Sub-O could throw at me. I would not be getting a bad report and I would not be dragging the rest of the watch down. But, as it happened, we didn't do any drills that day. We'd paraded and seen Green Watch get dismissed and disappear. We'd got out of uniform and into our overalls. The others had gone upstairs while I'd done the daily checks on the appliances. I'd got the last, stewed cup of tea from the pot when I went upstairs at the end of everyone's tea break and I was looking through the *Daily Mirror* when the call came in. The word 'Attention!' Then that two-tone warning sound. It cuts through you. I was on the pole and on my way to the engine before I realised I'd even moved. I don't remember putting down my tea. I've no idea if I left the paper on the table or dropped it on the floor. I was caught up in the wave of activity. We had a call to answer. Something had happened on a farm out near Preston Gubbals.

'It's a while since we've been up near there,' Charlie said as we waited for John to get back from the watch room with more information. 'North on the A49. Then it's just a question of finding the farm. They're not well sign-posted up there. Hopefully it's one of the ones we know.'

'So what is it?' Arfer asked when John was back.

'Someone's gone and fallen into a grain silo,' he said. It's terrible, but my first instinct was almost to laugh. I was so wound up and it sounded such a crazy, comic thing to happen. I could see from Arfer's face that he thought the same.

'They could suffocate or they could choke to death,' John said, bringing us all up short.

Arfer acknowledged the seriousness of the task with a brief nod as he finished rolling up the appliance room doors. He jumped on to the engine as we roared out towards the main road. 'So who is it that's fallen in? Is it the farmer or some dozy farmhand?' he asked the boss, not quite ready to give up on the joke.

John looked across at him grimly. 'It's neither,' he said. 'It's the farmer's son. He's eight years old.'

9

Against the Grain

'If you can drown in an inch of water then you can drown in a sea of grain,' Arfer muttered as we headed out of the station. 'It's a lie that drowning is a peaceful way to go. It's painful as heck. And that's in water. Doesn't bear thinking about what it would be like to drown in grain.'

'Well, then, don't think about it. And don't talk about it either. It's a little kid we're looking out for today. Let's just focus on that and watch what we say, right?' Arfer yelled back at him from the front of the engine.

We'd made it on to the main road and were heading towards Whitchurch when we hit a problem. A car had broken down on the Ditherington Road. Traffic was building up all around it – and we only got through because two elderly members of the public guided half a dozen cars on to the pavements and out of our way. Charlie gave a hoot of thanks on the horn and one of the men, who looked to be about seventy, stood tall and saluted as we passed.

We hugged the railway line as we passed the iron-grey stones of Battlefield church and the site of the Battle of Shrewsbury in 1403. Then we climbed up towards the North Shropshire Plain. Maybe it was the cooler temperatures but I wasn't feeling remotely travel sick that day. For a moment I allowed myself to hope that I'd kicked the problem for life. I twisted around and looked ahead of us. Charlie had switched the windscreen wipers on and he was accelerating strongly as we headed over the crest of Upper Battlefield. A scattering of low escarpments were dotted around the plain on both sides of us now. To the west a new front of heavy grey clouds was piling in. The wind had really picked up as well and the last few weeks of good weather suddenly seemed a distant memory. A few lone trees were swaying wildly out at the corners of the fields. This was not a good day to be waiting desperately for help from inside a vast, dark, metal drum, I thought. Especially if you're just eight years old.

'It's the third track on your right just out of the village. It's about two miles up the road from there. We're just a matter of minutes away now,' John called out to Charlie, folding down a slightly tired-looking Ordnance Survey map in the front of the cab. 'I can picture the farm. There's no gates, nothing complicated. We'll be fine.'

Those last few minutes felt as if they stretched into forever as we barrelled around the last country corners and Charlie blasted the horn to get all obstacles out of our way. We jumped out of the engine on the edge of a big, modern-looking farmyard. A corrugated-iron barn and a couple of lean-to buildings were to our right, surrounded by rusting farm machinery, tools, equipment, tractors, old cars on bricks and even a couple of ancient grounded caravans. To our left were three vast metal grain silos. They all had metal ladders running up the outsides – and an unshaven, dark-haired man in a long green waterproof jacket and jeans was jumping off the bottom rungs of the middle one as we approached.

'I'm Gareth. I'm his dad. I've tried to get a rope to him but he can't grab it. Every time he moves he sinks even further into the grain. It's hard to see him because there's no light down there. But he's almost up to his chest already. It's dusty as hell, too. Breathing's getting harder all the time. He's in a bad way.'

'How full is the silo?' John asked.

'Two-thirds full. He must be about there. Just above the logo,' the dad said, pointing upwards.

'And how did he get in?'

'There's an access hatch at the top. Russell was up there, mucking about with one of his mates. He's over there,' the dad said, looking around. A terrified, pale-looking and tear-stained face peeped out from the shelter of the barn door. The mate could only be six or seven, I thought. He was shivering in the cold. I made a note to go and find him and give him a coat or something once we'd got the job done. This had to be the worst day of his life so far. 'They shouldn't have been up there at all, but that's for another day. Somehow they got the hatch open and Russell fell in,' his dad finished.

I stood back to take a better look at the silo. It was cylindrical, about fifty feet high and had a one-foot square shoot at the bottom from where the grain could be funnelled into sacks or crushed in the milling machine. I felt a shiver, suddenly, as I imagined the damage a machine like that could do if you ended up in it by mistake.

'I'm going to take a look and have a word with the little lad. It's Russell, you say?' Joe asked, grabbing the first slick, wet rungs of the ladder and pulling himself up fast. Simon was hard on his heels, carrying two coils of rope and a torch. The rain was beginning to come down hard now, as the rest of us waited and tried to hear what was being said. 'The Fire Brigade's here, my name's John. I'm the man in charge and I'm going to get you out of there in two shakes of a rat's tail,' John shouted down the hatch. 'Can you give me a shout and tell me that you're OK?'

A few muffled words echoed through the metal.

'Can you see anything down there, son?'

We could hear a muffled negative.

'Well, I'm going to shine a torch on you now to see what's what. Don't panic, it's nothing to be afraid of and try not to move, son. The more you move the worse it's going to feel. Just stay still and we'll have this sorted in no time.'

After a short investigation Simon stayed up at the hatch to

keep the kid talking while John headed back down to talk to the dad.

'He's a brave boy. There's a lot of dust down there, a hell of a lot, so I could barely see him, even with the torch. I'd also say that the grain's getting well up his chest now. It's like quicksand. It can creep up on you, dragging you down. We need to get a rope on him fast.'

Our first attempt was with a lowering line. It did OK. The lad managed to get one of the built-in loops around the last part of his chest before he sank too low beneath the surface of the grain. The rope would hold him steady. Well, that was the plan.

'Can't we pull him out with it?' I asked Caddie as the others got the kit we needed off the engine.

'There aren't any anchor points up there. We canna get a pulley set up. All we can do is hold him where he is and stop things getting worse.'

'So what are we going to do?'

'We're gonna to listen to the boss,' Caddie said. I turned around. John was walking around the silo, looking it up and down. He yelled up and told Simon to stay where he was. Then he turned to the farmer. 'The best thing to do is to cut a hole in the side of the silo. We'll cut it just below where the boy is, then he can flow out with the top layer of grain. Are you all right with that, sir?' John asked. The cut would mean putting the silo out of action for some time, as well as wasting a heck of a lot of grain. I suppose there was always a chance the farmer might object.

'Do whatever you need,' the man said, quick as a flash.

John gave us the nod. We rushed to the engine to get the ladders and tools. Simon was shouting the good news to the boy from the top of the silo. We'd have him out in no time. Or at least that's what we thought.

*

'This is it. We cut it right here.' John was next to Simon on the ladders marking out the side of the silo. They'd got the zip gun up there with them, a sort of giant tin opener operated by compressed air. The idea was to cut three sides of a three-foot square panel – the top horizontal side and the two vertical edges. We could then pull it out from the top. The grain would start to flow and the boy could coast along on top of it towards freedom. And as we were folding it on the bottom edge he wouldn't end up being dragged over a raw, jagged edge.

Simon began the first cut at the top right-hand corner of our square. That's when we realised we had a problem. Zip guns aren't exactly stealth weapons. They make a lot of noise and even more vibration. The boy was terrified of both.

His screams were somehow loud enough to penetrate the silo walls and rise above the rain and the sound of the saw. Simon clicked it off so that we could listen.

'It's coming down on me! It's falling in on me!' we could hear the lad cry out through gulping tears and desperate gasps for air.

'Russell, lad, don't panic, it's just the sound of the saw we're using to get you out of there. It's not going to hurt you. It won't come near you. It's just cutting a hole in the silo like I told you before.'

'I dunna care. It's not the saw I care about it's the grain!' the lad called out in reply.

'What about the grain, son?'

'It's up to my chin.'

'We need a shroud,' Caddie said firmly as we all regrouped on the ground and tried to find a solution. 'Something to put over his head to stop the grain coming any further up his face.'

'What do you mean by a shroud?'

Caddie brushed the question away. His eyes were darting around the rain-swept farmyard. My own mind was working overtime, trying to work out what might help and what we should do. Caddie beat me to it. 'Hey, jockey, empty out that tea chest and fetch it over here,' he told me, pointing to a wooden box half buried in a pile of rubbish alongside the barn. I fetched it and Caddie tested its sides for strength. 'Bash the bottom of it out,' he said. 'Keep the edges smooth.' He held it up when I'd done so. 'It's gonna work,' he said. 'But it's not gonna be easy.'

We had a bit of a huddle, talked through our new tactics and watched as Caddie tied a line around himself. We couldn't get a pulley at the top of the silo to drag the boy up, but we could feed the rope to lower Caddie down. He was going to do a *Mission: Impossible* thing holding the tea chest. He'd suspend it over the kid's head then push it into the grain. 'It will keep you safe, pal. It will stop the grain moving around and falling in on you. It's gonna be like a shield,' Caddie shouted out as we edged him down to do the job. When he yelled up that all was well we got ready. On Joe's signal Simon got the zip gun working again. Inch by inch he cut out the three sides of the square. A few streams of grain and kernels began to leak out into the gloomy afternoon air when he got to the final cut. Then, when the saw had been lowered down to the ground, he got a wrench in at the top edge and began to peel the panel out. Nothing happened straight away, but after a few more pulls it began to jolt free. Simon almost disappeared behind a waterfall of grain and a huge cloud of dust.

'I'm sinking! Help me!' the kid cried from inside the silo.

'You're safe, lad, you're behind your shield and the grain won't come in on you,' Caddie told him from above. 'Keep going, Simon. Get us out of here.'

The waterfall became an avalanche. The cloud of dust became a fog. But through both we could finally see a tea chest, a fireman and a filthy, frightened eight-year-old boy. We had two ladders up against the silo at this point. Simon grabbed the lad and carried him down one of them.

I didn't see dad and son being reunited because, out of the corner of my eye, I suddenly spotted the other kid step fearfully out of the barn. He hesitated, frozen in indecision. It was as if part of him was terrified he would be in trouble if he showed himself, but part of him needed to be absolutely sure that his friend was all right. I headed over to him. He darted back into the shadows and disappeared. 'Don't worry, it's OK, I'm not going to hurt you,' I said, suddenly aware how tall I was and how terrifying I must have looked in all my kit. I crouched down by the barn door. 'Come on out. You can sit in the fire engine if you want. It'll get you warm. You can wear my helmet, too, if you fancy.' After a couple more promises he finally showed himself. His teeth were chattering. I couldn't decide if that was nerves or cold. He was looking past me, over across the muddy farmyard and at all the wasted grain, the ruined metal and the devastation this rescue had caused. 'I bet you'd rather be at school than looking at that,' I said after a while. 'Just promise me you won't climb up something like that again, eh?' He promised me, standing tall, the most serious-looking six-year-old I'd ever seen. And when I stood up he followed me out to join the others.

The farmer invited us all over to the farmhouse to get warm and dry. 'Hang your jackets up anywhere you want. We dunna stand on ceremony in this part of Shropshire,' he said in a huge boot room at the back of the house. Then he led us into an equally vast kitchen with loads of chairs and a table big enough for ping-pong. 'I'm just going to call this little lad's mam,' he said, indicating my six-year-old best friend who was sticking to me like glue.

'I ripped my shirt. My mam's going to kill me,' the lad said.

'Well, think on about the state of my grain silo. I might kill you first,' the farmer said. Then he gave the lad a good-natured whack over the head. 'No one's killing anyone, pal. You go and help yourself to a slice of cake from next door,' he said. Then he turned to us and pointed where the lad had gone. 'The larder's through there. If you can find anything just grab it and eat it. I'll be back in a minute to help. My wife's at work till three. She does meals down at the pub in Grinshill. She loves cooking. She'll kick herself, missing the chance to make a spread for all of you.'

The larder was like an Aladdin's cave of food. 'If you can find anything just grab it' the man had said, as if it might be a challenge. The real trick was knowing what not to choose. There were cold meats stacked up on huge ceramic dishes. There were about four loaves of what looked like freshly made bread – and each loaf was the size of a portable TV. There were dozens of jars of home-made jams and honey. Other jars were full of what looked like roasted tomatoes, peppers and all sorts of other goodies. There were fresh eggs, cheese and enough fruit and veg for a small stall. There was a huge ceramic jar full of home-made biscuits and, best of all, three-quarters of a big, fat Victoria sponge cake on an old-fashioned glass stand.

'Jockey, the man said take anything, not take everything,' John said with a smile as I came out of the room with a loaf, a plate of carved meat and a brick-sized block of cheese.

'There's a lot more where this came from. This is nothing,' I told him.

When he'd made his phone call, the farmer put a kettle on the Aga. 'Your mam's coming straight over,' he told his son's friend. Then he turned to us. 'She's a decent cook as well. She'll be able to find you something to eat if you have any problems.'

We were hacking into the bread and drinking tea when the lad's mother arrived. She gave him a hug and a bit of a telling off. Then she, too, turned to us. 'Has he left you to fend for yourselves? Typical farmer. Janet would be very upset if you didn't get at least something to eat after all you've done. It's lunchtime. Give me a few minutes and I'll rustle you all up some nice cheesy omelettes. Is it too late for some crispy bacon sandwiches?'

Nearly a dozen men assured her that it was never too late for crispy bacon sandwiches.

The clouds had lifted a little by the time we left the farm. We barrelled down the first set of farm tracks towards the village and the main road. If I was sick today I'd at least be able to blame it on overeating, not on the travel, I thought.

'So, who votes to sack Mabel and Betty and get those two in to cook for us instead?' Arfer asked as we headed south.

'That's a bit like saying who votes for another world war,' John pointed out. 'If you want to give Mabel and Betty their cards then you'll have to tell them. And I don't think you're man enough for that.'

'No one's man enough for that,' Arfer admitted ruefully. 'Anyway, maybe their cottage pie and their mixed grills are pretty hard to beat, when all's said and done. And I don't think anyone makes better custard.' Then he pointed out of the window. 'What pub did that man say his wife worked in? Was it that one? I'm coming here for my lunch tomorrow. And the day after that.'

My stomach gave a sudden lurch when he said this – and that had nothing to with travel sickness either. It was because I knew we could all come back here for lunch tomorrow if we wanted. Today was the last of our day shifts. Tomorrow we didn't start till six and that would bring my next big challenge. Was I ready to do my first night shift?

10

First Night

A rfer, Charlie and Woody had spent the past couple of days winding me up about the horrors of working nights. They'd done a pretty good job, to be honest. Almost every tea or meal break at least one of them would come out with a smoky story about some fresh horror that could go bump in the middle of the night. As usual, half of me was thrilled and up for the challenge of dealing with it all – while the other half was terrified that I might make a mistake and let everyone down. Looking back, it was crazy to be so spooked. There was no real reason why shouts would be tougher after dark. But the adrenaline was certainly flowing as the day watch was dismissed at 6 p.m. and the evening routine began.

'Number one crew, your drill will be to slip and pitch the 13.5-metre ladder to the third floor of the drill tower. Numbers one and three to enter with hose line consisting of three lengths, water to be delivered out of the window which faces the appliance room. Any questions?'

The drills had begun at 6.15 on the nose – barely giving us time to change out of our dress uniform and into our overalls. I was in number one crew and, as we moved towards the water tender to start the drill, I could tell that at least two people were watching me carefully. One of them, of course, was Joe, the Officer in Charge of the drill, the man who'd given us our instructions and would judge whether the crew had completed the task well enough or whether we needed to do it all again. The other pair of eyes belonged to Martin, my heavy-smoking friend from the mess room the other day. I was glad about that because I was ready for him. I didn't want him to miss a thing tonight. I was going to do all the drills as if I'd swallowed the textbook. I swore to myself that I wouldn't put a foot wrong.

An hour later I was feeling better than ever. My crew had performed perfectly. We'd even started to have some fun.

'Sorry, jockey, didn't see you there,' Arfer called out at the end of our next pump drill when a burst of ice-cold water hit me from behind. I turned and flashed a quick look at him. He was grinning broadly.

'Second time tonight. Bad luck, jockey,' one of the other jokers said a little while later when we were disconnecting the lines and I got another soaking.

Way back at training we'd been warned that jockey bashing was an occupational hazard. In some stations the new boys had raw eggs put in their boots, flour put in their helmets or walked through doors that had buckets of water balanced above them like a real-life Dennis the Menace cartoon. I'd have taken all that and more. As far as I could think, the worst form of jockey bashing had to be being ignored. If the rest of the watch couldn't be bothered to wind you up then what did that say about how you all got along? I knew I still had to prove myself in lots of ways, but at least everyone knew I could take a joke.

Still dripping wet from yet another 'accidental' hosing, I rejoined the rest of the crew on the squad line. We were dismissed after another successful drill. The second crew finished their next pump drill and we moved on to the situation drills. I stole a glance at my heavy-smoking friend. His face was quite red, I noticed. Maybe that was the real reason he hated the bread and butter drills. Maybe he wasn't quite as fit as he thought.

'Number one squad. That car has crashed into a lorry containing scaffolding. A pole has gone through the car and has pinned the driver into his seat. Your task is to secure the car and rescue the driver. Any questions?'

I put everything else out of my mind as I climbed into the truck and got ready to tackle this exercise. We took about forty-five minutes doing it, using a whole host of different cutting, lifting and rescue kit. We worked as a perfect team, sharing the loads, playing to each other's strengths, listening to each other's instructions. Our training dummy, playing the part of the car driver, was pulled out, carried to safety and left in the hands of an equally imaginary ambulance driver.

The air was starting to cool as we ran back towards the squad line. It was about half past eight, there'd probably be something good on the telly at home but there was no way I'd have swapped the station for a seat on the sofa at home. Nor would I have chosen to do anything else. My old school friends might have been boozing and having a laugh at a pub overlooking the river. I wouldn't have swapped with them either. I certainly wouldn't have swapped with a job in a factory or an office. Yes, this first night shift was spooking me out a bit. But it was always going to be better than the nine to five.

The second squad were finishing their grey-matter drill when we got the announcement we'd all been waiting for. 'Food on the hatch!' came the call from the mess room. Down on the drill yard twelve hungry men itched to be dismissed. When Joe finally gave the word there was the now familiar rumble of boots as we broke ranks, left our kit next to the appliances then headed up towards the mess room in our overalls. I was right at the front of the pack as usual and I had a particularly wide smile on my face – because this was going to be my second big meal of the night.

Back at home my mum had refused to believe that firemen knew how to cook. She certainly couldn't get her head around the fact that we might cook for each other. So at five o'clock she'd served up my favourite tea – a huge potato pie with diced beef, onions and carrots – to make sure I'd have enough energy to survive the night. Less than four hours later I was sitting down with a huge plate of Ben's fish pie with cheese sauce and vegetables. Not a bad result, all told, I thought to myself as I tucked in. And I have to say that Ben's pie was bloody brilliant. He was one of the most practical men on the watch. Ex-army, probably in his late forties, he had a huge handlebar moustache, armfuls of tattoos and I'd barely heard him speak. Before I joined the watch I'd have laughed if you'd told me that a gruff, silent man like that would also have been a great cook. Now I was starting to realise that everyone on the watch had hidden talents. People who are quiet in the mess room can sometimes take control when we're on a shout. I glanced over at Howard on the next table. He was keeping himself to himself, as usual. I'd barely heard him speak since I'd joined either – but I remembered how forcefully he'd kept the onlookers back at the pub fire. Then there was Andy, sitting directly across the room from me. He was one of the jokers who always seemed to be taking short cuts and pushing the line with the boss on the drills. But I'd seen him follow orders without question when we'd helped the old couple rescue their dog.

I headed back to the hatch with everyone else for seconds.

'I suppose we have to leave it all if we get a shout during dinner,' I said when we were back at the table.

'Yeah, but we can finish it up when we get back,' said Charlie. 'See the marker pen over there?' He pointed towards the dartboard. 'Write your name on your plate and whoever's left behind in the watch office will line them all up in the hot box while we're gone.'

If Ben's fish pie was good then his rhubarb crumble and custard was even better. It was bursting with flavour. The crumble was the tastiest I'd ever eaten. The custard was smoother than Betty's (though I would never have dared tell her). The whole thing was such a funny surprise. If Ben had come out of the kitchen on a unicycle I couldn't have been more shocked by his hidden talents.

Everyone on my table was in a great mood that night. Arfer was telling a long, funny story about lancing someone's boil on ship. 'I was head chef on a merchant navy ship,' he began. Charlie and Woody both rolled their eyes.

'Was that before or after you cured the common cold and won your gold medal doing the triple jump in Montreal?' Woody asked.

'Backin' cheek. Like I say, I was head chef in the navy. The ship's doctor was collecting his grub and he told me he had a patient with the biggest boil on his neck that he'd ever seen. The doc said he was dreading having to lance it.'

'Don't tell us. You did it instead,' said Woody.

'Course I did. I offered my services and the doc accepted. I said that if the patient was in the sick bay when my shift ended I'd head down there and do the business. "I'm an expert with knives, y' know. It'll be a backin' walk in the park for someone like me," I said to the doc.'

'So how did it go?' I asked, genuinely interested.

'It was a backin' nightmare. I was expecting something the size of a golf ball. It was bigger than a tennis ball. But I bust it for him. Blood and puss went all over the shop. But the doc was a good pal of mine. I even helped clean up.'

I didn't really want to dwell on that aspect of the story, especially over dinner. 'So when were you in the navy, Arfer?' I asked, trying to bring the story on to less gruesome territory.

'Before you were backin' born, mate,' he said. 'Twenty, thirty years ago. I played football for Millwall before that. I did a couple of good years there. I've been a lorry driver, I've been a referee, a milkman, a photographer.'

'And that makes you, what, a hundred and five years old?' Woody interrupted, trying to keep a straight face.

'More like a hundred and twenty,' said Charlie, with one of his characteristic giggles.

'Backin' cheek,' Arfer said again, happily slurping up the last of his crumble. 'If either of you two had ever done a proper day's work in your lives you'd be less of a liability on the watch today.' He turned to me. 'I don't suppose you've got any skills yourself?' he asked.

I was more than happy to answer that one. I'd never lanced a boil on a warship and I'd not done any of my jobs for very long. But in the six-month gap between getting accepted by the Fire Brigade and starting my training I'd certainly been busy. I'd read gas meters, been a postie, bashed out wooden pallets in a factory, driven a tractor, worked on a farm out at Haughmond Hill, done clerical work in an office back in the middle of Shrewsbury – I finished my list and looked up. Even Arfer looked impressed.

'Backin' hell, mate, you should be able to come up with a decent spiv number out of that lot.'

I smiled. I'd finally cracked the code and realised that a spiv number was a second job – and that back then almost everyone on the watch had at least one of them. Arfer ran a furniture removal business with George, the other Londoner on the watch. Charlie and Woody both worked as painters and decorators. The others were just as busy on their days off. It seemed that at any given moment the mess room could have rustled up a part-time plumber, electrician, furniture restorer, plasterer and mechanic. As well as a phenomenally good pie, crumble and custard maker in Ben, of course. I tried to think what I could do. I loved cars. I loved being outdoors so I'd really enjoyed my time out on the farm. But I wasn't short of cash back then. I was a teenager who lived at home so I hardly needed a second wage. Arfer and the others would probably have laughed their heads off if I'd have told them. But in truth if my main job was being a fireman then my ideal spiv number was simple – it would be being a fireman.

*

We lined up for seconds. We washed them down with tea and had a quick smoke. Then, while the officers sat talking at their top table, the rest of us headed into the kitchen to do the washing up. The whole thing was a bit of a scrum. And if anything went wrong it was clear where the blame would lie. 'If anything is not sparkling clean or if anything's put in the wrong place Mabel will be on the warpath tomorrow morning. And she'll know it was your fault, jockey. Even if it wasn't,' Charlie told me with relish.

'And if you break a plate Betty will break your face,' added one of the old hands who sat over at the furthest table from us. 'They do judo down at the WI nowadays, and I'm pretty certain she's a black belt.' I didn't fancy finding out whether or not this was a joke so I gave a sigh of relief when the last bits of china were put away and we began washing the cutlery. As usual I ended up wetter than everyone else. If water was going to be spilt on anyone it was going to be spilt on me. If anyone's head was going to take a hit when someone shook out a tea towel it was going to be mine. 'Sorry, jockey, I didn't see you there,' Woody said several times, just as he had done out on the drills.

Other jokes came thick and fast. 'This is Mabel's favourite crystal jug. Catch, jockey!' said Arfer at one point, throwing the jug at me and making my heart miss a beat before I realised it was made of plastic.

Ben emptied the bins after the last of the pans was washed, dried and put exactly where Mabel would expect to find it the next day. Then Arfer handed me a bucket of cloths and a mop. 'Do us proud, pal. Remember it's your funeral if it's not perfect,' he said, slapping me on the back and leaving me to it.

I spent almost half an hour tidying the kitchen. Every time I thought I'd got a surface clean enough, either Mabel's or Betty's face would loom up in my imagination and I'd go back and polish it one more time. At one point Ben came back to inspect my work. I supposed he was worried about getting some of the blame if the room was left in a bad state. 'Not bad. But don't let Betty's spectacles fool you. She can spot grime from twenty yards.'

Later on I stood by one of the kitchen windows and gazed out as the rest of the watch milled around next door. They all seemed to know exactly what they were doing and where they were going. I watched the headlights from a few cars as they lit up the main road outside. They danced with the red brake lights going the other way. The world outside was quiet and it somehow seemed a long way away. We were in a bubble at the station – but I knew we weren't cut off from reality. If I leaned out of the window and looked over to my right I'd see the watch room, almost directly below the far corner of the mess room. One of the officers was down there now. For all the joking around up here, we were all ready for action if he got a call. And at any moment he might. I wondered, suddenly, how on earth we were expected to sleep.

The sound of pints being pulled drew me out of the kitchen and back into the mess room. Pete had pulled up the hatch and opened the bar. He looked to have three different bitters on tap, a couple of lagers, a fridge full of cans and a shelf full of spirits. I felt a bit like a child in a sweet shop. I was only just old enough to be allowed into pubs. Now I had my very own pub open at work. It was just brilliant. It was also cheap as anything.

'It's sixty pence for a pint, young man, prices for the spirits are on the blackboard up there. Nothing's much more than eighty pence, we're not out to take all your wages from you,' Pete said. He'd served the first half-dozen or so people and was settling back on a bar stool with a copy of *Exchange & Mart*. I asked for a pint and a packet of peanuts – and we all got to see a few more inches of the topless woman when the bag had been removed from the board.

I carried my drink over towards the armchairs where most of

the other drinkers were talking. I knew that the only members of the watch who really had to pay attention to what they drank were the night's engine drivers. They weren't supposed to have more than a few pints when they were on duty, though judging by the speed Ben downed the one in front of him I'd have guessed he'd get to that point in, oh, ten minutes. It seemed strange that this amount of drinking was acceptable, and twelve years later it had completely stopped, but for the time being the atmosphere was just like a working man's club.

'Remember that time the Chief Fire Officer came in?' Arfer was saying just after sinking his first pint in little more than one go.

The CFO was the most senior member of the Fire Brigade in the county. He had the power to hire and fire any of us. I sat up a little straighter at the mention of his name.

'He only went and accused me of having had eight pints,' Woody explained, sounding most aggrieved. 'I told him I'd only had six. So he bought me my seventh and told us all to have a good night. He's a good man, the Chief.'

What looked like a very well established canasta school began just across the other side of the room from us. Woody had joined three of the old hands there. They were all hunched over an octagonal green baize card table, flicking their lighters and drawing deeply on their first few cigarettes of the night. In the far corner of the room, underneath a poster of Cheryl Ladd of the TV series *Charlie's Angels*, I watched Caddie fill and light his pipe. The mess room was full of smoke within minutes. I was hoping someone on the watch might be up for a game of darts, but at this rate we'd struggle to see the board.

I sat down as Howard turned on the TV. *Blankety Blank* was on and the first face we saw on the screen was that of Lorraine Chase. 'No, mate, Luton Airport,' everyone shouted out. Next up was Keith Harris with Orville so everyone started talking in stupid duck voices. I loved it and I was settling down for a real laugh of a night when John strode over. I recognised the look on his face. It was the same one he'd had when he'd caught me whistling in the kit room. I stood up, without being asked. When he spoke he didn't shout, as I'd expected. Instead his voice barely rose above a whisper. I had to lean forward and strain to hear him. It was far more effective. 'Jockey, this is not a youth club and you're not paid to loaf around watching television' was the gist of it. I can't believe many of the others were able to hear what he was saying but I could sense them all smirking. 'Get down to the appliance room now. There's work to be done,' he concluded.

I was given the last of my instructions when we got downstairs. 'I want this whole room and everything in it gleaming. I want the vehicle inventories checked. I want the breathing apparatus compressor checked. I want the room swept properly and I want the drive outside swept even better. Get to it.' I got to it. And it wasn't so bad, to be honest. I'd have liked a bit of music but it was OK without. I was in my own little world. I was cut off from the others, but I still felt connected. And I was clear about what I was supposed to be doing.

'So, enjoying yourself, jockey?' About an hour had passed when a familiar voice echoed round the metal walls and the concrete floors of the appliance room. It was rich, deep and low. It was Caddie. I jumped slightly, though I tried to pretend I hadn't.

'I'm OK, thank you,' I replied.

Caddie wandered slowly around the room and all the appliances. I stayed rooted to the spot, not sure if I should carry on cleaning, follow him around or what. For some reason I kept thinking back to what I'd said to him in the back of the engine on the way to the pub fire. Could that really have been just a week ago? It felt like a lifetime. And I still felt I needed to at least try to apologise for it, or explain why I'd said it. So should I do so now?

'You wanna get these really clean or the boss will be after you,' he said, interrupting my thoughts and pointing to the wheel arches. 'He notices them. And there's no point cleaning the locker doors from the outside and not opening them up and sweeping out the insides like this.' I fell naturally into step alongside him at that point. He led me around each of the vehicles. When he'd finished talking about how to clean and care for them he began again, talking for ten or fifteen minutes about all the kit they carried. 'You wanna always take a fireman's axe into a breathing apparatus job because you never know when you're gonna need one,' he said as we looked at everyone else's piles of equipment. He told me about a few times he'd needed an axe, then took a few steps further round the engine and began telling a story about knots. 'Take the rabbit up the 'ole, round the tree then back down the 'ole and it's always gonna be right,' he said, demonstrating a perfect bowline. We moved on a bit then stopped so he could tell another story or give a few nuggets of practical advice. I lapped up every word.

After one last tale he looked at his watch and headed for the appliance room door. I decided it was now or never for my belated apology. I went for it. 'I'm sorry for what I said on the way to the White Horse fire the other day,' I blurted out like a little kid. 'I know fire's not a game.'

Caddie turned back from the doorway. He didn't say anything for what felt like forever. Then he really surprised me. He told me a joke. 'Have you heard the one about the two bulls in the field?' he began. 'There's a young one and an old one. One day a whole herd of cows were moved into the field next to them. "I say we run in there and shag one of them," said the young bull. "I say we walk in there and shag them all," said the old one.' Caddie looked at me carefully. 'You're the young bull, jockey. Don't be in too much of a hurry. All this kit we've just looked at can make you feel invincible. But you're not. We needed a tea crate in the grain silo, remember? We didn't have that on any of the engines and I'll warrant they didn't mention tea chests at your training school either. However good all this looks, we've still only got a limited number of tools for an unlimited number of situations. Yes, you need to think and decide what to do fast. But while you get going on Plan A you should always be thinking of a Plan B. Experience is one thing you can't buy in a shop, no matter how much money you've got. But you'll get it, jockey. If you keep your head down and your eyes open you'll get it.'

I thanked him quietly. He shrugged it away.

'If you've ever got any questions just ask me. And the boss says you can come back upstairs at midnight,' he said. Then he pointed to a random part of the fire truck, told me I'd missed a bit and walked away.

The smoke was even thicker when I got back to the mess room just after midnight. The canasta players didn't look to have moved, though a lot more beer glasses were now lined up on the table. Woody was holding a pint in one hand and his cards in the other. He had the tail end of a roll-up in the corner of his mouth. I watched him take the final draw on it. He leaned back in his chair, held his head back so that he was looking up at the grimy Artex ceiling panels. He breathed in, long and hard. He sat still as a statue for what seemed like forever. Then the smoke finally fanned out of his mouth and nose, almost hiding his face and hair. Only then did he move. He jerked forward fast. He took the cigarette out of his mouth with his right hand and stubbed it out in the nearest ashtray. Then he reached out and grabbed a card from the player opposite. 'I've been waiting for that,' he said, lighting up another cigarette the moment the words had left his mouth.

Charlie was stretched out across two of the armchairs balancing an empty pint glass on its arm. Arfer was dozing on the next one across. The other seats were all pretty much occupied. Discarded copies of the *Daily Mirror*, the *Sun*, *Exchange & Mart* and various car and fishing magazines were carpeting the floor. In the far corner Pete was still manning the bar and Caddie was back in his usual spot alongside it, smoking away on his pipe. A couple of the old hands were getting a bit loud playing darts but no one looked to have touched the pool table. I picked up a magazine and pulled out a dining chair by the window. I sat down and opened it, then I tried to look beyond it and do a surreptitious head count. Had anyone gone to bed yet or were we all still here? The room was full. Pretty much the whole watch was happily sitting or lying around. I seemed to be the only one who was trying not to yawn, though that might have been nerves rather than tiredness. Either way, I knew I couldn't be the first to go to bed. Like everything else in the job I was sure there must be a pecking order about this. I guessed that early nights were seen as signs of weakness and of being a wuss. As the jockey, I knew I couldn't risk being branded with either label. I tried to get a bit more comfortable on my dining chair. I'd have to sit there reading about the new Vauxhall Chevette till the bitter end.

It was just after half past one when Charlie called me over. A few of the others had finally headed off for bed and there was room on the sofas. I put my magazine down and walked over, grateful for the company. I soon regretted it. Charlie, Woody and a couple of the other night owls had decided to have one more go at spooking me out. They were in competition to try and come up with the most shocking night-shift story. I sat there as they relayed bloodcurdling descriptions of midnight or early hours' calls. They revelled in reliving all the real-life ghost stories, all the blood and gore they'd dealt with. 'So, you ever seen anything like that?' Woody asked when he'd finished a suicide story about cutting a man's heavily decomposed body down from a beam in an isolated country cottage.

'I want to go and see *Friday the 13th* at the pictures. I read about it in the paper,' I offered lamely.

'That won't be anything like the real thing. In real life you don't just see dead bodies. You smell them. Even blood smells, especially when it's fresh. Sleep well,' Woody said laughing loudly and slapping me firmly on the back as he disappeared next door.

11

Little and Large

W here we all slept depended on who we were and what we were doing. Someone had to be in the watch room at all times in case a call came through. Tonight it was George, one of the hard-man old hands I'd not yet properly spoken to. He got to doze on a pull-out bed in the corner of the room. As Station Officer, John had his own room upstairs at the back of the station near the pole. That was a luxury, though in truth it looked a bit like a prison cell. It had a low, metal-framed single bed and one wooden chair. The only spare space had been taken up by a metal filing cabinet. There was one window, high in the wall, and one light, a single bulb hanging down from the ceiling. The Sub-O and the other leading firemen had their own small dormitory next door. The rest of us were in the main first-floor dormitory right alongside the mess room. Big wooden folding doors closed it off – apparently they were opened up once a year for the Christmas party so that we could squeeze more people into the station. When it wasn't being used as a dance floor the dorm contained twelve metal-framed beds. The ones against the far window were the most desirable, so I guessed I'd be waiting about twenty years before I got to test one out. The nearer you were to the mess room bar and the dartboard the noisier and the less desirable the bed became. Mine was just a thin piece of folding plywood away from the action – though apparently the real danger was inside the room.

'It's not the snores you want to worry about,' Charlie had said just before leaving the mess room at 2 a.m. 'Pete's farts could wake up a corpse.'

I took my time getting into bed about half an hour later. I'd been told that jockey bashing could get even worse at night so I was on full alert for hidden hazards. We were supplied with some bedding – a couple of rough-looking sheets and a grey woollen blanket with bright red stitching – but most people brought in their own sleeping bags or duvets. So that's what I'd done. I was well aware that they were an open invitation for mischief so I was expecting the worst when I finally crept into the dorm. It all looked OK, to be honest. My sheets were still on the bed, not hanging out of the windows in the rain. They hadn't been tucked round the bed apple-pie style to stop me getting in it either. Nor were there any unwelcome visitors. I couldn't find any dead birds under the blankets or any nettle leaves under my pillow. If they're planning anything they must be going to do it when I'm asleep, I thought. So I did my best to protect myself. I folded my clothes up neatly and put them on top of my shoes. Then I moved the pile as close to my head as possible in the hope that I'd wake up if anyone touched them. Legend had it that one jockey over in Telford had been fooled by a fake alarm on his first night shift. He'd pulled on his shirt, grabbed his trousers and pulled them on – only to find that someone had taken a pair of scissors and sliced the legs off them in the night. He'd slid down the pole in a very fetching pair of navy shorts. As if that wasn't bad enough, one of his colleagues had taken a photograph when he got to the bottom.

I lay still on my bed. The next risk was that all the others leaped up for a bit of late-night sandwich making: putting one of the other mattresses on top of me and then all piling on top till I was as flat as the proverbial pancake.

No one moved, however. Maybe they really were asleep. Maybe I was going to be OK. I opened my eyes and tried to look around in the gloom. I couldn't see much – but that didn't mean nothing was going on. The room seemed alive. A dozen men were snoring, snorting and wheezing up a storm. Would I wake them up and piss them off if I shuffled around too much getting comfortable? And how was I expected to sleep anyway? It wasn't just that all the noise was putting me off. I couldn't forget we were all here for a reason. We were on duty. Over some one thousand square miles of central Shropshire someone, some-where, could be picking up the phone and dialling 999 right now. I was wound up like a spring just thinking about it. I didn't think there was any way on earth I could sleep now that that thought was in my mind. I was wrong. I think I was dead to the world within minutes of my head hitting the pillow. For the rest of the night I'm sure I snored, wheezed, snorted and farted away with the best of them.

I woke just after 6.45 on my first morning in the station. A fair bit of snoring was still going on all around, but I could hear Dave Lee Travis on the Radio One breakfast show on the other side of the wall so I guessed some of the watch were already up. I reached gingerly for my clothes. They didn't seem to have been booby-trapped in any way. My trousers were still trousers, my shirt still had arms and neither my shoes nor my socks contained any nasty surprises. I headed to the loos down by the locker room to clean my teeth, straighten my hair and check that my shirt and shoes would pass the Station Officer's inspection. On the edge of the yard I could see some swallows nipping in and out of the trees and up towards the gables of the station. In the background I could hear some early morning motorists out on the main road. The good weather looked to be back, the sky was the palest of blues and there was already a touch of warmth on the breeze. I felt as if I was on a camping holiday as I put my toothbrush back in my locker. Then I headed back up to the mess room.

'An early riser. That's what we need in this job,' Caddie said.

He was sitting on one of the chairs doing a crossword. Two of the other old hands were on the chairs near him reading what looked to be the day's papers – we must have had a delivery at the crack of dawn. A big cloud of cigarette smoke was coming up from behind the *Shropshire Star*. It was Martin, my roll-up smoking critic from the drill ground. I looked warily at him but I was in for a bit of a surprise. 'Morning,' he said as he turned a page and nodded at me. It looked like a nod of approval. Staying up late had won me some points last night. With a bit of luck getting up early would win me a few more this morning.

The station's breakfast rule was simple. Whoever cooked dinner the night before cooked a full English at seven o'clock the morning after. 'It'll be your turn before you know it. Hope you can do more than boil an egg,' Ben said as I watched him fry what looked like a sackful of tomatoes and stack up about a yard of toast. I made a mental note to ask my mum for remedial cooking lessons as soon as possible. I'd expected to do many things in the Fire Brigade. But not to cook a two-course meal and then breakfast for sixteen.

Pete interrupted my worries. 'We'll be wanting your money soon as well,' he said. 'Grub costs £3 a week, paid in full on the nail every last night shift. No excuses, no credit. We draw up a list of what we need and if we've got a quiet afternoon a few of us will head to the Co-op on the truck to do the weekly shop.'

'We go on the fire engine?' I asked.

'Of course we do. There's plenty of storage room in the lockers at the back and if we get a shout we can answer a call from the Co-op just as easily as from here,' Pete said. I mulled it over as I took a look at the headlines in the *Mirror*. It sounded brilliant. I loved the idea of rocking up at the Co-op in a fire engine. I particularly liked the idea of walking up and down the aisles in full fireman's uniform. I was looking for a new girlfriend. If that didn't help get me one I didn't know what would.

The rest of the watch had started to appear from about 7.15 onwards. The latest we were allowed to get up was 7.30, but I'd only find that out when I somehow managed to oversleep one morning and got the bollocking of my life from the Station Officer. That first day there was a lot of scratching and stretching, a lot of moaning about Pete's lethal farts. The radio was cranked up a bit louder, there were a few tussles over the papers and almost everyone lit up a fag as they called out for coffee.

Then came the moment I'd been waiting for. 'Breakfast on the hatch!' Ben yelled out from the kitchen.

The usual stampede began. I got to the hatch pretty fast, as I always did, and I grabbed as much as I could lay my hands on. I've always liked a good breakfast – when Ben had asked me last night if I wanted the full English I'd been over the moon. Now it looked as if there was even more on offer. There was masses of cereal and toast stacked up and I tucked into all of it with a big grin on my face. Then I was back at the hatch to collect my main plate of two fried eggs, bacon, sausages, fried tomatoes, black pudding and, yes, even more toast. I couldn't believe how great it was. And I only realised everyone was looking at me as I pushed the last corner of toast around my empty plate to mop up a stray splash of egg yolk.

'What have I done now?' I asked.

'You either have the cereal or the full English, not both. What do you think this is, a blinkin' hotel?' Ben asked as the whole watch fell about laughing.

No surprise that I was put on washing-up duty after that little gaffe. I didn't mind, but I did have one question for Ben when he pushed me into the kitchen and prepared to leave me to it. 'Why did we all clean this place like our lives depended on it last night only for you to turn it into a bomb site this morning?'

'Because we could have been called out on a shout in the night. We could be called out on a shout right now. And if so we'd have left the place looking like a bomb site.'

'Which would have got us into a lot of trouble with Mabel and Betty,' I said, glad to prove I had finally got some idea of how everything worked.

Ben shook his head. 'It's not just them who'd have it in the neck for us. Our early morning cleaners will be here in about half an hour. And if you think Mabel and Betty are scary just you wait till you meet Babs and Bev.'

Babs was as skinny as a rake, which by comparison made Bev look like the size of a small car. I did a double take the first time I saw them. It's Little and Large off the telly, I thought, trying not to laugh. I couldn't work out how two people could look so alike yet so different at the self-same time. When they marched into the mess room that first morning they were both wearing identical blue overalls and they were both carrying mops like weapons. They were both almost exactly the same height, around five foot five. They both looked to be the same age, roughly their mid-forties. They both had sharp, dark eyes that didn't stay still for a moment. I'd soon find out why.

Babs had straight, jet-black hair and very pale skin. Her cheekbones looked as sharp as knives. When she was hurling insults at one of us – which tended to be most of the time – those cheekbones would gain spots of red. They were like warning lights that she was on the warpath and was ready for a fight. Bev, meanwhile, had a huge frizzy mass of pale brown hair. It burst out like an explosion. She almost always looked tired, but her hair somehow gave her life.

'Babs, Bev, we've got a toy boy here for you this morning. Fancy giving him a quick one in the cleaning cupboard?' one of the old-timers yelled out when the pair of them were halfway to the kitchen. I was thrust out into their path and was very nearly hit over the head with a mop. It was already becoming clear why Babs and Bev's eyes were constantly darting around the room. Mabel and Betty were off-limits because of their age, but a lot of the firemen felt that if any other woman came on to the station she was fair game. Women didn't need to look like Jaclyn Smith (another one from *Charlie's Angels*), though I would have pushed to the front of the queue if they had. No: the simple fact of not being a bloke was enough to get Babs and Bev attention. Dirty jokes, innuendos, dodgy banter. It never stopped.

'You showed me the ropes on my first morning, remember? Get your kit off and give the poor lad a day to remember,' came a call from the dorm room.

'I'll get your kit off and march you down to the police station as naked as the day you were born!' roared Bev. I hadn't expected her voice to be quite that loud, to be honest.

'I will if you will,' came the reply, to a hoot of laughter.

'And we all know that seeing you naked will give the whole town something to laugh about till Christmas,' said Babs. 'Now leave us be or we'll have the law over here. It's about time we saw a few real men in this place.'

The backchat continued to flow on and off for most of the next hour. It was better than any TV show I'd ever watched. I lost count of the number of times I thought one of the lads had said something unbeatably rude – only for Babs or Bev to fire back something even worse.

It was just gone eight when I was told to take another cup of tea down to Simon who had taken over in the watch room. He was a lot more talkative than George had been and I was able to ask him all sorts of questions about the way our calls came in. 'It's simple, but it works,' he told me. 'The call comes in on this phone. We need to get all the details written down fast – and written down right. The pad gives us four copies, all of which we need. We make the Tannoy call here and it works by pushing the button there,' he explained, pointing it all out. 'Then we open the hatch to the appliance room and hand the copies with all the job details to the officers in charge of each appliance.'

'It is simple,' I agreed.

'That's why it works. But it's got to be done right. You send an appliance to Roseberry Avenue when it's needed at Roseberry Crescent and lives can be lost. It's not a game, jockey.'

I slowed down a little as I headed back up to the mess room. Every day there seemed to be more to think about. I wondered when I'd ever feel I'd got it all.

In the meantime I started to count the minutes as nine o'clock approached. It wasn't that I wanted to go home or anything. Nor was I afraid of a last-minute shout. I was ready for anything and I'd have happily headed off on a job right up to the last second. But I felt that getting to the end of the shift got me past an important milestone. The first time I did anything I could tick it off my list of hurdles. I could feel a bit more secure afterwards. So I watched from the window as the first Blue Watch cars began to arrive. We all got into dress uniform to parade. Then, when we'd been dismissed, I changed back into jeans and a T-shirt and drove home with a huge smile on my face. I'd done my first night shift. I'd got through it. I'd not made a fool of myself, I'd not let anyone down. I'd even made a few new friends. Back at home, Mum and Dad had both gone to work and the house was empty. All my mates would be at work as well, so I had the whole day free to do whatever I wanted on my own. Mum had left me a note saying she'd be back at lunchtime, and did I want waking up if I'd gone back to bed? I didn't even reply. Why would I want any more sleep? I was all fired up. I had all the energy in the world.

12

Back Down to Earth

'Attention!' A week or so later that one word shot through me as the shadows were lengthening on the night shift. Immediately afterwards, the three warning tones were automatically played over the Tannoy to make doubly sure everyone had shut up and was ready to listen. That was when we were given the key details of the shout. 'Rescue pump and emergency tender to RTA, persons trapped, A458 just past Halfway House.'

It was just after seven forty-five in the evening. We had nailed a handful of drills and I was starting to wonder what Arfer was rustling up for us on his shift up in the kitchen. We never found out. When the call came in the gas turned off automatically and he slid down the pole almost as fast as we got off the drill ground and into the appliance room. On a night shift we had fifty-three seconds to get ready for the off – twenty seconds more than on days. We flung ourselves into our allotted positions. I was in my usual number five seat in the back of the fire truck. I braced my feet on the floor as the appliance room door was rolled up and we hit the road.

The emergency tender was hot on our heels as the engine raced down the Welshpool road to the RTA. I was trying to imagine what might be ahead of us. Until I'd started training I had imagined the worst car accidents came in winter when the roads were covered with ice. Up in Chorley I'd been taught that things are just as likely to go wrong in midsummer. There were the skidpans created when cloudbursts of rain hit hot, bone-dry roads, the head-on collisions caused when high-summer hedgerows stole everyone's visibility, plus all the times speeding locals who thought they knew the terrain like the back of their hands were suddenly forced to swerve around cyclists, hikers or even fellow motorists tootling along at a snail's pace on holiday.

'You ready for this, jockey?' Caddie asked, jolting me out of my thoughts as we hit a clear patch of road and the siren was temporarily stilled.

'I'm ready.'

'Well, remember we only get to see the bad ones.' His voice was low and firm. He sounded worried. I felt a jolt of fear.

'What you mean?'

'Think about it, son. If a driver can get out of a car crash on his own then he's gonna do it. If he needs a bit of help then there's almost always a member of the public who can give a hand. If it's more serious than that then the people in the ambulance will take over. They've got the training and all the medical equipment they need. If we get the call it means the medics can't get the guy out either. That means it's really serious. Remember the two bulls in the field, son, and you won't go far wrong.'

I reckoned I'd taken this on board by the time we'd arrived at the scene of the accident, but I hadn't. I didn't know that this wasn't just my first road traffic accident. It wasn't just my first night-time shout with the sirens and the lights on. It would also be my first encounter with death.

A police car, two ambulances and about half a dozen private cars were lined up on the grass verges and farm gateways just outside the beautiful village of Halfway House. A member of the public in a gleaming white T-shirt and shorts ran towards us as we approached the scene.

'We've left plenty of space free for you up there,' he said, pointing up ahead past the last of the vehicles.

Charlie took us a dozen or so extra yards to a wide grass verge just before the blind corner that must have caused the crash. Then, making sure there was room for the ambulance and police cars to get past if needed, he parked in the 'fend off' position, the rear of the engine close to the kerb, the front a few feet away from it. The man in the white T-shirt was back alongside us. He pointed forward when we jumped clear of the fire engine. But we hardly needed any help seeing the accident. Thick black tyre marks were slashed across the lane about fifty yards ahead of us. They were screaming out some awful, silent warning of horror. They ended where two cars were locked together almost as one. The first was a racing green Austin Allegro Estate, the second what looked to have been an already very battered, pale blue Vauxhall Cavalier. They must have crashed almost head-on, right on the bend of the road. They had been crushed and crumpled and were left head-to-head in an awful, vicious embrace. On impact, a mass of metal and glass and plastic must have exploded out like a short, sharp, summer rainstorm. It littered the road with tiny, shiny fragments of tragedy.

'OK, Charlie, get the tool dump ready,' John ordered. Charlie was already on it. He collected and laid out a green, reinforced salvage sheet on the ground in front of the engine, where the lights would be brightest. He and Pete began laying out the tools we were most likely to need in a road accident. Behind them Woody had got the pump working and was charging the hose reel with water. When it was done Woody pulled off the hose and dragged it towards the vehicles. We were ready for an explosion or for fire, though I could sense in everyone's faces that it was probably too late for that. It was too late for almost everything.

The rest of us walked forward as a group. Glass and plastic crunched underfoot, sounding harsh and unnaturally loud in this perfect country lane on this perfect summer's evening. Eight or ten members of the public were standing, heads bowed, just before the crash scene. None met our eyes. The police car, right up close to the accident scene, had its blue lights on, even though it was barely dark. They cast a cruel colour over the whole area. They left everyone looking washed out and empty. One woman began to cry as we passed. The man in the T-shirt and shorts put his arm around her and tried to persuade her to sit on the grass. She refused and he held her even closer.

The police officer stepped towards John when we got close to the cars. He was quite young, probably Woody or Charlie's age. He was tall and lean looking. His voice was low, his face grim. 'We're going to need your help getting the passenger out from the Allegro. His legs have been badly crushed by the car. We can't move it and we can't move him. The medics have given him some sedation as he was in a bad way. His life's not in danger. But we need to get him out fast.'

'And the drivers?' John asked.

'Both dead.'

We had reached the cars now. Pete stepped forward to 'block' them – putting wooden blocks under the wheels and the suspension so they wouldn't rock or move when we worked on them.

That's when we heard it. A moan of pain and horror and grief and fear. It's a sound that can still come back and haunt my dreams today. It was the passenger, trapped amidst death and desperate for our help. His cry was like a muffled, broken lamentation. He sounded like an injured dog, utterly vulnerable, unable to understand what was happening. Lost in some terrible place. Crying out for someone, anyone, to turn back the clock and take him away from there.

I couldn't not look, hearing that sound. The man was a bit older than me, but probably not much more than twenty-five. He was wearing blue jeans and a pale green polo shirt. His skin was clammy and his face was horribly pale. When he opened his eyes after letting out that cry he locked them on to me. 'Get me out of here. Get me out, please,' he screamed. But I could already see why this was proving so hard. His seat had been jammed right up against the engine in the impact. Every part of the car looked to have been forced into half as much space as it needed. He had been trapped in a steel cage.

I gave the man a thumbs-up sign to try and reassure him. Then I had to walk away. I took a couple of steps past him towards the other car. And that's when I saw it. Who wore seat belts back then? Not many people. Certainly not the driver of the Vauxhall Cavalier. First of all, he must have gone through the windscreen. Then, been thrust down on to the jagged edge of the glass. Probably when the car lurched back after the impact, he must have been thrown back into his seat again. His head had fallen against the head rest. His neck, terrible as it sounds, was open, like some feeding baby bird. From one angle you could see down his trachea and his oesophagus. From another you could see up into his mouth and into the poor man's brain. I saw both in those first awful moments. I admit I froze. I stopped quite literally in my tracks. I'd never seen such horror. I'd never anticipated having to act amidst it. All I could hear was the passenger, sitting next to one dead body in his car and directly facing the worse horror in this one. The man was moaning, pleading, crying. And how could he not be? I'd looked away from the driver the moment I'd seen him. But even as I looked at the road his mutilation was all I could see. The image had been forced into my mind. I couldn't lose it. I couldn't think. I couldn't move.

It turned out that Caddie wasn't the only one watching my back that night. Our Sub-O, Joe Morgan, had finished talking to the copper and was at my side inspecting the vehicles. He saw what I had seen, a split second after me. He had also seen how it had hit me. 'Go fetch the Cengar saw, jockey. Get it now,' he said sharply as I stood, rooted to the spot. It was only years later that

I realised what he had done and why. He had given me a job to do, a role to play and a few precious extra seconds to regroup and face up to the reality of the situation. He had told me to do something simple, achievable and useful. He'd saved me.

I strode back to the engine and the tool dump.

'The Sub-O has asked for the Cengar,' I said, picking it up. The Cengar saw was an air-operated hacksaw. We might need it to cut the passenger out of his seat. We'd certainly need it a little later when we had to get two dead bodies out of their twisted, metal tombs. I took a deep breath as I turned back towards the accident. I walked faster as I returned to it. I was a fireman. I was ready to help.

'Well done, jockey. We're going to start work and get the passenger out straight away,' Joe said as I arrived with the saw. His eyes were asking me a question. Was I OK now? My answer was to stand tall. I was ready. We all moved fast as a team, calling for and passing equipment up and down the line. Whoever was closest and most able did whatever job was required. We didn't have any of today's hydraulic spreading or cutting tools. The kit we had took longer to work and needed a lot more muscle. The Cengar saw helped cut through the three door pillars but wasn't enough for the door hinges. John called for the petrol-powered Stihl circular saw. It was passed to Woody. He moved forward without a word. The noise cut through the country air, rising above the hedgerows and spreading far across the fields. Sparks flew and we all gulped down that acrid stench of metal wrenched against hot metal. The passenger, whose name was Darren, was rigid in his seat. His eyes were closed. His face, washed out by the police lights but lit up by the sparks from the saw, was tight and afraid.

'That's it.' There was a thud as the grinder cut through the last of the hinges. The door came free.

'Try to stay still, Darren. You're doing fine and we're well on our way now. We're going to get the roof off, then push the dashboard away from your legs to make some room. Then we'll get you out of there.'

We were getting the saw ready to tackle the roof when Woody did something extra. He used a blanket to cover up the windscreen of the other car. We'd already put a sheet over the dead body next to him in the car we were working on. Now Darren would also be spared the horror of the other driver right ahead of him.

'Lift on the count of three.' The roof came off. We carried it away from the car and deposited it on the road. The metallic sound was like the toll of some terrible bell.

I was given the hand pump when we used the telescopic hydraulic 'ram' that forced the dashboard off Darren's legs. As it moved, giving him inch after precious inch of space, Pete slid a spine board down between the man's back and the car seat.

'We can move him now. On the count of three,' John called when the man was strapped into the board and his legs were free.

We pulled the loosened seat backwards into a reclined position. We lifted him out of the car and away from his dead friend. 'You're going to be fine. The doctors will sort you out now,' John said as we carried him towards the ambulance.

Darren kept his eyes closed. He just repeated the same two words maybe half a dozen times in reply: 'Thank you.'

The pace changed completely when we walked back towards the cars. The pressure had been intense when our live casualty had been there. We'd thrown everything we had at the situation to get him out within the golden hour. Now we'd done so, we were left with the two drivers. The two corpses.

'Is he going to be OK?' The man in the white T-shirt and the woman he'd been holding on to had got as close to us as the local policeman allowed. Both of them wanted – or maybe needed – to talk.

'He'll be fine. He's being looked after now,' John said. 'Did you know him? Did you know any of them?'

'No. But we heard the crash,' the man said. 'We didn't see it. We must have been a few minutes behind the green car. There was the sound of a dreadful skid, then the crash itself. We got round the corner and the cars were both there, steaming and twisted. It was terrible.'

'I stayed here on the verge,' said the woman. 'I tried to talk to the man you rescued while Robert drove off to find a phone and call for an ambulance. He was crying out so much and he must have been in such pain. It was horrible. I tried to tell him everything would be OK but I couldn't bear to look. I couldn't go any closer to him.'

'I told her not to get too close. We didn't know if the cars were safe. There was so much to think of. It all just happened so fast.'

'Should I have done anything else? Could I have saved one of them?' The woman was crying and shivering now. She was in a pale cotton dress. She looked about to fall.

'You did the right thing. Just hearing your voice would have helped that man. You couldn't have helped the drivers.' The ambulance drove past us as John spoke. 'Look, he's on his way to hospital now. And, if you'll excuse us, we should tend to the others and get the road cleared.'

The policeman led the couple towards his car saying he wanted to make some notes about what they'd seen. His voice was calm and business-like. It set the tone for the rest of the operation. We worked for about an hour and a half. The driver's door on the Vauxhall came off easily. With the roof already gone and the dashboard pushed back, it was relatively straightforward to lift him out and stretcher his body over to the second ambulance. The Allegro Estate was a tougher challenge. The car had taken more of the impact and was in a far worse state. The driver's condition made everything so much worse, of course. I kept thinking that in all the practice drills I'd done in training, and on the watch, the emphasis had tended to be on the car – where to cut, which saw to use, what to pull back, how to lift the top or the sides off or how to drag the whole vehicle out of danger. That night I learned that in real life a fair amount of the focus has to go on the body as well. Where to hold it. What to touch. How to support it. How to stop that almost severed head from detaching itself completely.

'Lift on three as usual.' Joe had taken over this part of the operation. He gave the count and the second driver was finally carried away from the place at which he had died. We left him in the care of the ambulance crew while the policeman took a final look at the accident site. We had one final set of tasks to accomplish once he'd finished. We separated the cars so that they could be loaded up on to tow trucks and removed. We cleared up the debris. I shovelled some soil from the verge on the worst of the spilled oil. We did a hazard check for any other potential problems. 'If I had my way I'd cut this whole hedge down so people stand a chance of seeing round the corner,' Woody said with an unusual seriousness in his voice. We didn't have the authority to do that – and in truth it's not certain that the hedge had caused the crash in the first place. We'd all been discussing the accident in quiet voices throughout the clear-up job. We'd looked at the skid marks, considered what the Good Samaritan couple had told us, examined the angles at which the cars had hit and come up with plenty of theories about its cause. We were still talking quietly when Joe told us to pack up the tool dump and get all the other hoses and equipment back on the engines. The tow trucks were on their way and the policeman reopened the road to traffic. Darkness had fallen so the skid marks were almost invisible. Drive past now and you'd never know that two men had died at this spot.

But I knew.

I took off my helmet, pulled off my tunic and sat on my usual makeshift seat, facing forwards, as we headed back to base. No one spoke. There were none of the usual jokes we usually shared after a shout. No one was showing off over something they thought they'd done well. No one was mocking anyone else for any stupid mistakes. The windows were open and air flooded the cab. But it tasted heavy rather than fresh. It was rich with pollen and, for the first time in weeks, I felt a wave of travel sickness hit me as we headed back towards base.

Pete opened the bar when we were back at the station. Everyone drank that night. I sank two pints fast. I smoked a lot of cigarettes as well. 'We did a good job tonight. You'll learn to snap out of these things, jockey. You'll learn how to put them in their place,' Woody told me before heading over to the canasta table. The TV was on and after a while things did begin to feel normal again. Some time after one o'clock in the morning I headed to the dorm. It was about an hour earlier than usual but no one took the piss. I slept well. I couldn't get the picture of that man's severed throat, the feeding baby bird, out of my mind. But it didn't haunt me. I didn't have any nightmares and I woke convinced we'd done a good job the night before. Everyone else was putting a brave face on things as well. The jokes and the banter were as loud as ever at breakfast – they might even have been just a touch louder than normal. Babs and Bev certainly seemed to get more than their usual share of catcalls and lewd suggestions when they arrived just before the end of our shift. One of the old hands had tried to wind them up yet again by swapping their vastly different sized overalls around in the cleaning locker. Life went on, I told myself. And, nine hours later, when we were back at the station for the second of our two night shifts, I was given an even bigger confidence boost.

We'd paraded, had a bit of a pep talk from John and a typically manic hour of volleyball. We did one long situation drill rather than the usual series of basic drills. I'd missed out on the tea break because John wanted me cleaning up in the appliance room. After about half an hour Woody came in. 'The boss says you can take a break,' he told me. 'And the rest of the squad has decided you can help us out with something.' He led me out across the parade ground to some spare bays beside the training tower. The lights were on and from inside I could hear the radio and a lot of talking and laughing. For the past few weeks I'd been wondering where everyone got to when I was sent into the appliance room to paint and polish anything in sight. It seemed that they finally trusted me enough to let me in on the big secret.

13

Caddie Reflects

The watch had decided to enter a massive raft race being held on the River Severn on the last weekend of August. The race was expected to be one of the highlights of the town's summer festival – and we wanted to win it. Apparently the gang had been working on various prototype rafts since the spring. They'd recently narrowed the job down to two far from basic designs. Full production had just begun.

'It looks like a tank,' I said when Woody led me across the drill yard and showed me the first of them.

'It is a tank,' Charlie said proudly.

'And this one's a missile launcher. It's an aircraft carrier. It's backin' brilliant,' said Arfer.

The second raft certainly looked capable of packing a punch. It was a real Heath Robinson craft. It was built around one of our so-called 'light portable' pumps. A suction hose would lie beneath the hull, they told me. Water would be fed into two places, first into hand-controlled branches aiming backwards that would power and steer the craft and second into two branches up top that we would aim at rival rafts. 'If anyone comes too close they'll get a soaking,' Arfer explained. 'If there's a bottleneck on the river we can use the firepower on this one to open up a whole channel of water for the tank. Once it's got through we can protect it from the rear. The whole strategy is foolproof. We're winning this race. That's guaranteed.'

It took about an hour for everyone to talk me through the

finer points of the two creations. No surprise that the crafts were already so ingenious and so well made – it would have been hard to find a more practical group of men. Everyone had a different skill to bring to the task. All our part-time plumbers, builders, electricians and mechanics had thrown themselves into this challenge. I wanted to join them – but it took me a while to work out how to do so. None of the short-term jobs I'd done between school and fire training seemed particularly useful. Out on the farm I'd learned how to drive a tractor and to make a cow walk forward by twisting its tail. When I'd been a postie I'd learned how to distract dogs and get from front door to gate without losing any of the skin on my legs. I wasn't entirely sure how these skills might help us construct a raft. So I decided to focus on tactics instead.

'So who else is in the race?' I asked as the dinner call rang out and we all thundered upstairs in our usual herd-of-wildebeest charge.

'Every backin' blighter in Shrewsbury,' Arfer said as we jostled for position at the hatch. Pete was cooking and he'd done a pile of spaghetti bolognese that looked bigger than the Wrekin. When we sat down Arfer added a bit more detail. We were expecting several Young Farmers' groups, lots of pub teams, some football clubs, student groups, factory workers and even some groups of nurses from the Royal Shrewsbury Hospital. The local police and ambulance crews were also expected to be building rafts – as well as several other fire stations.

'The Rolls-Royce people will be a challenge if they're taking part. They might get real engineers working on their rafts,' I mused.

'Real engineers? What? Are you trying to say we're not real engineers or something? Backin' cheek,' said Arfer, swatting me round the back of the head as usual.

I shrugged it off. 'I know a couple of people who work over

there. They're mates from school. I'll ask them if they know what anyone's planning. Maybe we could sabotage it.'

'Sabotage is cool,' said Charlie. 'There's no rule saying we can't do that.'

'I'll go up to the Royal Shrewsbury and sabotage some of the nurses' rafts, if you know what I mean,' one of the others yelled over from the next table.

'You wouldn't know how, mate. You need a real man for that,' Arfer shouted back. We carried on like this for most of the rest of the night. I could hear the insults fly from outside when I was sent down to repaint the station step. Later on we all did a sandwich on a couple of people who dared to go to bed early. After that I slept like a baby. I'd got the hang of the routine now. I'd left my kit ready in case we had a shout in the night – having followed Caddie's advice and taken my T-shirt, shirt and jumper off in one go and left them like that so I could put them all on quicker in an emergency. But I didn't let the thought of a late-night shout spook me. And when I tucked into my full English the next morning I realised something else had changed. This time around I was looking forward to our four-day break. I was starting to feel like a proper fireman.

The next day I spotted someone I knew by the carp pool up at Picklescott. It was Caddie. He couldn't have looked happier or more relaxed. He was sitting on a blue, striped deckchair, his feet resting on his bait box and his face half hidden by pipe smoke. I wandered over, feeling oddly shy. 'Good morning. I didn't know you came up here,' I said, a bit too formally. He looked up at me through the smoke. I'm pleased to say he didn't seem unhappy to see me.

'It's a good place, lad. I didn't know you were a fisherman yourself.'

We talked about the carp and about some of the other local fishing pools for a few minutes, then I decided I should leave him in peace. I headed right around the pool and found myself a pitch out of eye-sight from Caddie. I got my kit together, cast out and sat back in my own chair. I felt even more connected to the Fire Brigade now I knew that Caddie was just around the corner from me. Now that my time off was in sync with the rest of Red Watch I didn't need to sit up here and worry I was missing out. I could relax and smile when I checked the time and guessed what the other watch might be up to in our place. I could picture them extending that 13.5-metre ladder up to the third floor of the training tower, trying to find a way to break in to the spare bay unnoticed so that they could sabotage our rafts, and being bossed around by Betty. I could imagine them lining up for lunch when she called. I could almost hear Mabel ticking them off, telling them to mind their language and not to make a mess on her nice clean linoleum. I could also imagine what the rest of Red Watch were up to while I counted dragonflies on the water and whiled the day away in the sunshine. I knew that Arfer and George had a big removal job on. We all knew it, to be honest. 'It's from Shelton to backin' Ludlow. And it's out of a top-floor flat in Shelton. We'll be sweating like sick pigs by the end of it,' Arfer had moaned about twenty times a day for the past four shifts. Charlie and Woody both worked as painters and dec-orators on their days off. They were always moaning that they were 'brassic' because there was never enough work in the summer. But they were also boasting about one big job they'd got in a house over in Belle Vue so I didn't think they'd be going hungry any time soon.

It was nice to think that Caddie didn't need a spiv job to get him through the week, though. I liked the fact that the Fire Brigade was enough for him. I'd heard from the others that he had a nice wife, no kids, a dog, and that he made model aero-planes when he wasn't fishing. What more would you want out of life than that?

'Thinking of something funny, son?' Caddie was suddenly at

my side. What was it with firemen? We were the biggest, heftiest people, but we could creep around like mice sometimes.

'Nothing in particular. I'm just enjoying the day.'

'Mind if I join you?'

'Not at all.'

Caddie had brought a flask of tea. He poured us both a cup and we sat gazing out over the still waters. 'I caught a two-and-a-half-footer here once,' he told me. 'It took a good half-hour to get her out. Well worth it, though.'

'I used to come here as a kid, with my dad. We hardly ever caught a thing.'

'But you can't beat it. Look at that view.' Caddie started to talk about the hikes he'd done over on Long Mynd and the fossils and quartzite rocks he and his dog had found all over the Shropshire hills. He talked about all the old tin mines and smelting works over at the Stiperstones. He knew a huge amount of local history. My county, my beloved Shropshire, came alive when he opened up. He talked about the Celts and the Romans. He talked about hidden hill forts up on the Wrekin. He talked about the Danes and the Normans and all the half-forgotten shades of history they had left behind. Then, as we stared companionably ahead of us, he finally stood up.

'Time I headed back to see if there's another two-and-a-half-footer waiting at the end of my line. I'll be seeing you on Thursday, lad,' he said before heading back to his own pitch. After he'd gone I realised we hadn't said a single word about the Fire Brigade or about any of our colleagues. I liked that.

Arfer, Woody and Charlie were all full of their various spiv number successes on Thursday when we started our next tour of duty with two day shifts. 'She only had a piano,' Arfer began over a cup of tea when he began to tell the story of the great Shelton to Ludlow house move. 'She never mentioned that when she made the booking. A backin' piano. Down three flights of stairs. And when we got to the new place she only wanted it taken down to the basement. Where there was a hell of a turn on the stairs. We'd still be jammed up on that staircase today if I hadn't had the foresight to get the backin' pedals taken off beforehand.'

'Did you know about the pedals from your time as a concert pianist? Between the time you did the moon landing and became a high court judge, wasn't it?' Charlie asked.

'Backin' cheek. You know I was never a high court judge.'

Charlie and Woody seemed to have done OK on their decorating job as well. 'I told him, two weeks won't be nearly enough. We'll need a good month in there to get it the way he wants it,' Woody said.

'I could have done it in a weekend. But a month it is,' Charlie said with a happy smile.

Mid-morning I took a break from my own, unpaid, painting and decorating in the appliance room to see how the rafts were progressing. Both looked pretty amazing, truth be told. 'That tank could take on the Russians,' I said. I just hoped it would float.

John had taken over from Joe and was running the drills for the next few days. He was working us hard and his eyes were moving around even faster than usual. My heavy-smoking, red-faced friend had been right that I'd be the main focus of all his attention. I guessed the thinking was that Joe had trained me up. Now John wanted to see if I'd taken it all in. He had a lot to say when we lined up at the end of each drill. He yelled 'Rest!' several times so that he could stop us mid-drill and point out some error or imperfection. But after two days of bread and butter drills – the bullshit ones – he gave us a brilliant, full-squad situation exercise involving the training tower, a vehicle and just about every bit of kit we had. We got dismissed after a short debrief that nearly – very nearly – included a few hints of praise. My heavy-smoking, red-faced friend could hardly have failed to notice that. If we got sent back to bullshit drills in the future it was surely clear that I wasn't to blame.

Back then my favourite part of each shift was the very end. It wasn't because I wanted to leave. I was still happier in the station than almost anywhere else. I'd still have happily stayed and done a second shift back to back if asked. No: the fun bit was watching the others. Arfer, Woody, Charlie and the rest of the gang would zoom past me, faster than a rat with the runs at knocking-off time. Their cars were heading for the main road before I'd even shut my locker door and got outside. It was the same, but in reverse, at the start of each shift. I'd almost always be one of the first to arrive. I'd park my HB Viva in its usual slot, check up on the appliances and wonder what the off-going watch had been up to. Then, as the others gradually began to arrive, I'd wander into the locker room to get ready for work. But in the first week of August things were a little different at the start of our next set of night shifts. When I arrived for work the appliance room was empty. The fire engine, emergency tender and water ladder were all gone. The station itself looked deserted. The day shift must have been called out to a shout. A big one.

'There's been a farm fire way out in the sticks in Ellesmere,' John told me as I stood around all on my tod in the empty appliance room. He was the one person who was always on the watch before me. He'd been in the watch room reading up the notes.

'Is it a bad one?'

'They'd have been back here long since if it wasn't,' he said laconically.

I kept my mouth shut after that. I knew from hearing everyone else's smoky stories that farm fires on dry summer days can be terrifying prospects. August wasn't exactly the hay-making season but we were in the middle of a long, hot summer so most farms would be full of tinder-dry fuel. Sparks could fly a long way on windy days. One blaze could easily trigger another. Fires could jump like kangaroos. In the isolated south Shropshire hills, where water sources could be hard to find, fire crews could easily be overwhelmed. Our job was to protect property as well as people. If we failed then whole livelihoods could be ruined – and lives could end up being lost.

John headed inside and I poked my head around the appliance room door to check the board. As usual, it showed where we would all sit on the engines, had they been present, and what our roles on a shout would be. I was in my usual number five slot. If we'd had an engine to sit on, Caddie and Woody would have been alongside me at the back in positions three and four, with John and Charlie as one and two up front, as usual.

Caddie was next to arrive, just as John and I stepped back out on to the drill yard. 'Looks like there's been trouble. Is it out at Ellesmere?' he asked as he walked over from his car. John looked at him. His worried frown was temporarily replaced by a good-natured smile.

'How the heck do you always find these things out?' he asked.

'You've got to keep your ear to the ground in the country,' Caddie said. 'So it is Ellesmere? Is it Hickman's place?'

'It is. Let's hope Blue Watch were able to find it all right.'

Caddie turned to me. 'The farmers like to keep a low profile out there and Hickman's one of the worst. They're stubborn little buggers who don't welcome visitors and don't like change. They'll give their farm a name but getting a full address out of 'em is like pulling teeth. It's like they wanna keep the world at bay. It can't be much fun for the poor sods who have to deliver their post. It's not much better for us. You don't wanna be on a night shift trying find somewhere like that on the Ordnance Survey. Still, happen you'd have a few flames to use as a guide if the place was on fire. And Blue Watch must have found the place in the end.'

When the others had all arrived John gave us a full briefing on the stroke of six.

The fire had begun just after eleven that morning. The farmer had been doing a bit of DIY welding outside one of his barns and hadn't been too bothered about all the sparks. Not until they'd set his hay alight, that is. Instead of beating down the flames on the surface of the bails he'd tried to pull the hay apart and put´it out with water. It hadn't really worked. After about half an hour he'd run back to his farmhouse and dialled 999. By the time he got back to his barn the fire was out of control. Blue Watch had headed off with two appliances. When they'd arrived one squad had fanned out to check there weren't any unexpected people trapped or hiding out in any of the nearby barns and farm buildings, another had tracked down the nearest water sources for when the engine tanks ran dry. They'd got ready to organise an engine relay – with one heading down to fill up at the nearest hydrant while the other went back up to the farm to fight the fire. They had doused down the outer perimeter, checked the prevailing winds and got ready to take action if the fire started jumping. Then they'd begun doing the beating down that the farmer should have done at the outset.

'It took them a while to get to grips but the last message we got said Les reckons they've finally got it beaten. They've been up there for seven hours now and they won't have had any grub. Let's go give them a hand,' John concluded. Everyone gave a roar of approval. We got our kit together and squeezed into the nine-seater fire van we had for when the engines were otherwise engaged. I was squashed on the back seat as usual, pinned in by Charlie on one side and a pile of equipment on the other. It's funny, but I remember noticing how relaxed everyone else seemed to be. There was normally a fierce, contained tension in the air on the way to a shout. Today everyone seemed in surprisingly high spirits. In a couple of hours' time I'd find out why.

14

Picnic at Hickman's Farm

O ur route took us out to the north of Shrewsbury and past all the steam and the noise coming out of the Northern Lights-style roof of the Rolls-Royce factory. 'One hour earlier and we'd never have got past here. If we get a shout around knocking-off time it's murder. Hundreds of men are pouring out like ants out of an anthill. They're all over the shop. Driving, walking, biking, getting in the way, causing confusion and blocking all the roads. It's like being on the dodgems weaving through 'em all,' Charlie told me as we passed the main factory gate.

I looked at him blankly. 'Shut up. Stop talking. Don't say another word about traffic,' I wanted to say to him. Because for the first time in several weeks my travel sickness was back. It must have been the new vehicle. My brain, my body or my stomach must have got used to the fire engine. But they didn't like this van one little bit. Waves of nausea were hitting me like kippers. I held my helmet tightly in my lap, ready to use it if I threw up.

'It was worse down here,' Woody yelled from the row ahead as we accelerated away from the factories. 'Do you remember that shout we had to swerve round the horse box? When we ended up nearly going into a tailspin on the roundabout?' he asked. 'That was you driving, wasn't it, Charlie? Before you had your secret eye op?' I started to gulp for air. I looked desperately at the back windows. There was a yellow and black sticker on the main one. 'Open in Emergency Only' it said. Did this count?

'We did the tailspin on market day. They're a killer. You don't want to be here on market day, jockey,' Charlie continued helpfully. 'It feels like every tractor and cattle truck in the county is here. Manoeuvring through all of that's no picnic. We have to go up and down the kerbs, round the outside of all the cars. It's crazy driving. *Gumball Rally* stuff.'

I slumped back in my seat, hoping Charlie wouldn't notice I was as green as the Incredible Hulk. I tried to do what helped me in the engine – to focus on the far horizon. Our route took us north-west of the North Shropshire Plain into the countryside where the rich green rolling hills were littered with little hillocks called drumlins – it was Tellytubby land, some twenty years before they had even been invented. Unfortunately for me, drumlins weren't good for my stomach. Nor was it any better when we dipped into Shropshire's little Lake District. The roads were narrow and twisted wildly. This was my worst nightmare. How could I be in such a beautiful place and feel so terrible? The early evening light was shining right into my eyes now. My head started to ache almost as much as my stomach. Surely this couldn't get any worse?

It could. We left the last of the village roads and began to bounce over farm tracks – some of the worst maintained farm tracks in Shropshire. 'Hang on tight in the back!' George yelled from the driver's seat. We crossed a cattle grid and hit some serious potholes. The farm track then swung upwards and to the left. The van was being shaken like a child's toy as we headed back down and then followed alongside a greenish, mossy stream held back by surprisingly big reed beds. 'Where the hell is this farm?' I was thinking as we bounced on even further. I'd seen the smoke a while back, a grey, soul-destroying haze drifting out across the hills. We had to be close, hadn't we? I looked down and my knuckles were as white as powder as I held my helmet tight on my lap. It suddenly occurred to me to wonder what I'd wear on the shout if I did throw up into it. 'Next time, bring a plastic bag,' I told myself. If there was a next time. I loved every bit of being a fireman. Every bit except for the journey to and from each job.

After what felt like a dozen more hairpin bends and sudden dips in the road we made it to Hickman's farm. John headed over to get briefed by the Officer in Charge of Blue Watch as we all took a look around. It's funny but however bad I felt on the drive out to a job I managed to recover the moment we arrived. This was no exception. I snapped out of it immediately. I put my helmet on, took a deep breath of smoky, country air and felt absolutely fine.

The fire had certainly covered a lot of ground and done plenty of damage. It looked like an old five-bay Dutch barn had taken the worst of it. Not much more than the barn's frame was still standing. A few beams were poking through clouds of white smoke. It looked a bit creepy, like the setting for a ghost story or maybe the backdrop of a disaster movie. The fire had certainly been jumping in the day as well. If this was like any normal farmyard it would have been jam full of junk and kit and equipment. Not much was left now. The hedgerows and fences all around had taken a hit as well. They'd have been dry, in mid-summer, but even so the fire must have been pretty furious at its peak to have done that much damage. Blue Watch had done well to contain it. We stood by our vehicle as they walked around and completed their duties. A couple of the men were carrying pitchforks. Every now and then they'd come across another smouldering bale of hay or straw. They'd open it up and stand back as the fire got the oxygen it craved and sprang to life. 'It's such a waste. Some of those bales look fine,' I said as the flames reared up and yet another bale disappeared.

'It's got to be done. The more it burns the better,' Woody said at my side. 'Getting rid of a load of ash is a hell of a lot easier than getting rid of several tonnes of half-burned bales. And if it's hay or feeding straw it has to be burned anyway. Animals won't touch it if there's even a hint of smoke in it. Picky eaters, those blinkin' cows.'

John called us all together. 'OK, lads, Blue Watch are standing down and going back in the van. I want the equipment checked fast. It's going to be a long night and I want us to carry on their good work.'

When Blue Watch had gone we set off to patrol the perimeters of the fire. The good news was that it hadn't spread out on to the fields or travelled to any of the other farm buildings, or to the ramshackle old farmhouse about 200 yard further up the lane.

'Is the farmer not even going to come out and speak to us?' I asked Caddie as we kicked some soil over one set of embers.

He shrugged. 'Like I said, they're buggers, these country farmers. They don't like admitting they can't handle anything on their own. Hickman won't have wanted to call the Fire Brigade in the first place. He'll reckon it makes him look weak. He'll be holed up in there with his family, telling them it's someone else's fault. Happen the family would love to come and see us, though. They go weeks without seeing another living soul, I'll warrant. Funny old lives they live out here. Funny people, funny lives.' He gave a snort of laughter all of a sudden. 'He'll also be insured well enough, though. He won't be that shy of the modern world. I don't think we need lose much sleep worrying about him.'

We reached the others who had been walking round the fire's edge from the other direction. We stood still and gazed over it for several minutes. It was one of the most beautiful, peaceful things I'd ever seen. There was power there, certainly. There was an underlying threat in all of those slow-burning flames. But there was also something utterly magical. At first I could only see the oranges and the reds. Then I saw all the other colours. The ever-shifting blues, blacks and even the whites. The patches of violet and mauve. The subtle gradations of each colour. There were sudden explosions of magic, times when the whole palate changed and re-formed before my eyes. Staring at it was like being hypnotised. It was alive somehow. It was mesmerising. I could feel myself drawn in. It was as if I was in a different place, on a different planet. The summer night was already warm. The fire made it balmy. When you stood upwind of the smoke you could still breathe in rich country air. This was Scout camp, Bonfire Night, all sorts of other good memories all rolled up in one. And it was about to get even better.

John had done a patrol of his own. He rejoined the rest of us and agreed we were in the right place for the watching brief. 'This is where we stay. I want two of you doing a walk round every half-hour. But I think it's going to be a quiet one. So, lads, it's time to get the specialist equipment out.'

The others gave a cheer. It jolted me out of my reverie. My stomach lurched as I looked away from the depths of the fire. I had no idea what kind of equipment he meant. I also had a terrible feeling that I'd get the blame if we didn't have it. I tried to think back to all the lessons I'd learned at training school and all the drills we'd done out in the yard but I drew a blank. I pretended to readjust my left boot to buy a bit of time and see what the others did. The engines had been brought out by Blue Watch, so in theory I could blame it on them if anything was missing. In reality I knew I would be in the firing line. I always was. So what had I missed? What was it the others were moving round to the back to collect? And how much shit would I be in when they realised I hadn't known to pack it?

I stood up and watched Arfer pull open one of his bags. He grabbed something, turned around and headed my way. In the evening light, lit by the warmth of the fire, it looked a bit like a big, silver hand grenade. 'Baked potato,' he said with a grin.

Charlie was next. He had two sliced white loaves with his

foil-wrapped potato. Then Caddie appeared. 'It wouldn't be the same without baked beans,' he pronounced, carrying a four-tin pack and a billycan as well as his own two foil-wrapped spuds.

The potatoes were buried in the ashes straight away. 'They'll cook faster than in any kitchen,' I was told. We gave them forty-five minutes then began the rest of our meal. We toasted the bread by stabbing the slices on the end of a pitchfork and balancing it on a low wall right next to the fire. The beans were bubbling away in minutes. Then we retrieved the potatoes. Mabel and Betty themselves couldn't have made a better meal, though none of us would ever have dared to tell them so.

The next couple of hours were magical. The glow from the fire was as captivating as ever. Every now and then a new patch of embers would hiss, crackle, fizz and die. At one point I lay back on the hard, dry earth. I gazed up through the smoke towards the thin, straggling clouds. We were miles from the lights of any town so we owned the whole sky. Every now and then I could see a faint patch of stars.

'Jockey, I think it's time we had one last look around before lights out,' John told me just before midnight. We paced around the perimeter of the fire in companionable silence, walking through patches of colder night air and sudden waves of warmth. The fire had dampened itself down dramatically. The blackness of ash had swallowed up most of the earlier colours. It wasn't as attractive now. But somehow it still held the eye.

John spoke up when we got back to our little camp. 'George is staying in one of the engines to monitor the radio. I'll be sitting out here. The rest of you can have a bit of kip if you want,' he announced. The old hands had first dibs on a couple of soft, unburned bales, Charlie reckoned he'd found a perfect patch of grass and Woody didn't even move. As usual, I was left scratching around for anything that was left, but in the end I got lucky. After rooting around for a while I found myself an old wheelbarrow down by the gate. I rolled it back towards the others. It wasn't very clean, but tipped back on its handles it made a very comfortable bucket bed. I was asleep within minutes.

It was just after three in the morning when John woke us up, gave the call to knock off and head back to base. The wind had fallen practically to nothing and a slight dampness in the air was probably in our favour as well. The farmer was up, John said, and he was happy to see the back of us. I stretched and tried to wipe the back of my uniform clean when I got out of my wheelbarrow. I'd been dreaming a good dream. But I was already losing all the details the way you always do. Everyone helped pack up the engines but someone else had to pick up all the dirty pots, the empty beans cans and all the other rubbish we'd made earlier on at dinner. As usual that someone was me. I carried as much as I could and headed back towards our engine. George had turned the headlights on and I was halfway towards them, bang in the middle of the spotlight, when I stumbled on a clod of earth and dropped the lot.

'If you lose anything or anything's dented you'll pay for it out of your own pocket, Windsor,' yelled George as the rest of the watch laughed like drains from the shadows.

Hopefully the headlights were bright enough to bleach the colour out of my cheeks as I rooted around on the ground picking everything up. But in truth I wasn't blushing because I was embarrassed – I was blushing because I was proud; Windsor ... Windsor Castle. George had just given me a nick-name. That had to mean I was finally and officially one of the gang. I grinned like an idiot all the way back to town. What I didn't realise was that the old hands still had one last test up their sleeves.

15

Swimming Lessons

'Jockey, get on the end of the ladder. Right now!' I had a horrible feeling this was going to end badly, but I did what I was told anyway. We were back on days and the whole watch had driven off-station to do some drills on the turntable ladder. We'd parked the vehicles in the delivery bay at the back of Woolworths, just off Ravens Meadows. The loading area was pretty empty so there was plenty of room for us to work. And, while the back of Woolies was pretty much a windowless brick wall, that didn't mean we were short of an audience. It was another nice early August afternoon. Plenty of people had spotted us arrive and were hanging around to see what we got up to. I wasn't over the moon at being the star of the show, but I didn't have much choice.

I pulled myself up on to the base of the turntable ladder and started to edge along it. It was ancient, one of the oldest and most rickety bits of equipment in our arsenal. The aluminium ladder, made up of four extensions, had clearly taken a battering over the years. So had the rough metal guides that were supposed to hold each extension in place. Every time I'd cleaned this kit I'd wondered when it had first seen service. The sixties maybe? Or even the fifties? I was about to find out if it had been built to last.

I got in position at the end of the ladder and hooked in my safety belt. 'Show us a clean pair of heels,' Woody shouted. I lifted each foot away from the ladder in turn and shook it. The idea was to show to everyone else, and to remind myself, that my feet were safely on what's called the drop-down step. If they weren't I could lose toes. They'd be sliced off like bacon when the ladder was extended.

'Be a pal and take it slow, Woody,' I was thinking. Then I realised Woody wasn't the one driving the apparatus. One of the leading firemen, a serial joker called Paddy, got up on the operating console and fired up the turntable instead. My bad day looked set to get a whole lot worse.

The ladder began to move. It goes out horizontally at first. I was carried with it as each of the four extensions jolted and juddered into place. What I'd like to have heard someone yell at that point was: 'You're doing well, jockey. Just hang on in there.' I would even have been OK if I'd heard the boss yell something along the lines of: 'Not like that, jockey, keep your arms bent and don't put all your weight on your legs.'

What I didn't want to hear, though, was this: 'Paddy, you'll effing kill him if you do that. That turntable's not been fixed, remember? It's not strong enough.'

Nor did I want to hear Paddy's reply: 'It'll be fine. He's got to learn, hasn't he? Odds are it won't break again.'

I glanced behind me towards the control turret. There was a manic glint in Paddy's eye and an equally wild look on his face. Oh, and his hand was on the elevation lever. I saw him tense his arm and prepare to pull the lever sharply towards him. I turned away, faced the ladder and focused on my grip. The appliance began to roar. The ladder jerked into life. I was going up in the world . . . fast.

'Paddy, those extension guides are too loose!' Woody yelled from what felt like a hundred feet beneath me. Oh, great. So the turntable really was as rickety as it looked. As if all this wasn't bad enough, I knew that if each of the four extensions was loose then the overall effect would be magnified fourfold by the time it got to me. I was effectively on the end of a very long, very flexible, fishing rod. One small movement at the bottom would create a horribly big one at the top. And I was at the top.

I clung on with all my might when I sensed that the ladder was close to the maximum 75° point. The good news was that at that point the turntable's safety mechanism should have cut in and stopped the ladder going any further upright. The bad news was that if the extensions were as loose as they felt then I'd carry on swinging well over the vertical point. If that happened, Paddy wouldn't just have scared me – he might end up killing me. All I could think of was the crumple of mangled metalwork as the turntable collapsed. All I could hear were the shouts of panic from everyone down below. And all I could do was inadvertently let out a little whimper of fear as I shut my eyes, maybe for the last time in my life.

That's when I realised it was all a big joke.

'We heard that, jockey! The intercom is on, remember?'

'We had you going then, Windsor!'

'How's your underwear, Castle? Need a fresh pair yet?'

I wasn't quite sure whether to laugh or cry. In the meantime I cursed the fixed intercom system I'd forgotten was even there. The intercom that had now humiliated me in front of my colleagues and what felt like half of my home town. Hoots of laughter kept on rising up from the squad as the worst of the swaying began to die. In the control turret I could hear the loudest whoops of all coming from Paddy.

'Did you think you were going home in a box?' he shouted at me through the blinkin' radio.

'Are you kidding? I knew it was a wind-up all along,' I lied.

'Well, happen you didn't know about this!' he yelled with another manic cackle of laughter. Before I could take stock he put the turntable in gear and started rotating it around the loading bay at a breakneck pace. It had been bad enough swinging on the end of the ladder when it was yanked upwards. Clinging on to it as the ladder was swung up towards the solid brick wall of Woolies was like being on the worst fairground ride in hell. The game continued for about ten minutes. Ten minutes during which I vowed that nothing on earth would let me be sick, wet myself, cry out or show any sign of weakness. At one point I even had the bravado to take one hand off the rung and give Paddy a very obvious V sign. I got a roar of approval for that.

When Paddy had finally had his fun and turned off the engine I began the 115-foot climb down the fully extended, very shaky and almost vertical ladder.

'You're a blinkin' maniac,' I told Paddy when I was back on the ground.

'Well, you're nothing but a big girl, whining like that with all the world to hear you,' he said. But when he clipped me round the ear I swear I could see him give a wink of approval. I'd not fallen off the ladder. I'd not fallen apart completely up there. I must be doing OK.

We'd got our next call. We were heading towards Shrewsbury Town football ground to try and stop a suicide attempt. A man was threatening to end it all by jumping off the nearby railway bridge into the River Severn. I could imagine exactly where he must have been standing as we piled on to the engine. When there were games on they always sat a man in a coracle in the river to paddle out and collect any stray balls. The river was wide and the bridge was pretty impressive. Constructed in the middle of the nineteenth century, it stood on a series of huge metal legs built on to hefty stone plinths. It was covered in dome head rivets – so if you had a mind to try it was pretty easy to climb. Could you really kill yourself if you jumped off the top? I wasn't sure. The bridge was probably about 40 feet tall at its highest point. There wasn't exactly any white water or thundering rapids to worry about in the middle of sleepy old Shrewsbury, but it was probably the widest that the Severn gets in Shropshire and the banks are pretty high. So if the man couldn't swim, or if he was too drunk or drugged up to pull more than a few strokes, he might still go under and die before anyone could get to him.

'We fish around six or eight dead bodies out of the Severn every year,' Woody shouted across at me in the back of the engine as we headed through town to the location. 'We'll tell you more about them later. It's not a pleasant job.'

I said I'd look forward to it – and I knew that it would probably be my job next time we faced it. In the meantime we steeled ourselves for the forthcoming challenge.

John wanted us to approach the scene discreetly – well, as discreetly as five uniformed men on a vast red fire truck can approach anything. We didn't have any bells, sirens or hooting of the horn to see us through the last bits of traffic. But as it turned out our efforts at subtlety were in vain for one of the local bobbies was already on the scene – and he was well on his way to ruining everything.

'Bloody hell, it's Pierce. I reckon he's deaf as a post. He's going to be as useful as a backin' chocolate teapot,' Arfer muttered as we climbed out of the engine to survey the scene. I'd known PC Pierce by sight for years – everyone in Shrewsbury did. If central casting had ever wanted a classic village bobby from years ago then they'd have done worse than to give him a call. He looked a bit like something off *The Muppet Show*, to be honest. His uniform struggled to hold in his round, barrel-like stomach. He didn't have a beard, but his white hair was always showing from under his helmet. He wore little metal-framed glasses and he walked around a bit like a bird. Forget police brutality: I doubt he'd really have the energy to clip someone round the ear. But he was a nice old codger and you could see why the force would want him kept on till he retired. He was always smiling, always helping lost tourists, chatting to the locals and giving stern looks at motorists he thought were going too fast on his streets.

The man on the bridge was younger. He looked to be in his

early forties, roughly my dad's age. He was quite smartly dressed, wearing a pair of dark brown cords, a brown jacket and a white business shirt. He had climbed right out to the middle of the bridge and was perched there, holding on to the edge behind him. His eyes were on the water beneath him. And a little way back on the riverbank Constable Pierce was approaching fast.

'Stay calm, climb back towards me and let's sit down and have a nice chat about what's been going on,' Pierce called out in a phlegmy voice but in his friendliest manner. I found myself smiling at the kindness of this man. But I couldn't stop myself from agreeing with Arfer. If Pierce was on the case who knew what could happen.

'Get any closer and I swear I'll jump!' spat out the man on the bridge.

'What's that you say, sir?' said Pierce, edging closer.

'I said I'll jump!'

Pierce cupped his hand to his ear. 'I'm sorry, sir, I didn't quite catch . . .' he began. At which point . . . . the man jumped.

'Jockey – get your jacket off. You're going for a swim!' John had given the instruction almost before the man hit the water. It certainly wasn't the hottest day of the summer and the Severn was blinkin' freezing when I waded in. I took a deep breath and did a mini dive when I was thigh-deep and could feel my boots starting to sink into the mud. The cold encased me, stealing the air from my lungs. But I got used to it in an instant. I loved swimming. I was glad I'd been chosen for this. So I set off downstream of where the man had hit the water. He was on the surface now, splashing around, and it looked as if he could swim well enough. All I had to do was to guide him or get him to safety. Unfortunately that turned out to be easier said than done. I remembered from life-saving classes at training school that dragging another body across the water was tricky, even when the body in question is your best mate. When it's a man who doesn't want anything to do with you and couldn't care less if he drags you under with him then it's that little bit harder.

'Grab his jacket!' Charlie yelled from the riverbank. The whole watch was following us as the man kicked out at me. No surprise that rent-a-crowd was there as well. It was the middle of the school holidays and this was easily the best free show in town.

'Get his arm!' someone shouted.

'Grab his balls or whack him on the head,' offered a woman's voice. She was shouting so loudly, and her advice was so specific, that I couldn't stop myself from treading water and trying to see exactly who she was. It was a woman I recognised from the fish bar just down from Shrewsbury Castle. She must have been sixty if she was a day. She normally seemed perfectly pleasant. 'Do what I say – whack him on the head!' she repeated, even louder this time. 'Or just grab his bloody balls and have done with it!' I made a mental note never to mess with her when I got my Friday night chips.

The man seemed to have calmed down while I was treading water so I headed back towards him. 'Come on, mate – can't you just swim to the bank?' I shouted between gulps of air and mouthfuls of Shropshire's finest untreated water. 'If you don't I'm going to have to grab you – and drag you back there myself.'

'Eff off,' he yelled back.

'Look, I can't leave you out here. One way or the other I need to get you back to the riverbank.'

He spat out some water, kicked out at me again then began to paddle furiously away. I headed after him – and the further into the river we got the colder it seemed to be. I shouted more and more instructions at him and in the end I think I finally wore him down. He swore a few more times but he stopped resisting. He looked to have drunk far more river water than me and it wasn't doing him much good. As he was unlikely to have spent his days playing volleyball and doing ladder drills he probably wasn't as fit as me either. 'Come on. Let's get to the side,' I said as he finally allowed me to grab his jacket and drag him towards one of the reed beds.

I got him there, somehow, and tried not to slip in the mud as I pulled him through the reeds towards the riverbank. When I'd done so, Woody and Arfer took over. They got an arm under each shoulder and scooped him out of the shallows and on to the grass. He was coughing, spluttering and maybe even crying. He was filthy. His clothes were ripped and clinging to him. He looked thin, bony and horribly sad.

I'll not forget what happened next, or who took charge. Of all people it was Paddy, the manic-faced joker who had forced me up on the dodgy extension ladder the day before. Paddy, who was always the first to laugh at everyone else back at the station and who was always looking for some sign of weakness to exploit with a snide comment or a sarcastic aside.

That day, though, Paddy was serious. For him this wasn't an irritating man in a river who was wasting our time and putting on a show for the lunchtime crowd. It was a man with severe problems. A man who fifteen minutes earlier had been so desperate he'd jumped off a bridge because he wanted to end it all. 'There's an ambulance on its way. They'll look after you, mate,' Paddy said. 'Get your jacket off. I'll look after it. We've got blankets here as well. Pull one around you. It'll keep you warm. You need to stay warm. It's important.' His voice, I noticed, was a lot lower and quieter than it had ever been at the station or out on the drill yard. And he hadn't finished surprising me yet. Paddy was the first to notice that the crowd had begun to creep up on us on the riverbank. 'Don't worry about them. I'll move them on, mate,' he told the jumper. Then he stood up and walked away, arms outstretched to shoo everyone else back. When what looked like a tourist got out his camera Paddy put his hand right in front of it. 'No, mate. Not now,' I heard him say. The man was pushed very firmly away. If he hadn't moved I didn't doubt for one moment that Paddy would have clocked him.

We all stood guard until the ambulance arrived. The crew checked that the jumper hadn't injured himself in the fall or the swim. And it was only when the man had been driven off for a proper check-up in hospital that Paddy reverted to form. He looked me up and down like I was a piece of dirt. 'You swim like a girl, Castle,' he said. But I'm certain he was smiling as he walked away.

For the rest of the shift the lads talked about all the other river rescues they'd done over the past few years. Most of the stories involved corpses – mainly the dead bodies of men who had got drunk, stood on the riverbank or on a pontoon to have a pee and had then fallen in. If you're wearing heavy winter clothes when you hit the freezing winter water then you can be dragged down fast, apparently. And the summer's not much safer. The others reckoned unfit, middle-aged men in particular could still get 'cold shock' when they fell in, especially if they'd been drinking and sweating beforehand.

The worst story of all came from Woody the way it normally did. The guy in question had been missing for several months. The police had done a major search at the start of the summer but hadn't found a trace. It turned out he'd been in the water all along. He'd fallen in and been taken way downstream where he'd been caught in a makeshift dam of broken branches, reeds and rocks called a strainer. That's where he stayed till the bigger autumn waters finally dislodged him. His body began a new voyage, floating down towards Atcham where he rested underneath a bridge and was spotted by a couple of kitchen workers from the Mytton and Mermaid Hotel. I spotted a very unusual look appear on Woody's face as the story developed. He almost looked bashful – and I was intrigued to know why. 'It did not end well,' he admitted ruefully. 'Five of us got ready to lift the guy and carry him over to the body bag. It was one person for each leg. I had the head. For some reason everyone else was waiting to lift after three. I lifted on three.'

'So what happened?'

'His head came off. The whole body was bloated and it was so rotten that the neck snapped in two. The effing head came off in my hands. It was like something out of a horror film. There I was, on the edge of a misty riverbank, holding on to some dead geezer's head. That was not what I signed up to the Fire Brigade for. And the stench. It was rancid, disgusting, like nothing on earth.'

We'd paraded as normal at nine o'clock on Saturday morning. We'd heard the day's notices, done the full weekly check of the vehicles and left them all on charge. We'd had our first mug of tea of the shift and I was up in the mess room, itching to hit the volleyball court and spike some balls.

But something else was afoot. 'Hey, Windsor, get yourself into the appliance room fast. The boss is in a good mood today. It's been a while but we're finally going to get to play ice hockey again,' Charlie said with a laugh, giving me yet another hefty thump on the back as he passed. I followed him down the pole. I'd forgotten all about the promise of Saturday morning ice hockey. I didn't believe for one moment that we'd actually be playing it. It had to be code for something else, as usual. But whatever it was I knew it would be fun.

The rest of the watch were already gathering in the appliance room when Charlie and I arrived. George, Woody and Pete were driving the various appliances out into the yard. Paddy was plugging the hose into the hydrant outside and soaking the concrete floor of the appliance room. Then Caddie and Joe came out from the store room with a stack of bars of soap and a whole bundle of brooms and brushes. Everyone else was pulling on their wet legs and gloves. I stood there, grinning like a blinkin' idiot. We really were going to play ice hockey. The soap would be our puck, the brooms our hockey sticks. This really was the best job in the world.

'There's only one rule. Don't get injured or you'll spoil it for the rest of us,' Charlie yelled as open warfare broke out. Our volleyball games were tiddlywinks at a vicarage tea party compared to this anarchic madness. Everyone went hell for leather. Someone blew a whistle and up to a dozen of us lunged for the soap all at once. We threw ourselves at each other, using every ounce of our bodyweight to push each other aside. The slick, wet, soapy floor was as fast and hard as ice. We slammed into each other at every opportunity. We whacked each other with the brooms. And we faced a whole lot of other hazards as well. The metal edges of the appliance room doors were blade-sharp, I noticed, when I was jammed up close to one of them. I gave an involuntary shiver as I pictured someone – most likely me – going into that face first. Then I just got back into the game.

After an hour-long, anarchic and crazily high-scoring contest everyone left the room knackered, wet, pumped up and ready for anything. Plus, of course, we'd given the appliance room floor the first stage of its big weekly clean. Joe told me to hose the soap suds away, stack up all the brooms and wind back the hose before heading back upstairs where, if I was lucky, there might be one last stewed cup of tea left in the pot. There was, and we all had a bit of a laugh reliving the best bits of the game while we loafed around. The whole thing was brilliant fun. Ice hockey was fantastic. Saturday mornings, I decided, were my favourite time of the week.

Comparative calm descended on the station for the rest of the morning. When I'd had my tea I headed to the drying room on the ground floor to hang up my kit properly. As I looked at it I knew I needed to do a bit of housekeeping. John expected every bit of our uniforms to look as good as new at all times – and my plastic leggings were starting to look worryingly tired. Could you iron plastic? I was wondering about this when one of the chaps named Keith popped his head round the door. 'Wrap them up in a towel. Then iron them through that,' he said kindly. I gave it a try and managed to get the job done without melting them or setting anything on fire. While I was doing it I knew most of the watch had headed out to the spare bays to put the finishing touches to our rafts. So when I thought John wasn't looking I nipped over to see it all for myself.

The tank was pretty much finished. It really did look like something out of World War Two. The painted, plywood struc-ture was attached to a tough-looking set of barrels. It even had a fake gun turret. Our second raft, our key fighting machine, was looking just as good. Every inch of it was painted yellow – the exact same shade as the station's hydrant paint, funnily enough. 'We'll be able to take out anyone with these beauties,' Charlie said, waving the two hoses around and aiming them at all sorts of imaginary enemies. I watched the group tinker around with the pump mechanism for a while then headed upstairs.

In the mess room Pete was busy cleaning the pipes on the bar while George was taking a look at the books. 'We took £55 on Wednesday night. I think there were only twelve of us on watch. That's not a bad result,' he said.

'The record's £70 – and that was back when a pint was at least ten pence cheaper,' Pete told me proudly. 'Whoever decided that if we can't go to the pub on a night shift then the pub should come to us deserves a bloody medal.'

I glanced out of the windows. Two of the other old hands were out tending the flowerbeds on the road alongside the station. I doubted they were being paid or had been told to do it, but I understood it completely. I was proud of my job and that translated into pride in the station. I was feeling utterly relaxed and was on the point of going down to help them when the Tannoy clicked to life. I froze, just like everyone else.

First we heard the word 'Attention!' Then came the three

warning tones and the brief details of the shout. I was on the pole before I'd even realised I'd moved.

The standard thirty-three seconds later we were out on the road and I was as fired up as ever. Our destination was a bank, right in the middle of Shrewsbury. But as it turned out, there wasn't a fire. Nor had there been a hold-up. None of the cashiers were trapped in the vault waiting for us to cut through the reinforced metal doors to let them out. No, that day our emergency call-out was for something altogether different. The silly season had begun.

16

Catch the Pigeon

'A pigeon? We're on a call-out because of a backin' pigeon?' Arfer yelled from the seat next to me as we were radioed more information on our way into town.

It seemed that we were. Apparently the bird had flown into the bank branch just after opening time. Three hours later the manager wanted our help getting it out.

'Could they not just open a bleeding window?' Arfer continued, appalled at the whole situation. 'Or shoot the thing? They're vermin, after all. Pigeons are just rats with wings. Everyone hates them. One less of them in the world wouldn't bother anyone.'

He turned out to be wrong on that final point, for the first people we met outside the bank were two volunteers from a local animal charity. They seemed to know a lot of us quite well – and they certainly didn't hate pigeons. 'The poor thing's getting badly distressed. We couldn't free it on our own, we knew you'd be happy to help,' said the first of them, a lady of about forty who was wearing several very colourful silk scarves and looked mildly bonkers. I got the feeling that the rest of the watch had long since taken the same view.

'It's flown into the walls a few times now and it's losing a lot of feathers. It's in a bad way,' added her colleague, a far more reasonable-looking man of about thirty.

'It's a bleeding pigeon, who gives a backin' stuff?' I heard Arfer mutter from just behind me. I tried to hide my smile.

'Well, let's just go inside and see what we're dealing with,' said John taking control the way he always did.

When we got inside I found out why the bird hadn't been able to get out on its own – and why even the long-handled nets the charity people had been using weren't really fit for purpose. The bank was unique. It was more like a stately home than a place of business. The cashiers sat at desks in front of what looked like wood panelling. There was an oil painting on one wall. The chairs customers sat in wouldn't have looked out of place in *Brideshead Revisited*. And above it all was a huge central dome. It had big glass windows all round it. And there, flapping and crapping away some twenty-five feet above the customers' heads, was our pigeon.

'I'm the manager. I'm so glad you're able to help us out,' said a smart, efficient-looking man in a dark blue suit and tie. 'We're one of the few branches that are open on a Saturday so we don't want to close. But it's not easy to serve customers with that thing up above us. There have been,' he paused for a moment, then drew his right hand across the top of his bald head, 'there have been, well, accidents,' he concluded, reddening slightly. This time we found it even harder to hide our smiles. By the look of it the young cashiers were finding it just as difficult.

'Well, let's work out what we can do to help,' John said. I wondered, yet again, how he managed to keep his face straight in front of the public when all the rest of us were on the point of laughing like drains. Maybe it was because he was always thinking ahead. He pointed towards the windows just below the top of the dome. 'Do those open?' he asked. They didn't. 'And there's no other access up there?' There wasn't. 'Not even from outside?' Not even from outside.

With most of his usual twenty questions exhausted I can't say I was surprised about what he said next. 'Jockey, I think this is going to be a job for you.'

*

Ten minutes later I was climbing a ladder high above the bank's polished marble floor. The charity man had handed me his net – and while it looked like the kind of thing you'd use to catch butterflies rather than birds I was still quietly confident of my chances. I would be pretty close to the bird when I got to the top of the ladder, so I'd have a good chance of catching it, right? Wrong. I soon found out that it didn't matter how slowly and unobtrusively I cast the net. The blinkin' pigeon was having none of it. Its horrible beady eyes could see it coming from all angles. It would fly away soon as look at me. The noise of its wings was magnified by the shape of the dome. The flapping was so loud it was as if there were a dozen birds up there. I kept thinking of that horror thriller *The Birds* in which the woman gets pecked to death in a lighthouse. I stayed as still as possible for a few more moments hoping that the bird would calm down. When it perched on one of the window frames I swept the net across yet again. Yet again it flapped away at the very last moment. The game had already been going on for too long. There seemed to be no end in sight.

'Try offering it some nuts,' Arfer shouted with a snigger after yet another failed attempt.

'It's not a blinkin' budgie,' I shouted back down.

'Move the net from underneath it, not from in front of it.'

I gave it a go but those beady eyes didn't miss a thing. The charity pair began to suggest some tactics of their own. The man's ideas were good, but ineffective. He thought I might stand a better chance if I stepped down the ladder a little and tried not to scare the bird so much. He also thought I might catch it if I left the net still for as long as possible in the hope that the bird decided to investigate it of its own accord. His colleague's ideas were, well, downright barking. 'Why don't you talk to him,' she said at one point in stage whisper straight out of amateur dramatics. 'If you can earn his trust then I just know that he'll come to you. Sing a lullaby. It's so hard to tell from down here but he might only be a little baby bird. A lullaby might be just what he needs to hear.' I did talk to the pigeon, as it turned out. But I'm not sure that the nice lady from the animal charity would have approved of my language. And I certainly didn't sing him any blinkin' songs.

I was starting to sweat after about ten minutes up under the dome. I was starting to hope Arfer had managed to sneak in an air pistol when I suddenly got lucky. I wasn't doing anything different. But all of a sudden I got the net round the bird's body. Two things then happened. The first was that the bird flapped like crazy – and it had so much power in it that I was nearly pulled off the ladder. The second thing was that all the staff and customers in the bank gave me a huge round of applause. The sound of that echoed round the dome like a thunderclap. It gave me such a fright that, yes, I nearly fell off the ladder.

'Coming down,' I shouted when I'd got my breath back.

'Oh, look at him, what a darling! Look at that poor little frightened mite!' the charity lady said as I handed the bird and the net over to her.

'She means you, jockey,' said Arfer with a laugh.

The manager gave me a very formal handshake when we'd brought the ladders down, carried them back out to the engine and allowed his bank to get back to business as usual. 'I don't suppose there's a reward. Some free money, perhaps?' Woody asked cheekily. The manager, who didn't seem to have anything resembling a sense of humour, told us that there wasn't.

We said our goodbyes, threw some of our most heroic smiles at all the cashiers, and headed out into the square. The charity lady had carried the bird to the other side of it where she'd been checking it for injuries. Apparently it was fine so she got ready to set it free. 'Don't fly back into the bank, my lovely,' she told it. It wasn't that stupid. It shot up like a bullet from a gun, fluttered about for a moment then disappeared in the direction of Ludlow.

It was a clear day and we didn't have anywhere to rush off to so we hung around for a while. There are five centuries of history preserved in the buildings in the middle of Shrewsbury. The old town square is as beautiful as anything you'll ever see. Ornate, top-heavy stone buildings lean in on one side of it. Ancient black and white, half-timbered houses lean in on the other. At the back is the old Music Hall where Charles Dickens once gave a reading of *A Christmas Carol*. All around were the signs of wealth that the wool trade brought to the town under Elizabeth I. Best of all was that in our time there was a friendly little café on the north corner that had been run by the same family for about a hundred years. We were right outside it. 'Coffees, gentlemen? White with sugar?' asked the owner, just the way we'd been hoping he might. John looked at his watch. 'I don't mind if we do,' he said. 'White with sugar all round would be very much appreciated.'

'Do you remember the parrot?' the charity man asked once the coffees had arrived and we were all still standing tall and trying to impress the waitresses. The others let out a groan.

'It was a few years ago now. This parrot had escaped from someone's house over by the river in Atcham. Its owners were beside themselves. They called the police,' the man explained to me.

'The police thought he was having a laugh but they called us just in case. When we got there we called you,' he continued.

Arfer took up the story. 'What the beggar's owners couldn't get into their heads was the fact that the backin' bird was as happy as Larry. He was free. He was in a tree for the first time in his life. The reason he wouldn't fly back to them was because he didn't want to. The last thing he wanted was to go back into some tiny cage in their front parlour.'

'So what did you do?' I asked.

'We got the turntable ladder out. Our job's to help the public when they're in need. And this crazy couple weren't just in need, they were desperate.' Arfer turned to Charlie. 'You were the jockey back then, weren't you, mate?'

'I was and I'll tell you now that the jockey bashing was worse then than it is now. You don't know you're born, Windsor.'

I thought back to the time Paddy had scared the life out of me on the turntable ladder at Woolies and didn't quite believe him. 'But how did you rescue the parrot?' I asked.

'We didn't,' he admitted, looking a tiny bit bashful. 'There's a whole line of willow trees running along the river down there. Every time we got the turntable up and I got close to him on one tree he'd only go and hop off to the next. We had about three attempts to get him but after about an hour we had to leave him be. We'd shown willing. We'd had a bit of a laugh, to be honest. But I wouldn't be surprised if that parrot's not still out there somewhere having a high old time.'

We finished our coffees, thanked the café owner and climbed back aboard the engine. 'See you boys next time,' the charity lady trilled out as Charlie turned on the ignition.

'Not if we see you first,' mumbled Arfer.

We were back on nights – and everything was going well. We'd sweated up a storm and nearly killed each other on the volleyball court. We'd had a top-notch meal of toad-in-the-hole, thick onion gravy and peas cooked by none other than Woody, followed by four huge lemon meringue pies all courtesy of Mr Thom. I'd got in the way a bit in the raft room and had been sent out to tidy up the already immaculate appliance room. Now I was left to daydream a little and count my blessings. I sneaked out on to the drill ground and lit up a crafty cigarette. I had a bottle of Brasso, a cloth and some wire wool at my feet, just in case anyone came along and accused me of shirking. But I had a feeling everyone else was feeling just as mellow.

It was one of those perfect summer's evenings. It was still light, just about. It was still warm. But everything felt deliciously slow. I looked out towards the main road and saw hardly any cars going by. It was as if the whole of Shropshire had gone to ground. Maybe everyone was sitting on a deckchair on a freshly mowed lawn. 'This is thinking time,' my grandfather used to say when what he really wanted to do was doze off. I was happy just to think. I wondered what it would be like to do this job for the rest of my life. Pretty good, I decided.

I threw my cigarette butt away and watched the orange glow die on the concrete slabs of the drill yard. It was nearly ten o'clock and after doing a final check of the appliance room I headed upstairs. The bar was open and most of the watch seemed to be crowding round the telly ready to watch *The Professionals*. I tried to find a space to join them. But John stopped me. He was about to give me one heck of a wake-up call.

'Sure you've got time to watch that, jockey?' he asked.

'What do you mean?'

'You're still on probation, remember. You could be booted out in the New Year. Don't tell me you've forgotten about your exams?'

17

Of Spuds and Chip Pans

From that moment on I pored over my books on each and every day off. I took to bringing them into the station so that I could read them on shifts as well. While the rest of the watch were working on the raft, playing darts, washing their cars, watching telly or generally pissing around on night shifts I got in some quality study time. I needed it. I wasn't the most academic person in the world. I'd got six GCEs but I'd lost interest by the time my A levels came around. I took two of them and got a U in both. If there'd been exams in common sense or life experience I reckon I would have walked them. But ordinary exams? I can't say I really took to them. I hated that they had suddenly become the most important thing in my life.

'It's tough and not everyone makes it,' the instructors had told us before the first tests we'd taken at training school. Back then I might have been able to cope with failure. But that was before I'd joined the watch. That was before I got the Fire Brigade bug. No way could I walk away from this job now. No way could I work in a factory. And I couldn't imagine working on a farm where I'd have to watch another set of firemen turn up in triumph in an emergency.

The exams themselves were part of a long process. My first ones were due in December. I was due a second set eighteen months into the job and a final set on my second anniversary. Oh, and the Fire Brigade had one final trick to keep its new recruits on their toes. Apparently it wasn't enough just to pass every exam. You had to get a higher mark in each one as well. 'So if I fail in December I'm out, but if I do really well I'm in just as much trouble because I'll have to do even better from then on,' I moaned to my mum and dad back at home. They didn't really have an answer to that little conundrum.

No one could really help me at the station either. Everyone I talked to seemed to have a different opinion.

'Exams? You don't need to worry about the exams. Charlie here passed them and he's as daft as a brush. I swear I've swatted gnats with bigger brains. The tadpoles in the pond in my back garden have got bigger brains than Charlie. If he can pass the exams then you're going to be fine' was Woody's initial comment.

No surprise that Charlie disagreed. 'Don't believe him, mate. Those exams were the hardest thing I ever did. You do need to worry about them. If you fail I bet they'll never let you back in. Get ready for the worst. The tests get tougher every year. I heard that over in Welshpool last year more than half of the candidates got the chop.'

I kept on asking questions though. Every lunch, tea or dinner break it was the only thing on my mind. 'So what do I need to concentrate on?' I'd asked Arfer one day.

'Everything. Backin' everything,' he replied. One thing I knew was important was the exact measurements, weight and dimensions of each bit of kit the different fire engines all carried. I repeated the figures to myself all day every day. 'I think I've got most of them,' I told Charlie after he'd sat and tested me one afternoon.

'So where was the 13.5-metre ladder made?' he asked.

'What do you mean?'

'It's not a trick question. Where was the 13.5-metre ladder made? One of the jockeys on Blue Watch over in Telford says that kind of thing is in the exam as well now. Want to take a look?' The pair of us spent the next hour examining the back or bottom of every piece of kit for its country of origin.

Arfer began firing questions at me every day after that – often when I least expected it. He followed me into the toilets one morning and started to run through the correct routine for a ladder drill from the other side of the cubicle door. Caddie did the same, though he never questioned me in the loo, just in every other room in the station. It all helped, of course, but it added to the pressure as well. Some days I was convinced I was learning too much too soon and would forget it all by December. Other times I thought I'd already left everything far too late and couldn't possibly get through all the books in time. Mostly, though, I just worried.

If you parked our engines on the main road and pointed them in the direction of the hospital I swear they could have driven there on their own. We were being called over there all the time that summer. Some super-sensitive new automatic fire alarms had been installed and they'd go off at almost anything.

'So, what do we think? A real fire or someone on the geriatric ward farted while he was being wheeled past the backin' sensor?' Arfer asked as we raced through the streets of Shrewsbury.

'Maybe one of the nurses had a smoke a week ago last Thursday and the alarms picked up the smell on her uniform,' offered Charlie.

Or maybe it's thunderflies, I thought to myself. They were the bane of my life that summer. I seemed to spend half my time cleaning them off the windscreens of the engines. Now we found they could set off the new automatic fire alarms as well. The basic job was to turn up to the location in question and confirm that nothing was alight. Then, when we'd located exactly which detector had gone off, we had to begin the complex task of resetting the system. Which basically involved taking the detector apart, blowing hard to dislodge all the dead flies, then reconnecting it and waiting for the next time.

The Royal Shrewsbury Hospital was a hotchpotch of 1960s

concrete buildings divided into north and south wings on either side of Mytton Oak Road. It was an easy journey and having a few extra trips there was no bad thing, as long as we weren't missing lunch. We'd leap off the engine, two of us in full breathing apparatus, the rest of us all heroic and ready to get the equipment ready. Then, when we found out the alarms had been triggered by a fart, a smoky uniform or a cloud of thunderflies, we would stand down and get to flirt with the nurses. They seemed to smoke just as much as we did. They were always ready to sneak outside for a quick drag, a cup of tea and a chat. Most of them were young – they were closer to my age than to any of the others so for once I felt as if I fitted in. Winning them over was a little tricky, though. Because the rest of the watch were normally in full mickey-taking mode I couldn't relax for a moment. Paddy loved telling the story of me 'whimpering like a baby' on the end of the turntable ladder. 'It was one whimper. If that,' I'd say.

'He was so scared he nearly had a heart attack. He was this far from being one of your patients,' Paddy finished with a flourish.

Then Woody or Charlie would pitch in with a story about how I'd got injured in the course of my duty the previous week. The nurses would look impressed. But I knew what was coming. 'He only went and jumped down the pole without a shirt on. He got a friction burn all down his front. Come on, Windsor, show it to the nurses,' they'd say.

Then, of course, someone would start on the story about the pigeon. I could hardly have seemed less heroic if I'd tried. And to think that on this latest visit I'd been on the point of asking the girls where they all went drinking of an evening. I stood back a bit, determined to show that I could at least take a joke when the atmosphere suddenly changed.

'It's your boss and he doesn't look very happy,' the prettiest of the nurses said.

We all looked over. John was heading our way fast. Our next call had just come in over the radio. It sounded serious.

'There's someone on a farm up in Alberbury who's caught his hand in a potato harvester. It's jammed right up to his armpit, he's lost a lot of blood and they can't get him free,' John told us. Everyone on the watch winced.

'You'll want some of us to come with you then,' said the pretty nurse.

Regret was heavy in the air as John told her we couldn't carry passengers. 'We will be wanting an ambulance crew to come out as well, though. Maybe you could get yourself on to that? We could meet you up there?' he suggested, hopefully.

It didn't happen. But we did talk about the girl for almost the whole trip out to the farm, so she was certainly with us in spirit. The engine headed west out of town towards Welshpool.

The roads became clearer as we headed further over towards our destination. Our patch covered more than a thousand square miles, from Whitchurch in the north to Ludlow in the south, and included all the villages and towns in between. This farm was on the edge of the Welsh hills, right on one of the furthest corners of our area. It was beautiful but isolated.

'OK, we're getting close now,' John called back, folding up the old Ordnance Survey. He jumped down to get us through a couple of gates, we thundered over some cattle grids, round a dozen sharp corners and then, over the top of a high hedge, we could see the farm. The barns were quite modern and ugly, but the farmhouse itself was surprisingly beautiful. I've no idea how old it was, but it must have been built in the days when they really cared about such things. It had a real balance and elegance to it. The door was right in the middle, there were wide, well-maintained bay windows top and bottom on either side. It was made of warm Shropshire stone and was protected by a classic Welsh slate roof. 'Looks very nice,' I said as we approached.

'It looks it. But it's not one of the places where you want to say yes to a cup of coffee,' Arfer advised drily as we lurched over a final set of potholes and parked in the yard.

'Why not?'

'You won't like the look of the mugs,' Woody interrupted. And as Woody had never struck me as the kind to worry too much about personal hygiene or cleanliness, this had to be saying something. 'Some of these farmers don't see another living soul from one day to the next – one week to the next sometimes,' he continued. 'They get a bit set in their ways. I'll bet this guy lives in no more than two rooms of that whole house. There's no real reason for them to wash every day so they don't. They certainly don't wash up every day. The spoon he uses for sugar is likely as not the same one he uses for the dog food. So think on before you tuck in.'

'That's why we need to be ready if we get a call from them,' Caddie added. 'They're even more self-sufficient than the ones over in Ellesmere. These ones really don't like asking for help. To be honest, they don't need help all that often. If they do then it's serious.'

A small welcome party stepped out of the barn to greet us as we jumped out of the engine. The first person was a man in his sixties who looked as strong and resilient as the Shropshire stone itself. His face was weathered and walnut-brown. His hair was shockingly white and neatly combed in a formal side parting. Sharp eyes of the faintest ice blue glinted from beneath deep folds in his skin. He was leaning heavily on a silver-handled walking stick – but despite that he still looked as fit as a flea. A few paces behind him stood what must have been his son. The man, who looked roughly around forty-five, had the same pale blue eyes and the same dark, craggy skin. He was in a very different mood, though. He was clearly angry. His hands were never still. He clenched them into fists, he twisted them around, he put them in and out of the pockets of his ragged jeans. Last in line was a lad in his early teens – he must have been the latest generation of the family. He was taller than his granddad and almost as tall as his dad. And while his dad couldn't keep his hands still, the son had a similar problem with his feet. He was constantly hopping from one foot to another. He stepped forward, then back. He was the least relaxed kid I'd ever seen.

'You'll be wanting to see him straight away. He's over there in the barn,' the older man told us succinctly.

'And it's the last time he'll be on my farm. He's not working here again. He's had his last chance. When you get his arm free he's on his way,' the son spat out.

'It's my farm, and while it is I'll be the one to decide who works on it,' his dad told him quietly. The boy kept his head down.

'A bit early for a potato harvester, isn't it?' John asked as we followed the old man's lead into the barn.

'It's a beet harvester. He was moving it for me.'

'Messing with it, more like. What was he doing moving it in the first place? Turning it on when he's no business. It's his last day on this farm, I'm telling you that.'

Walking out of the August sunshine into the darkness of the barn was momentarily disorientating. It took more than a few blinks before we could see easily. The barn itself was chock-full of every type of equipment – but it wasn't a mess like most of those we visited. There seemed to be method in the madness of all the stacks of kit. Somehow I got the feeling that if we'd asked the old guy for a specific tool or machine he'd have known exactly where it was. This was his kingdom. He seemed to run it well.

We headed towards the far left corner, to where the harvester was. I knew them well from all the farm work I'd done earlier in the year. Harvesters like that one were towed and powered by tractors. They picked up the beet as they were driven down the rows of the field. Each bit of veg went between the blunt teeth of a series of strong, heavily sprung rollers to knock off all the earth. Small rocks in the soil were normally spat out without any problems. Bigger ones could get jammed. That must have been what had happened here. The man must have put his hand in between the teeth to try and dislodge a stone that had been left there from the previous year. What had happened next was obvious.

'You need to get me out, mon. I've been bleeding like a pig. My arm's gone dead. I can't move it. I can't feel it any more. You need to get me out!' The farm worker was desperate. He seemed barely older than me. He was fair-haired, had a face full of freckles and very scared eyes. He was wearing blue overalls, a bit like ours. His right arm was trapped well inside the rollers. The springs had snapped them shut. The ripped-up material of his sleeve was meshed in with the flesh and muscle of his arm. No surprise that the man was deathly, desperately, pale.

'What's your name, son?' John asked.

'Jamie.'

'Well, Jamie, how long ago did this all happen?'

'Half an hour? Maybe longer? I don't know,' he said. Fair play, I suppose. The poor chap could hardly look at his watch to check.

'This lad called you twenty-five minutes ago,' the old man told us, pointing to his grandson. 'Jamie was trapped in the machine for ten minutes before then. So thirty-five minutes all told. No more. No less.'

John looked back towards the barn door and the empty yard outside. 'Well, there's an ambulance on its way. I'm surprised it didn't beat us to it but it'll be here soon. When it is, we can get him out.'

'You can't keep me waiting like this! Just do it now. I don't need no ambulance. You're the effing Fire Brigade. Just get me out!' Jamie was straining against the machine now. His eyes were bulging. And even before he started tugging at his arm again it was clear that his injuries were worse than they'd first looked. I knelt down to look into the harvester and winced. Woody did the same. It was clear that the upper arm hadn't just been crushed by that first pair of rollers. The second set had been sprung as well. They looked to have snapped his forearm and done a heck of a lot of damage to his elbow and upper arm as well. Everything looked bent and horribly damaged. The man must have lost a lot of blood before his body shut itself down. He wiped his face with his free hand as we examined the situation. His eyes were wide and wet. I tried not to meet them. I could imagine the joy he must have felt when he had seen us arrive. He must have thought his ordeal would be over in minutes. But my first aid training told me it wasn't going to end this quickly.

Funnily enough, I'd been reading up on that sort of thing a couple of nights earlier. Every now and then we had to do what was called 'ambulance aid' as part of our various drills. It was a step beyond basic first aid and included mouth-to-mouth, heart compressions, wound dressing, back injuries and so on. Two nights ago, when we were all gasping for breath after finishing a pump drill, the officer in charge had fired out a load of questions about crush injuries in car accidents. We'd had to shout out the answers and demonstrate the action we'd take if we had to deal with it on a shout. Afterwards Joe had given me some extra medical books to look through and some chapters on crush syndrome had caught my eye. It seemed that the good news was that your body can apparently go into some form of shock when you have a really bad injury like this. It can practically stop you bleeding altogether. One of my textbooks had an eye-watering passage about someone being able to carry his own arm away from one car crash like some sort of living Frankenstein's monster. It said some bad stuff as well, though. I was racking my brain to remember the worst of it – something about toxins in your body that got blocked while your arm was crushed but could kill you when it got released and they could overwhelm your body and cause liver failure. I couldn't remember the exact details. But I had a feeling that while we could free the man straight away we had to wait till the ambulance crew was there to inject him or do something else the moment he was released. So where the heck was the ambulance?

'Go back to the house, Harry. Sit by the phone. Come out and tell us if the hospital rings us up. Happen the ambulance has broken down,' the old man told his grandson. The lad ran off to do as he was told.

'Please just get me out now. Please!' the worker said. This time he was begging, the poor sod. He also looked close to tears. John stepped closer to him, put his hand on his good shoulder and explained that we needed some medical people here for when his arm was free. The man started shaking his head and moaning in pain. I headed outside to see if the help was coming. It was a couple of minutes before I saw it. Far down the valley, at the end of the farm track, was an ambulance. I gave John a thumbs-up sign from the barn door.

'The cavalry's here, Jamie. Not long to go now,' John told him.

I could hear the man sniff and could sense him trying desperately hard not to cry when I headed back towards him. He begged us to get the job done fast. We said we'd do it as soon as the medics were alongside. And we would have done if the farmer's son hadn't tried to stop us.

John briefed the two-man ambulance crew as they strode across the farmyard and into the barn. They asked Jamie a few questions, took a good look at the wound, checked out his blood pressure and things and agreed that we'd been right to wait. They hooked up a saline drip to start to dilute the toxins before the internal free-for-all his body would face when his arm was released. The younger of them headed back to the ambulance to get a special tourniquet ready to tie to the top of his arm as well.

He was new to the job and this was his first emergency call-out, he told me as we walked back to the patient. I stood up a little straighter at the news. It felt good not to be the new boy for a change. I tried to walk like an old hand.

'Got a rod up your arse, jockey?' Arfer asked, watching me cross the yard. My old-hand act could clearly do with some polishing. I shrugged and waited for John to list the tools we needed. That's when the problems began.

'Hey, stop right there. Alligator jaws? Are you kidding me? I want you to just put the machine in reverse and get his arm out that way. I'm not having you damage my beet harvester. There's no way on earth you're ruining that.'

It was the farmer's son. John turned to him. 'If the machine could go in reverse I expect you'd have done it long since. We need to prise it apart. This is the only way to get the lad out.'

The farmer gave a short laugh. 'I don't care if it's the only way to frickin' Tipperary. It's not going to happen. The frickin' idiot shouldn't have been fooling around with it in the first place. Messing around, wasting my time, that's what he was doing. And now you want to destroy a perfectly good beet harvester? I'll tell you something for free. This is my farm and that ain't going to happen.'

The older man stepped forward. 'This is my farm,' he said very quietly.

'Look, old man, it's your fault as much as his. Moving the harvester around inside the barn? Turning it on when it's not needed? It's the stupidest thing I've ever heard. This place is going to rack and ruin. I'm not buying a new harvester just because you two Ronnies here have broken my old one.'

'This is my farm,' the old man repeated just as quietly, but with a whole lot more feeling. Some heavy-duty eyeballing went on between father and son for a few moments. Then John stepped in. 'Look, you can sort this out between yourselves another time. But you ought to know that we're the Fire

Brigade. We have a duty to save life and property. We have the right to do whatever is required to fulfil that task so we will be pulling this harvester apart to save the lad's arm. You don't have to help us. But shame on you if you try to stand in our way.'

The old man had won the eyeballing contest with his son. He gave him one final glare and turned towards John. 'This is my farm. It's my harvester, that's my farmhand and it's what I say that goes. You do whatever it is you need to do.'

His son spat at the ground in front of him then turned on his heels and strode out of the barn. His grandson, I noticed, took a few steps back and waited just outside the door. The poor sod can't have known which side to be on. We got to work – and to be honest the job didn't take long. I manned the hand pump, providing the hydraulic power to operate the alligator jaws. Woody put blocks in place as the space between the rollers opened up. When they were wide enough John gave the man the call to pull out his arm. He didn't need to be told twice – but he did get a hell of a shock the moment he was free. There were medical reasons for all of this, I was told. But, basically, the real pain only hit the guy when the rollers were no longer crushing it and the blood began to flow again. Judging by the noise he made, the pain must have hit him like a ten-tonne truck.

The more experienced ambulance man supported his patient while the new recruit tried to get the tourniquet on to his upper arm without knocking out the drip. The man was still howling in agony when they led him slowly across the yard and sat him on the back step of the ambulance. 'Just calm down here for a few minutes. Get your breath then we'll check you out properly,' they told him.

We packed up the kit, tried to do a bit of a repair job on the harvester, and headed back to the engine. The old farmer stood quietly by as everyone busied themselves. 'You'll all be wanting cups of tea, I'll warrant,' he said after a while.

Arfer flashed a look in my direction. I saw a flicker of a smile on his face.

'We're good, thank you,' he said.

The new boy from the ambulance clearly hadn't heard about the likely state of the cups and spoons. 'I'd love one. White, no sugar,' he said straight away. About five minutes later Arfer's smile was even broader when we saw what the farmer had brought out.

'I'd not be surprised to hear he'd been using that mug as a flowerpot not ten minutes ago,' Arfer whispered at the ambulance man knowingly. 'I hope you've got a strong stomach, lad. Happen you're going to need it.'

We were having a bit of a sing-song in the back of the cab as we bounced down the road alongside Onslow Park and back towards Shrewsbury. It had been a busy morning, what with the pretty nurses, the game of unhappy families up at the farm and the poor sod in the beet harvester. But it was only just gone twelve thirty when we reached the outskirts of town. We still had enough time to get back to base before Betty and Mabel got cross and tossed up deciding whether to leave our food under the hotplates or in the bin.

That's when the radio fired up. Shouts, I was starting to learn, are like buses. You wait ages for one then three turn up at once. A sharp, clear voice from the control room told us there was a house fire on a housing estate near the RAF base at Shawbury.

'Chip pan,' Charlie announced firmly. He was still obsessed with chip-pan fires.

'How do you know?' I asked.

'It's lunchtime. Mum puts the pan on. She calls the kids in from the garden. One of them refuses to come in. She goes out to crack the whip a bit. And next thing you know the curtains are on fire and it's spreading round the house faster than a rat with the runs. Trust me. It's a chip pan.'

The street wasn't hard to find. About a dozen kids were waiting at the entrance to the estate. They were jumping up and down in excitement – and I couldn't blame them. I'd have been jumping even higher if something like this had happened on my street when I was eight. I was still feeling pretty pumped up about it at eighteen.

'Go up to the end and turn right, mister!' the spotty little ringleader shouted out at us. He and his gang then raced alongside us. The house was pretty easy to spot as well. A big black tide mark had mushroomed up above the front window. The kitchen window, by the look of it. It probably had been a chip-pan fire, just like Charlie had said.

Caddie and Woody jumped out of the engine in full breathing apparatus. Charlie hit the ground and started to work on the hoses. I jumped out to man the board while John strode up to speak to the pretty young mum who was holding on to two little kids in the middle of the garden.

'I think it's out. I tried to put it out with a wet towel. I shut the kitchen door after us when we left. That's right, isn't it?' she asked, her eyes wide and her voice high.

'That's very good. That could have made a big difference,' John told her. 'Is the front door unlocked?' It was, so he turned and gave Caddie and Woody the nod to go in. I was slotting their tallies into the board and marking it up when one of the kids began to cry.

'I want my lunch, Mam,' he said. His mum gave him a bit of a slap.

Caddie and Woody weren't in the house for long. Caddie took John aside and talked him through what they'd found while I updated the board. A few minutes later the two of them took off their breathing apparatus, replaced the cylinders, stowed them and we all headed into the house to take a look around. The acrid smell of a house fire wouldn't be going away any time soon. But the mum had managed to contain the fire and keep damage to a minimum.

'If you'd not shut the door you could have had black smut and grease on the ceilings and going right down all your walls to the floor,' John told her through the kitchen window – he'd wanted her and the kids kept outside just in case we had a flare-up. 'It would have got upstairs as well. Your whole house would have been ruined.'

'It doesn't look great as it is,' she said, looking up at the smoke stain on her front wall. 'Where does all the blackness come from? How am I going to get it cleaned up?'

The bad news for her was that we were about to make it all a whole lot worse. As usual, we had to bash about a bit to make sure nothing was smouldering in some hidden corner – or up in what were now very greasy, grey ceiling panels. John was feeling particularly finicky that day and he wanted the electrics checked as well. He had the others pull a few of the wall panels off, too – which didn't go down so well with the mum.

'You know my husband's going to kill me when he sees this,' she said. 'Maybe I should have let the fire burn. I might finish the job and torch the place once you've left. That way the insurance will at least buy us a new one.'

She got her sense of humour back when I was sent to shoo off a swarm of local kids who were getting a bit too close to the fire engine for John's liking. She even hung around with us for a while when we'd given her kitchen the final all-clear and were having a quick cigarette in the street before heading back to the station. 'I'd offer you lunch, but you've destroyed my kitchen so I can't,' she declared, cadging a second ciggie off Charlie. My stomach was rumbling badly, but I'd have hung around that housing estate all day if necessary. It wasn't just the kids who were all wide-eyed and impressed with us. Their young mums seemed just as keen to have a butcher's at us as they walked by, popping in and out of each other's houses far more than seemed strictly necessary for a midweek afternoon. I was as happy as Larry with all the attention. I was just so pleased to be a fireman. I also had a strong feeling that this was the start of a whole new phase in the job. I was convinced that this small fire was only the start. We'd be real heroes from now on. I leaned back against the engine, took another big drag on my cigarette and smiled. Any day now I was convinced that I would be carrying that beautiful blonde woman out of a burning building. Any day now.

18

Messing About in the River

'Emergency tender and water tender to a cow in the river at Montford Bridge.' The call was put out at the start of our next tour of day shifts. I was in my usual number five position on the rear seat but I didn't feel travel sick. Instead I felt confused. A cow in the blinkin' river? This wasn't what I'd spent the past few days dreaming about. It wasn't the kind of heroic story I'd wanted to tell my mates down the pub. Especially as I already knew that if anyone was going to be forced to jump in and do some sort of rescue then that person would be me. I consoled myself with the fact that we did at least get to do another emergency run through town. It was the tail end of the rush hour and the roads were still surprisingly busy. I got a huge thrill out of racing towards a wall of heavy traffic and seeing the roads magically clear for us – more than thirty years on I still do, to be honest.

Montford Bridge is a little village a few miles north-west of Shrewsbury. The bridge itself is beautiful – it's a couple of hundred years old and it's got three shallow arches made of local red sandstone. When we arrived that hot August day we saw a very distinctive farmer waving at us from a field a few hundred yards upstream. 'Blimey, it's Captain backin' Birdseye,' Arfer muttered when we first saw the man. He was short, wiry and weather-beaten and he had the richest, thickest white beard I'd ever seen.

The farmer strode forwards when we climbed down from the

engine. Joe held out his hand but the man didn't seem that bothered with introductions. 'Er's in 'ere, mon,' was all he said, pointing just upstream towards the cow in question. To be honest, 'er didn't look that bothered. It was another scorching August day. The last bit of road we'd driven along from the village had been sticky with the melting bitumen in the tarmac and the field we had crossed to approach the river was hard as concrete. Out in the river the cow was up to her neck in water and was probably feeling a whole lot better than the rest of the herd stuck out in the fields. Her big, vacant face looked lazily at us as we stood on the riverbank. She was chewing away at something. She could hardly have looked happier.

'I need 'er out, mon. I can't risk losing 'er. She's a good milker, mon, and money's tight,' the farmer declared. I stole a glance at the nearly new Land Rover we'd parked the truck alongside. His definition of hard times was clearly very different from mine. We fanned out a bit to try to assess the situation.

'How do you think she got in?' I asked as we stood watching the sun glinting off the top of the water. The riverbanks were high and there was no easy path down into the water.

'A racing dive,' offered Charlie. 'Or maybe she broke the rules and did a bomb. That would have been worth watching.' We had a bit of a giggle in the shade of a lone willow tree. It was that perfect pale green colour, its branches dancing down to the water's edge and shimmering, ever so slightly, as the water tried to drag the leaves downriver.

'Won't she get out on her own if we just leave her?'

'Not in this part of the river. The banks don't get any easier as you go downstream,' Charlie pronounced. 'It would be a bit of fun to let her float off through town but I doubt the boss will see it that way. My guess is that we rope her up and pull like crazy. It's going to be a long afternoon, jockey.'

Charlie was right. John had us throwing lassos out to the cow, reminding me of poor old Brandy the racehorse back on my first day on the job. But this time our Roy Rogers act wasn't as successful. The cow was too far away and she was too good at moving her head just as the rope came close. After half a dozen or so failed attempts John finally said the words I'd been waiting for all along. 'Someone's going to have to go in and get her. Now, who's the tallest and the youngest here?'

Everyone looked at me.

'Hope you packed your swimming trunks,' Arfer said wickedly. I hadn't, but I was at least wearing clean underwear. I got my kit off in the shadow of the fire engine then strode off towards the water's edge. 'It's a hot day and I'm being paid to go for a swim in the river,' I was telling myself as I did so. 'This is a good thing. This is OK. It's not embarrassing at all.'

That's when I heard the first of the wolf whistles. I looked up towards the bridge. Oh, my God. Where the blinkin' heck had they all come from? A whole gang of builders or road diggers or some other workers were lined up on top of it. Cars were stopping on the road to see what was going on as well. Whole families were there looking down at me. I heard someone tell her husband to get the camera. Everyone was hooting with laughter.

I tried to ignore the catcalls as I slipped and slid my way down the muddy bank towards the water. I felt the rush of cold as it reached my stomach. 'Get in, Malcolm, just go under and get it over with,' I told myself. I did a shallow dive and when I came up for air I heard a bit of clapping from the bridge. It was a lot better than the laughter. John threw me the rescue line and I swam off towards the cow. The river was surprisingly deep in parts. I'd expected to be able to walk right across it but in places I could barely touch the bottom. The light was also dazzlingly bright as the sun hit the surface. I could have done with a pair of sunglasses, but wasn't going to ask for them while I had an audience.

If the cow had stayed where she was then I think I'd have been all right. Getting the rope round her wouldn't have been very dignified but it should have been quite straightforward. But 'er didn't want to stay put. It seemed that 'er wanted to go swimming as well.

'Go after her, Castle!' one of the watch yelled out from the riverbank.

'Give her the kiss of life, mate!' came another voice from the bridge where two dozen people appeared to be simultaneously splitting their sides with laughter. Unfortunately for me they would carry on doing this for quite some time.

Cows, it turned out, can be pretty handy in the water. This one was an Olympic-standard swimmer. Whenever I got close she just changed direction and paddled away at surprising speed. And if getting close to her was tough, then getting a rope around her was almost impossible.

'Swim underwater. Catch her unawares next time,' Charlie suggested from the shade of the willow tree when my latest attempt to get the rope around the cow's neck had failed. 'Try doing backstroke so she doesn't know you're coming.'

'Try swimming like this,' Arfer offered instead. I managed to tread water for a moment and look at him. He looked like a cross between an injured seagull and a malfunctioning helicopter as he mimed some bizarre, unrecognisable stroke.

'Distract her – like this,' offered Charlie, miming something very similar.

I won't repeat what Arfer suggested as a surefire way to per-suade the cow to move forwards. To this day I'm still trying to forget the way he acted out his idea up on that sunny riverbank. I doubt the group of three elderly ladies who had just got out of their car on the bridge will forget it either. Though, as Charlie said later on, there was a good chance they wouldn't press charges.

I'd swum and splashed around in the river for about twenty minutes when the cow finally decided that this strange, half-naked man had bothered her enough. She edged her way towards the bank – and was at last within easy reach of the others. They tied one end of their rope to a nearby tree and got the other round her neck. It wasn't easy to drag her out without harming her, not least because, having got so close to the bank, she then decided to dig her hooves in and refuse to take the final few steps to freedom. For a while I could see her point. All the workmen from the bridge had run across the field to see if they could help pull the ropes. I got some more catcalls when I climbed out – and John told me to get back in just in case the cow went into reverse. She didn't, fortunately. After about five minutes of pulling we won the tug of war and she finally deigned to edge up the steep bank and back on to dry land. I snuck out just behind her. She then stood on the river's edge for a moment and carried on chewing while the lads got the ropes off her. Then she ambled off to join the rest of the herd without a care in the world. Or a single moo of thanks.

No surprise that I didn't get much praise either once I'd dried off and got my clothes back on. 'Messing around in the river on a sunny day. You should be paying us, Castle,' John told me. The others then pitched in by listing all the far tougher jobs they'd allegedly carried out in the past. 'Cows are backin' child's play compared to sheep,' Arfer told me on the way back to the station. 'You'll have something to say once you've pulled a sheep out of a mine shaft, mate. Sheep kick like hell and because their legs are short they're bloody hard to get hold of and tie back. You rescue a sheep and you're getting somewhere. Stick to cows and horses and you're nothing but an amateur.'

Fortunately the grim-faced, busy-bearded farmer came good, though. He turned up at the station the following day and gave us a bottle of very nice malt whisky to thank us for our work. 'Thank you very much,' I said, reaching out for it. Arfer, moving faster than Concorde, swooped in and took the bottle before my fingers had even brushed the glass.

'I'll be looking after that, jockey,' he said, disappearing behind the bar.

'At least the cow must have learned her lesson. She won't be going in the water again any time soon,' I said as the farmer shook my hand and turned to leave.

He shook his head resignedly. 'No, mon, 'er's already been in again,' he said, a note of pride in his voice as if he was talking about a naughty but much-loved child. 'To be honest, 'er went straight back in after you all left. 'Er loves the water, 'er does. Every year she has a little swim when it's hot. Happen you'll be back in there for another swim before the summer's out.'

We opened the bottle and toasted the cow's health on our next night shift – we'd christened her Dozy and she got a mention for the next week and a half until the bottle was empty.

It was organised chaos at the station for the rest of our tour of duty. The town festival was only a few days away – the great raft race of 1980 was about to be run. No one wanted a shout to interrupt the final tinkering that was designed to turn our rafts into world-beaters. We had endless tactical discussions. We spent forever trying to work out what the rival rafts might be like. We couldn't have taken more care of the creations when we transferred them to the riverbank on the day if they'd been made of glass.

But would we win the race?

Someone from the council had asked if we'd bring one of the fire engines down to the fairground for the duration of the event. 'So we're going to be on duty? How can we do the race if we have to be on the engine within thirty-three seconds for a shout?' I asked Arfer the day beforehand. 'Anyway, Saturday's our day off. I thought that was why we were doing this year's race in the first place.'

Arfer looked at me as if I was a total idiot, the way he always did.

'We won't be on duty, mate. White Watch will be working nine to six on Saturday as normal. The council have got other ideas. They don't want the engine down there in case there's a fire. They want it there as part of the entertainment. Mark my words, it'll be a giant climbing frame for every grubby-fingered, snotty-nosed little brat in Shropshire. Parents will use us as some sort of babysitters. They'll drop their little horrors off, tell them to play at being firemen then disappear into the tea tent on their own for half an hour's peace and quiet. Meanwhile, we've got to stop the little blighters from killing each other. More's the pity.' I smiled. Arfer's views on children were legendary. 'If women gave birth to teenagers they'd only ever have one child and all their friends would make damn sure they had none,' he'd proclaimed the other day. Now it seemed he was equally wary of younger kids – and I soon found out he was right. The moment we got the engine to the fairground a swarm of kids began wiping their dirty hands all over it. Six months ago I'd have laughed my head off if you'd said that kind of thing would bother me. Why would I care about a few little fingerprints? On race day it was a totally different story. I flinched whenever I saw one of the blighters touch our fire engine – *my* fire engine. I wanted to set off the bell and scare them all away whenever one of them approached holding a toffee apple or a bag of greasy popcorn.

When I took a break and wandered across the fairground the first person I saw was Mabel. She was sitting on a picnic rug surrounded by a vast, extended family – a whole heap of sons, daughters, grandchildren and even great-grandchildren. 'This is Malcolm. He's one of my boys. He's tall but he's too skinny. Don't you agree he's too skinny?' she asked two of her fortysomething daughters when I went over to say hello.

On the other side of the river I saw two other women I vaguely recognised from somewhere. I was trying to find my mum and dad but the women just ahead of me looked so familiar that I couldn't look away. They were coming towards me fast. One of them was fat and round like a football. The other was skin and bone, like a walking toothpick. It was only when they said hello that the penny dropped. It was Bev and Babs.

'Hello. You know what? I didn't recognise you at first,' I began.

'Because we've got our clothes on!' Bev interrupted as they both fell about giggling. 'This young lad's never seen us with our clothes on before,' she told a complete stranger walking by.

'I've never seen them with *normal* clothes on,' I said hastily. This would not be a good moment for me to find my mum and dad. 'I normally see them wearing —'

'Nothing but a smile!'

'Overalls,' I blurted out.

We talked for a while once they'd both stopped sniggering. It was funny to see them out of context and out of uniform. I suppose I must have looked just as different to them. 'So, no girlfriend for us to meet?' Babs asked at one point.

'Not yet. But if you know anyone I'm interested,' I told them.

'Well, I know a really big girl called Bev,' said Babs.

'And I know a real goer called Babs,' said Bev.

They were laughing so much at that I'm sure they never noticed me slip away and head back to the relative safety of Arfer at the fire engine.

'So how are the grubby brats? Brained any of them yet? Any blood been spilled?' I asked him.

'It's come close, mate, it's come close.' He was looking out through the crowds in search of someone. 'Charlie is supposed to have got back here ten minutes ago. He's taking over from me. I'm backin' starving and I want to get to the beer tent before Caddie and his mates drink it dry.'

You know how you sometimes say things without thinking first? I didn't think first before saying I'd watch over the fire engine if Arfer wanted to go and get a drink. He was off as fast as a rat up a drainpipe, leaving me alone on the fire engine. Alone, except for about a dozen monkey-like kids who seemed determined to cover every inch of my fire truck with fluorescent pink candy floss and the remains of their ice creams.

'Hey, kids, you can't play hide and seek in there. Are your mum and dad not back yet?' I was saying to one batch of them when I realised reinforcements had finally arrived. Charlie was there, with George and Paddy at his side as back-up. All three gave a huge, theatrical roar and battered their hands against their chests like crazed lions. With delighted shrieks of excitement every one of the kids ran away. 'I should have thought to do that hours ago,' I said.

'It all comes with experience,' George said. He turned to the rather stern-looking woman at his side. 'This is my wife, Kate,' he said. 'Kate, this is —' he stopped mid-sentence. I realised, suddenly, that he didn't know my first name. Ever since we'd met nearly three months ago I'd been 'Jockey' or 'Castle' or 'Windsor' to him, nothing else. The silence continued – and I suddenly realised that Paddy didn't know my name either.

'I'm Malcolm,' I said, in the end. Kate gave me a knowing smile and a satisfied nod as she reached out to shake my hand. George and Paddy, I'm almost certain, looked just a little bit bashful. Charlie leaned over to me and whispered in my ear, 'Well done there, Windsor, Kate measures all jockeys by how they handle themselves on first meeting. You did yourself proud, she's not a woman to cross I'll tell you.'

The rafting was due to kick off at 2 p.m. In theory the course would take everyone from the county cricket ground to the Pengwern Boat Club in the town park. In reality the whole thing was a lot less organised than this. It turned out to be less of a race and more of a free-for-all. It was a bit like a floating version of our daily volleyball games back at the station. At the sound of a starting pistol thirty or forty teams of rafters just leaped in and went for it. Each raft had actually been given a start time to turn it into some sort of time trial. But really it was just chaos. Woody and Charlie were manning our main raft, the tank. They'd decided to get into the spirit of it by dressing up like Freddie Starr's Hitler lookalikes. They weren't around for long, though. The tank turned out to be dangerously top heavy. It turned turtle within about twenty seconds of its launch. The top half then fell off completely and either sank to the depths of the Severn or floated away down the river far faster than Woody and Charlie ever would. 'Get on top of the barrels! You can still win this!' we yelled from the riverbank as the pair of them did just that. Somehow the base of the raft had held together. The lads did manage to climb on to it and paddled away like fury with their hands.

As if seeing that raft fall apart wasn't bad enough, the lads were also beaten by a group of nurses. The girls had done their raft up to look like a hospital bed – one lucky man was lying on it while four scantily clad nurses tried to steer him down the river. To be honest, Woody and Charlie weren't just beaten by this rival craft. They were so badly distracted by the nurses that they forgot to paddle for a while.

We got our own back with our second raft, though. That one set off just after a flurry of other teams – the first one we tried to beat was made up of Elvis lookalikes, the second was kitted out to look like a giant squid. Overtaking them wasn't easy but what we lacked in speed we made up for in firepower. Our pump worked a treat – just as well, as spraying water was our business, after all. It soaked all the other competitors and Arfer and George then took aim at all the people lined up on the riverbanks. The pair of them were both dressed as pantomime dames – I can't remember why – and got some of the biggest cheers of the scorching afternoon. Everyone knew they were the Fire Brigade team and they coasted along on a wave of goodwill. I'd never felt prouder. I ran up and down the banks with the rest of the watch, yelling encouragement and insults at Arfer and George and generally acting like an overgrown kid. Did we win the race? I'm not sure that the organisers went as far as naming a winner amidst the chaos. A couple of hours later, though, knocking back the beers in the Boathouse pub, I convinced myself that we'd not only won, but we'd done so because I'd been the captain of the ship. Better still, the rest of the watch were too drunk to say any different. It was the perfect day – and back at the station three days later for our next shift we looked set to have the perfect night.

Simon had brought in a brand new video player. 'I've got *Convoy* and *Jaws*,' he said proudly as he connected it up to the TV in the mess room. The whole watch crowded around after dinner like they'd never seen a TV before. The whole watch apart from me; of course I was sent downstairs to study as usual. But later on I found out they'd watched both films back to back – every now and then taking advantage of the new-fangled 'pause' button so everyone could top up their pints.

Down in the appliance room I was testing myself on the weight of all the ladders and feeling a bit sorry for myself when John strode in. He threw a series of questions at me and nodded his approval when I got them all right. Then he sprung a surprise. It seemed that I wasn't going to be the new-boy jockey for much longer. Someone else was joining the watch, someone fresh out of training school. When John had gone I turned back to my books with a big smile on my face. I'd really enjoyed learning from all the old hands on the watch. I hadn't cared about all the jockey bashing and the jokes at my expense. But it was going to be brilliant finally to work alongside someone my own age.

19

And Then There Were Two

O ur new recruit was a nineteen-year-old local lad called Matthew. He was a lean-looking whippet of a character. He had short, dark hair, he couldn't seem to sit still and his eyes were constantly darting around the room looking for something new to talk about. He'd gone to school on the other side of Shrewsbury to me but we still knew a few of the same people. He'd been working in a hardware shop in town but he said it looked so cool when the fire engines shot by outside that he'd applied to join up. He'd done his training just after me in Chorley. He was just as keen as me now he'd been given his first posting. It was brilliant to have him around.

'We're both on hydrant duty,' I told him firmly on his second afternoon in the job.

'What's hydrant duty?' he asked.

'I'm not sure.'

John soon put us right. As the Officer in Charge he was in the passenger seat of the fire engine as usual. Woody was driving for a change. Matt and I were in the back with Arfer. We headed east, over the English Bridge towards Shrewsbury Abbey, the thousand-year-old building practically cut in half by Thomas Telford when he wanted to build the London to Holyhead road. Woody parked us up when we got to Underdale and John got the file out to see where all the relevant hydrants were located. When he'd identified the first of them, Matt and I leaped down and carried the standpipe over to it. The idea was to open up the hydrant, screw the standpipe on to it and then to use the key and bar to turn on the water. The main part of the task was to sort things out if anything stood in the way of this procedure. Sometimes the hydrants had silted up since they were last inspected so we had to dig them out and clean them up before checking the water flow and passing them as effective. Sometimes the false spindle – the part that actually turned the water on – was missing and we had to replace it so that it would work in a real emergency.

When each inspection was finished we would call it out to John so that he could mark it on the file. Then we'd get the paint bucket out and paint the post yellow, front and back, as well as the hydrant lid.

'I want you to go right up to the edges on the lid. And woe betide you if you go over the edge. If you can't even paint right you're no use to me on this watch,' John said ominously when we had finished our first inspection of the day.

Job done, we would get back in the engine and head off to find the next hydrant. Then the one after that. The inspections had been neglected a bit over the summer when everyone had been working on our rafts. Now autumn was on its way we had a lot of catching up to do. And Matt and I were more than happy to help out: because we'd found a great way to make the time pass faster. 'Hey, take a look now, over on your right at three o'clock,' we'd whisper to each other, like naughty schoolboys, whenever we saw a pretty woman approach. We were in our overalls rather than our full uniform on hydrant duty. We probably looked more like escaped convicts than fire-fighting super-heroes but we still felt pretty cool. So we made the most of it. 'Good afternoon, ladies,' one of us would say, sometimes with a little salute, always with what we hoped was a blindingly heroic smile.

'Please excuse these two children, they don't know how to behave,' John told one of the women at one point, though I did notice he had puffed out his chest quite a bit before speaking. Then, to keep us on our toes, he fired off a few questions about the streets we'd just worked and the location of other hydrants all over Shrewsbury. To be fair, this was a useful exercise. The whole point of this duty wasn't just to keep the hydrants in good nick. It was also a good way to learn exactly where they all were. We always had a list with us in the fire engine, alongside the Ordnance Survey maps and plenty of other information. One set of lever arch files in each cab contained the 'risk information sheets' that gave masses of detail on various key properties. The most detailed sheets had plans of the premises, a description of what the buildings were made of, where the best staging point was for fire engines, whether they contained any hazards like flammable materials (in the case of factories), or whether they were likely to be full of elderly or handicapped people (in the case of hospitals or residential homes). The information was always worth going through. I was constantly being handed the files and told to mug up on them, partly for my exams and partly because it was important in its own right. When the pressure was on and we needed water fast we didn't want to be flicking through the pages of some directory. We didn't want to find that the page we needed was missing – or that someone had spilt tea all over it. Far better to know where to go and what we faced long before we arrived. Forewarned was forearmed – yet another of the many unwritten mottos of the Fire Brigade.

Back at the station John couldn't have been too annoyed at the way Matt and I had tried to chat up some of the local housewives – because he had allocated us some even better jobs for our next tour of afternoon shifts. We started off with some 11d. inspections.

'Which ones are they again?' Matt whispered to me when we'd been given our orders for the afternoon.

'The good ones,' I replied. The Fire Brigade has always had

the legal right to go wherever it needs to help protect people and property. Buildings don't need to be on fire before we expect owners to open up the doors for us. In fact it was a lot more useful to see places on an ordinary working day. If an empty building was on fire at three in the morning then we wanted as many people as possible on the watch to know the lie of the land inside. So we did our 11d. inspections to find out where the staircases were, what was through all the main doors, what sort of hazards might lie in wait for the unwary.

When we'd done a fair few of those we moved on to our next set of visits – Fire Prevention, or FP, Inspections. These are more about giving advice and we started off with a couple of cafés and restaurants in the town centre. Thankfully the fish and chip shop run by the sixtysomething 'grab him by the balls' lady from my river rescue didn't have any hidden nasties so we didn't risk incurring her wrath. A few other places weren't so well designed, however. John gave several stern lectures about the best and worst places to store gas canisters and other horrors. At first I thought he was also proving to be uncannily accurate about predicting which restaurants would be found using their fire extinguishers as door stops. After a full afternoon of inspections I spotted his secret. They all did it.

'Well, gentlemen, I think we've done some good today so I suggest we finish off with something just a little bit different,' he said as the Market Hall clock showed 4 p.m. just behind him. The clock was one of the least liked so-called architectural gems of Shrewsbury. Built in the early 1960s it's a four-sided, several-hundred-foot-tall, stark, square and ugly as heck brick tower. 'That's where we're going,' John said with a smile. 'Last one to the top is a girl.'

It's hard to imagine a better challenge than that for a bunch of super-competitive, testosterone-fuelled firemen. We were out of the engine in record time. It's a very good job there were no stray shoppers wandering around between us and the clock tower door. I'm not sure they'd have survived. A caretaker was expecting us and he held the door open. We slammed past him and hit the stairs two or three at a time. The iron staircase twisted around six or seven times inside the windowless interior. And we were all wearing regulation steel-capped fire boots. The noise we made running up there must have been heard across the whole county. The echoes could have triggered an avalanche. Maybe they did, far, far away.

'Yes! Done it!' Charlie yelled, first to reach the platform at the top of the staircase.

'It's not over yet!' John told him. He reached up, pushed open a trapdoor and pulled himself up through it to claim pole position in our little race. This time I was hard on his heels. And getting outside took my breath away. The view over the rooftops of Shrewsbury, down towards the river and on across the parched, brown countryside beyond was stunning. The top of the tower itself was a precarious place to be. An enormous twenty-foot spire loomed up from the middle of it. The rest of the roof was almost entirely flat and covered in lead. There was no lip on the edge, let alone any barriers. The very last thing that roof was designed for was five big, rowdy firemen playing chicken and daring each other to stand with their toes over the edge.

'I'm stuck, call the Fire Brigade!' Charlie yelled out with a laugh, leaning forward over the edge and scaring the heck out of all the shoppers down below.

'I'll take your picture, boss,' Woody said to John, pretending he had a camera in his hand. 'Just stand back a bit. A bit more. One step more.'

When we'd come up with every joke we could think of we finally threw ourselves back down through the hatch, had another race down the staircase and nearly flattened the poor caretaker waiting at the bottom.

For the next week or so the relaxed mix of hydrant duty, 11d.

and FP inspections continued whenever we were on days and had an afternoon without a shout. We headed down into the vaults of one of the high street banks, we went into the projection room of the town's only cinema. We even got to walk through one of the sewerage tunnels that runs under the River Severn – a bit whiffy but still a brilliant way to spend half an hour. Best of all, though, was when we did a visit of my old school – and I got to go in the staff room! I'd enjoyed school. I can't claim I had scores to settle. I didn't have loads of teachers who'd said I'd never amount to anything to stride up to and make a point. Instead, I just wanted to see where they'd all been hiding on lunch breaks. I wanted to see what it was like to talk to them as equals. It was good, to be honest. We had a lot of laughs that day.

The only bad thing about Matt's arrival was that we were back on the bullshit drills every morning. I could already see why the old-timers had hated doing so many of them when I'd joined just a few months earlier. 'Thirteen point five to the third floor!' We had to carry that ladder so many times I started to hear those seven words in my sleep. We carried and lifted so many ladders and rolled out and rolled up so many hoses our brains went numb. 'Forget hearing it in my sleep, I reckon I could *do* it in my sleep,' I moaned to Charlie one tea break.

He looked across at me. For once he looked serious. 'Well, that means you've got it, mon,' he said quietly. 'Well done.'

Our long hot summer continued. It was like the summers I remembered from when I was a boy. It just went on and on. Week after week of long, slow, hot days. And just like when I'd been a boy I got to spend an awful lot of it outside. If we didn't have a grass fire or some other shout to tackle during the lunch hour then we got to spend a lot of time out in the yard. When we'd bolted down our grub everyone had their favourite spots to catch the sun, snooze, read or listen to

Walkmans till we got back to work. If we had an emergency call at that point it was as if a pack of meerkats suddenly popped up. Heads appeared from flat roofs, secret corners and all sorts of unlikely places. Then everyone moved in a cartoon-like blur and converged on the appliance room within the allotted thirty-three seconds.

If I wasn't busy – and even though I wasn't officially the jockey any more I was always given some job or other to do – I liked to take my books and study alongside a dilapidated barbecue behind the breathing apparatus room. It was a sun trap. None of the others wanted to be on that side of the building because it backed on to a nearby office block and anyone sitting there was in full view of all of its workers. After a while I saw that as a good thing, though, because about two weeks earlier a new face had suddenly appeared at one of the office windows. A pretty, young female face to be exact – and we saw precious few of those on the station during working hours.

Looking back, I might have known I wouldn't be able to keep the girl a secret for long. The others spotted her when we were in the middle of our next ladder drill. And they all seemed to have a lot more confidence than me when it came to attracting her attention.

'Morning, gorgeous!' Arfer would yell as we headed out for volleyball.

'Got a smile just for me today, love?' George would try. I'd normally be the one smiling as I watched everyone flex their muscles, blow kisses and do all the stupid things teenagers might do, not middle-aged men who mostly had wives and teenage kids at home.

Fair play to her, the girl at the window put up with it all with good humour. She looked embarrassed a lot of the time. She looked particularly mortified one day when two of the watch had acted out some crazy Shakespearean love scene in front of her. But she did always smile quickly before turning back to her desk. For my part I always tried to look sympathetic as the others had their fun. And then, about a week after the others had first spotted her, I gave her a very quick wave as well.

She waved back.

20

Matt's Misunderstanding

I t was just after ten at the start of what looked set to be another very hot day shift. I was trying to put the girl at the window out of my mind and to focus on John. He had started to give Matt and me a daily briefing or pep talk. This one seemed particularly important. We'd had very little rain since early May and the countryside was as parched and brown as I'd ever seen it.

'What's likely to be one of our biggest challenges of the next few weeks?' he asked. 'Standing corn,' he said, answering his own question the way he always liked to do. 'It's going to be dry as hell now the sap has gone down. And what could set it ablaze? Almost anything. The main worry is the harvest itself. The machines can cause any number of problems. Sparks from the exhaust pipes, stray cigarettes from imbecile drivers, you name it. Then we've got all the hikers out there, all the people thinking the middle of a field is the perfect place for a summer barbecue – all sorts of idiots doing all sorts of stupid things and leaving us to carry the can.

'Think about corn, for a moment,' he continued. 'Think about what it looks like. There's so much space and air between every stalk. That air is the oxygen, the corn itself is the fuel. All that's needed to set it off is an ignition source. Could we have designed anything that could catch fire quicker? No, we couldn't. When corn is tinder-dry it's like gunpowder.' He looked over at Matt and me. 'Fire can rip across a field a lot faster than you two jockeys can run. A thermal gust can send it in a different direction before you can take in your next breath. You can get trapped. Forget how dangerous it is in a burning building. You can just as easily die in a cornfield. Worse still, we can lose a fire truck if it's parked badly. So think on. Be ready if we get the call. Do you remember cooking those potatoes up on the farm fire back in June, Windsor? Of course you do. Well, a corn fire on a summer's night is nothing like that. Nothing. If we get a call you'd both better be ready. Dismiss.'

Up in the mess room the others were happy to add their own two penn'orth to the subject. 'I'll tell you the other bad thing about a standing corn fire,' Charlie said when we were sitting down with mugs of tea and the latest after sell-by treats from the Thoms. 'It's the noise. Why do you think popcorn is called popcorn? It might sound fun in your kitchen. Out in the fields, in the dark, it's like you've got low-level gunfire all around you. It's like you're on a battlefield.'

'It's like hearing your own death rattle,' Woody added gruesomely. 'And you know that burning corn can smell like burning flesh sometimes as well. Pass the biscuits, can you, mate?'

Matt and I managed to spend much of the rest of the day talking about what burning corn might really smell like. We also talked about how great it would be to get called to a really big corn fire – and about all sorts of other rubbish as well. We talked about the charts and the telly and where all the most beautiful girls in Shrewsbury went drinking. Neither of us had girlfriends at that point, though I had my girl from the window and Matt was hoping to get lucky at a wedding on the Saturday night – even though we were supposed to be working on Saturday night.

'So do you think the boss will give me time off?' he asked when the two of us were in the kit room polishing our boots. I shrugged. I was so keen on the job I'd hardly even thought of asking for any time off. So far I'd barely taken a day of my annual leave. If I'd been pushed I'd have said Matt's chances of getting a last-minute night off that weekend were about zero. But I didn't really give it much thought. Matt didn't mention it to me again and I forgot all about it until Saturday just before six.

Matt's car hadn't been in the car park at the drill yard when I'd arrived. That wasn't unusual, to be honest. I was still so keen that I was always one of the first to get to the station. But Matt wasn't in the muster bay ten minutes before parade either – and that was unusual. So was the fact that someone new seemed to have joined us for the night. It was another lad of about my age.

'Who the devil are you?' John had barked as we stood in line in the muster bay.

'I'm Bob,' the stranger had said.

'Well, I don't recognise you. Where are you from?'

'I'm from Shrewsbury.'

'I mean what station are you from?'

'I'm not from any station. I'm Matt's mate. I'm a plumber and I work over on Porthill Bank. Matt said I could come along and work his shift for him.'

John stood there, unable to speak for several seconds, before he unceremoniously sent the luckless Bob on his way.

He was just as speechless the following Friday, our next day shift, when Matt was asked to account for himself in front of the whole watch. 'But I asked you if I could have the night off. You said it was OK as long as I got someone to cover my shift. I asked my mate Bob to cover it. He's a good bloke. He works for a company near my house,' Matt said. His face, as he talked, was a picture. Obviously he knew he'd done something wrong. Equally clear was the fact that he couldn't quite work out what it was. After a pause, John, well and truly, put him straight.

'When I said "ask anybody" I meant ask anybody off the other three watches, you bloody fool. Not just any Tom, Dick or bleeding Harry off the street. Get in line and try not to make an idiot of yourself for at least the next nine hours.'

*

I could barely speak to Matt for the rest of the shift – because every time I looked at him I wanted to fall about laughing. And I did have plenty to smile about. His arrival had helped push me below the radar. I could focus on my exams while Matt took all the heat as the new boy who couldn't put a foot right. As the poor sod continued to prove almost every day.

In early September we were sent out on a shout to a beautiful country house way out in the sticks. It was a stunning property, probably hundreds of years old, set in glorious grounds and owned by people with more money than I'd ever see in my life. They'd called 999 after a fire had broken out in an upstairs study and we'd raced across the countryside to help. On the way John had gone through the file and checked the status of the property. We had what were called salvage guidelines for some of the county's finest homes. They are the half a dozen or so houses dotted around our patch where the contents are deemed to be just as valuable as the buildings they're in. It's not an exact science and we didn't have to stick rigidly to the script. But if we were called to a fire in these properties and no one's life was in danger then our primary task was to go in and try to salvage as many of the pre-specified valuables as possible. That meant oil paintings, sculptures, tapestries, all sorts of things like that. Only when these treasures were safe were we expected to cover the place with water or foam and try to douse the flames.

Up in number one position on the passenger seat John folded the salvage list away. He put it back with all the other maps and information sheets in the box beside him. The building we were heading to that day wasn't on the list so our task was simple. We had to check that no one was trapped or in danger. Then we had to put the fire out PDQ. As it happened, it wasn't that tough a shout. The residents had been clever. They'd done their best to put the flames out, then they had shut the door on the fire and helped contain it. They'd called for help straight away so we arrived before it spread into any other rooms. So, less than an hour after arriving, it was all sorted.

'They were blinkin' lucky it was that room, not the one below it,' Woody had said when we were checking the exterior of the building a little later. He was right. The fire had broken out in a room in what must have been the old servants' quarters, one storey above a huge hall the size of a ballroom. That lower room had an enormous, multi-coloured stained-glass window that took up almost the whole of its wall. 'God only knows how much that would cost to replace if it had got damaged,' Woody continued. 'The heat alone from a fire would have destroyed it. And you'd never find anyone who could mend something like that nowadays. Charlie, I reckon you and your cowboy builders would make a right pig's ear of it. These people don't know how lucky they are.' What none of us knew was that their luck was about to run out.

The salvage operation was handed over to Matt and me while the others had a cup of tea with the owners. As usual we had to rip out anything that was damaged, dangerous or both. We'd set aside a patch of garden just outside the window for all the rubbish. Matt and I threw out half-burned chairs, rolls of soaked carpets and all sorts of other junk to be collected later. We also threw out any electrical items. They're not safe once they've suffered smoke, water or fire damage. So out went a part-melted record player, a desk fan, a couple of standard lamps – and a big, three bar electric heater.

To this day I can still picture Matt carrying that heater to the window and lobbing it out. What neither of us had known was that it was still plugged in – and plugged in very firmly. So instead of landing on the pile of rubbish in the garden along with everything else, the heater was jerked back towards the house by its electric cord. To be exact, it was jerked back towards the vast stained-glass window on the floor beneath us. The crash, as the heater smashed through the window into the previously undamaged ballroom, could probably be heard in Wolverhampton.

Fortunately someone else managed to embarrass himself even more than Matt did with the electric fire. It was a cocky sixteen-year-old lad trying to impress the girls in Shrewsbury Quarry, the huge, flower-filled park carved out of one of the loops of the River Severn right in the heart of the town. The lad had been playing around on a swing in the kids' play park – and he had somehow got himself jammed into one of the baby seats. When he couldn't pull or break himself free one of his mates decided to call the Fire Brigade. And, as usual, wherever we went rent-a-crowd would follow. It was a lovely evening, more late summer than early autumn, so there were plenty of people walking around admiring the flowers and taking in the air. They were all more than happy to come along and ogle. The lad had an audience of around two dozen when we arrived. A service or an event must have just ended up in St Chad's church at the top edge of the quarry as a steady stream of people was wandering down from there to see what all the fuss was about as well. By the time we entered the play area there must have been about thirty people having a bit of a snigger at the kid's expense.

'You've got yourself into a bit of pickle, haven't you, son,' John began in a kindly voice when he first approached the teenager. I won't repeat exactly how the kid replied. Suffice it to say that he wasn't particularly happy. He swore, spat and at one point even tried to kick out at the very people sent to help him. That was a bit of a mistake. John asked him to calm down and had pretty much the same response again. So we took the obvious course of action. We had the tools that could have freed the kid in less than five minutes. We made sure the job took nearly an hour.

Back at the station I looked up at the office windows as we

piled off the fire engine and headed upstairs for a cup of tea. My pretty girl wasn't there. A little later I invented a reason to head out to my car to get something. This time she was back at her desk. So this time I gave a proper wave and a bigger smile. She did the same. I stood there, still as a statue for a moment as I tried to work out what to do next. Her window was closed so she wouldn't be able to hear me if I shouted – though the lads in the station wouldn't have been able to miss it and any Romeo and Juliet impression from me would probably give them something to laugh about for a decade. I decided to do a mime instead. I made a gesture like having a drink, then I shrugged my shoulders and spread my arms out as if I was asking her a question.

She gave her biggest smile yet. She nodded her head and gave me a big thumbs-up sign. It looked as if I'd got myself a date.

21

Lovely Louise

M y mission for the next few days was simple. It was to do something heroic. That way I'd have something to talk about if I did get to take the girl out for a drink. That way I'd impress her. Trouble was, the county fire service seemed determined to thwart me at every turn. Heroes weren't always required back then. Instead the whole town seemed to be full of jokers.

'What do you know about owls, son?' John had asked me when I was getting ready to parade at the start of our next day shift. As usual he'd been in early, checking how the night shift had gone, reading the reports and checking up on any news from the other stations.

'Owls? As in twit twoo?' I asked. My exams felt really close and I'd been up early that day doing a quick hour of extra revision. This was yet another subject that never seemed to come up in any of my textbooks.

John did mean twit twoo. A non-urgent call had come in just before our shift had begun. He decided that we should give up our volleyball game and our drills to take it. And when we arrived on the scene it was a little bit like a Shropshire version of a major incident. The police were there trying to decide whether or not to close off a street. Our two friends from the local animal charity were there. An unusually large rent-a-crowd of gawpers was there. Then we were all there.

The owls in question were trapped on the roof of a very busy pub right in the heart of the town centre. It was a beautiful old Tudor building, one of the many ancient structures crammed in on a street called Mardol and on all of its equally narrow neighbours. 'I know my birds and I know they shouldn't be there in the daytime,' an elderly, very smartly dressed man told us confidently as he stood on the other side of the road, looking up and squinting against the mid-morning sun. 'I saw them from my house opposite. You can come up to the top windows to see for yourselves if you want. There are three of them, maybe four. They should be asleep, especially at this time of year. Something must be wrong. They must be trapped. Either that or they're ill. I didn't want to disturb anyone or make a fuss but I felt something had to be done. I thought someone should get up there to help.'

'He did the right thing,' the charity lady said. She was wearing another set of floaty silk scarves and was holding a dark green felt hat. 'We're here to help in any way we can, but we don't have the equipment to get on to the roof. If you get the birds down we can transport them to the sanctuary so that they get all the care they need.'

We all looked up, but we couldn't get far enough away from the pub to see on to the roof. We'd have to take the old gentleman's word for it that the owls were there. And while it did seem a bit crazy to be rescuing birds from the sky, you had to concede that he had a point about the time of day. As far as I could remember from nature lessons at school, owls were only supposed to come out at night. Maybe these ones really were in trouble.

'Well, whatever's going on we'll be wanting to get someone up there to investigate,' John said. I knew that someone was going to be me – and I'd not have wanted it any other way, to be honest. We got to work, but the job didn't turn out to be as easy as it sounded. There was no other access to the roof so we needed to use ladders. The first problem with that was that Mardol was one of the narrowest streets in the middle of old Shrewsbury. We'd need a 13.5-metre ladder to get to the pub roof, but the street wasn't nearly wide enough to lay it down and extend the usual way. Instead we planned to try a confined pitch – we would lay the ladder down with the bottom roughly where we wanted it to be and the top wherever it fitted. We would then under-run it up to the vertical before swivelling it round into the right position.

That's what we would have done had it not been for problem number two. This was that cars were parked all the way down the one side of the street where we wanted the ladder to be. Pitching the ladder over the top of all of them added to the challenge. But we did it. And after about fifteen minutes I was on my way up. The old guy who'd first spotted the owls had found something else to get excited about. He'd decided they were a family – and his bird book said it was very rare to see them all together. 'Please don't go too close or distress them,' he called out as I reached roof level. Looking at the state of the tiles I had to say I had no intention of doing so. They looked as wonky as a witch's teeth.

'What can you see, jockey?' John yelled up from below. 'You've got quite an audience now.'

I stole a quick look down. The street had become even busier. The whole of Shrewsbury wanted to see the fireman rescue the four sick owls. So it was a bit of a shame when I finally got myself on to the roof only to find that they didn't need my help at all. They were all made of plastic.

I brought them down to the street in case no one believed me. The old gentleman was so embarrassed that for a moment he could barely speak. Then he could hardly stop. If he apologised once he apologised a dozen times. 'New glasses, I must get myself some new glasses,' he kept repeating. Then he asked the question which was in the back of all our minds. 'Well, if they're plastic then who put them there? And why?'

The pub owner told us about fifteen minutes later when he turned up for work – totally unaware of the chaos that had been going on around his pub. 'I had them put up there at the weekend to stop pigeons damaging the building and swooping on the food in the rubbish bins,' he told us. 'And if you don't mind I'd like you to put them all back.'

'Can we at least keep one of them as a mascot?' I asked before I climbed back up and did just that. He agreed and Ollie the owl had pride of place on the front seat of the engine as we drove him back to the station. He lived in our yard for years – alongside the pigeons which weren't fooled for a moment.

The girl from the office window was called Louise. She was a secretary in a typing pool. She was seventeen, blonde, petite and infectiously friendly. After my mime act out in the drill yard I'd checked what time the local office staff normally went home. A couple of days later I'd snuck out to the edge of the station drive – the furthest any of us were really supposed to go in case we had a shout. I loitered around outside the office till I saw her. I was ready for her to run a mile – maybe I'd got the signals mixed up, and maybe she was sick to the back teeth of all us firemen waving at her, after all. It turned out all was well. I got a flash of her big smile when she saw me. She walked towards me and I took my career in my hands and took a few steps past our station perimeter and towards her. 'I thought I'd say hello properly. My name's Malcolm,' I said, slightly worried that, at six foot four, I towered over her like a beanpole.

'I'm Louise,' she said, not seeming to mind at all.

We chatted nervously for a few moments. Then I asked if she'd like to come for a drink some time soon. 'I'm on days again on Thursday so I finish at six. We could go to the Bear Inn over at Hodnet if you like? I've got my own car – I could pick you up at seven.'

The Bear was a real gem. If the weather was good we'd be able to sit out in the garden where there were loads of romantic benches dotted around under the trees. If it was raining there were plenty of cosy corners amidst all the old oak beams inside. The owners normally had a fire going, even in summer, so the whole place always seemed romantic. It wasn't the kind of pub for big groups of lads or heavy drinkers. It was perfect for couples. But would Louise say yes? She gave me a big smile out in the street that night. It was better, close up, than through her office window. She said yes.

For the first time in my life I worried about what to wear when our big date came around. I think it was because after three and a bit months in the Fire Brigade I'd got used to being told what to wear at different points of every day and night. Being free to make my own mistakes felt a bit of a challenge. But I decided I couldn't go wrong with jeans and an open-neck shirt – in Fire Brigade blue. Louise was waiting at her house when I pulled up in my HB Viva, glad she probably wouldn't know how small its engine was. I asked her lots of questions about her job and her life on the drive out to Hodnet. Then she turned the tables and began to question me as we settled down at the Bear with our first drinks.

'So, you're a fireman,' she began with another big smile.

'Yes, but I'm just a regular guy underneath,' I said. Then I rushed to explain myself. 'That's the line one of the men on my watch always uses when he's out on the pull. "I might be a fireman, but I'm just a regular guy underneath" is what he tells the girls.'

'Does it get him anywhere?' Louise asked, laughing.

'Not with the women. But it gets him a lot of stick back at the station. We all think it's hilarious.'

'So what's it like? Being a fireman?' she asked.

It was my big moment. I'd spent so long practising all my heroic stories, most of them exaggerated or fictional. But in the end I decided to tell the truth. I just told her how much I loved it. I said how hard the training had been and how worried I was about the exams in December. 'So what's the most dangerous fire you've had?' she asked a little later.

'It's not the fires that are scary. It's the cows that fall in the river that you need to watch out for,' I joked. She laughed as I told the story. And the two of us barely seemed to stop laughing from then on. We had exactly the same sense of humour. As it turned out we both worked with people much older than us so we had plenty in common on that score as well. Best of all, Louise was beautiful. She had a little bit of make-up on her cheeks and round her eyes, but she was really just naturally pretty. The night flew by and I remember I almost had to pinch myself as I drove her home. She was seventeen and I was just about to turn nineteen. Life couldn't have been more perfect. I was a fireman. I had my own car, and now I had a beautiful blonde girl to drive around in it. Could life possibly get any better?

22

Beating a Fire Out?

The day after my date with Louise I was still smiling from ear to ear when I rejoined the watch. But no one had time to notice let alone comment on it. Shropshire was burning. A couple of days earlier Green Watch had spent six hours dealing with a barn fire out in Harnage. Then they'd had a major warehouse fire over near Rolls-Royce. Up in the mess room I had sat, spellbound, when they'd relived both incidents. I'd wanted to hear every detail – and I'd ended up spending half my night off in the bar with them so that I could hear as many of their stories as possible. I always felt a bit cheated when any of the other watches got the most exciting shouts. I always wanted them to get called in on my watch, not theirs. But at the end of September I got my wish. A farmer up near the wilds of the Stiperstones had dialled 999 in the early evening. He said that the heathland up there was ablaze – and that the fire was spreading fast.

'What do you reckon it was? A campfire? Kids? Arson?'

We were in the engine heading south, a second appliance hard on our heels. 'It could be a campfire, but it's a bit late in the year for that. It's too far out for kids. Nothing but grass and gorse bushes to destroy so I can't think it would be arson. It could be hikers who left a cigarette burning. But we'll never know for sure,' Caddie said as we pulled on our tunics and leggings.

Charlie swung us off the Bishops Castle Road and we began the slow climb up to the Stiperstones. It wasn't an easy journey as village roads turned into single-track country lanes. Some of the time there were just drystone walls on either side of us, but in other places there were tall hedges, still in full leaf and impossible to see through. While we were high up enough to see around most of the worst corners it wasn't the same for any cars coming the other way. We might be bright red and the size of a caravan but they might not see us until it was too late. As usual, Charlie had to get the balance right. He needed to drive fast enough to get us to the shout quickly, but not too fast so as to trigger an accident. The last thing we needed on roads like these was to come face to face with another driver – especially one who was going too fast or not paying enough attention.

As it turned out we did meet another driver that day. She wasn't going too fast and you couldn't accuse her of not paying enough attention to the road ahead. But she was still a big problem.

'Oh, bugger, an old woman,' said Charlie as he hit the brakes after yet another hairpin turn. The three of us in the back craned our heads to be able to see. Ahead of us an elderly lady in a purple hat and matching gloves was driving an equally elderly blue car. The road wasn't wide enough for both of us. She had to reverse. That wasn't something she did very often, it seemed. Nor could she do it in a hurry.

'Move, you need to go back!' Charlie said, gesturing at her from the driving seat. The lady looked behind her to see what he was referring to. 'No, there's nothing behind you, love. We need you to move. Go back. We need you,' he pointed directly at her, 'to go back there.' He pointed back towards a wider part of the lane. Even from our vantage point, and through two sets of windscreens, the look of horror on the old lady's face was clear for all to see as she finally realised what he meant. She nodded and appeared to gulp. She looked behind her one more time. She checked her wing mirrors. She took a little while getting her car into reverse. She revved the engine so loudly that birds flew up out of the hedgerow. She gulped again, a look of fixed concentration taking over her face. But she didn't actually go anywhere.

'What is she doing?' Charlie asked, exasperated.

Woody, of all people, tried to calm him down. 'Just wait a second. If you hassle the old bat it'll make it worse and she'll stall,' he said.

'Well, she could hardly go any slower.'

A sharp intake of breath echoed around the truck as the lady, as predicted, stalled the engine. She looked up, a picture of embarrassment and confusion. She nodded several times, as if to tell us she knew we were in a hurry. She went through all her old manoeuvres, even going as far as adjusting the rear-view mirror. More birds flew up when she revved the engine as loud as a plane. Then she stalled again.

'Someone's going to have to go down there, get her out of the car and reverse it for her,' Arfer said in the end. 'Jockey. Go out and charm her.'

As it turned out John beat me to it.

He climbed down from the truck, all of us watching avidly from behind him. John's a decent man and I guessed that he had his best, friendliest smile on his face as he walked towards the car. The old lady looked utterly terrified. A discussion took place as John leaned in towards the driver's door. The lady locked it. She didn't even want to wind down her window. But she did try to move the car. It moved forwards with a sudden, unexpected lurch. Then the engine died yet again.

'You know what? This isn't funny any more. It's getting serious,' Woody said as we watched John try to persuade the lady to open her window so that she could hear him better. The clock was certainly ticking. Heath fires spread fast. The longer we were stuck in this lane the more damage this one would do.

'It's only a backin' Ford Fiesta. We could take a corner each and lift it back up the road to a passing place,' Arfer suggested.

But at the last moment John appeared to have had a breakthrough. He was standing back a little and the lady restarted the engine. He gave her a thumbs-up sign and she gave him a determined little nod. The motor roared as she revved up a storm. A full minute later the car was shaking violently but not moving. 'Handbrake! *Take off the handbrake!*' we could hear John shouting in frustration. The lady did so. The car lurched back so far and so fast that John nearly hit the floor. And something amazing was happening as he regained his balance. Not only did the lady manage to drive without stalling, she also managed to drive with style. The car swung to the left, to the right, to the hedge, to the ditch and back like some real-life Wacky Racer. It was like mad cartoon driving. Every few seconds it had us convinced she was going to hit a tree. But every time she pulled back from the brink. And she kept on going.

'Blow me, she's only gone and done it,' said Arfer, a note of shocked admiration in his voice. The lady had slotted herself neatly – perfectly, in fact – into the space in front of a farm gate. She had covered the last few dozen yards so accurately it was as if she was on rails. Stirling Moss could hardly have done it better. John ran back to us, climbed aboard and we were finally on our way. 'Don't any of you say a word. I'm going to pretend that never happened,' he said. And the last thing we saw as we sped ahead was a cheery wave from a purple, gloved hand.

Everyone got a lot more serious as we carved up the last few miles and approached our destination. The road had climbed and twisted sharply. The various hamlets and houses were spread ever further apart. And there was smoke in the air.

'This is going to be a big one, lads,' Charlie predicted as we arrived outside the Stiperstones Inn, a white-walled, red-roofed country pub perched on the edge of the honeycomb hills of south Shropshire. Its car park looked the best place to use as a base. We jumped out of the truck as the second appliance parked alongside us. The second crew joined us on the tarmac. Smoke was blowing down to us on the wind and we all knew that this was very bad news. The wind would be our biggest enemy up there. It would also be the biggest threat to the pub and all the other isolated buildings up on the hills.

'About time, too,' a man shouted out from the pub doorway. He was middle-aged, tweedy and overweight. He had a pint in his hand. I disliked him immediately and I wasn't the only one.

'You got a problem, mate?' Arfer yelled back, his hackles up.

'The fire's been burning since tea time. We could have done with you an hour ago.'

'Arfer, I'll deal with him,' John said curtly. He strode over to the man. A very short, very intense conversation took place. The man turned and went back into the pub. 'I don't think he will still be here when we get back. Now, let's get to work,' John said. 'Charlie, I want you staying here with the appliances for now. Everyone else, grab a beater. We're going to fight this one by hand. It's going to be as hot as hell up there but we need to be protected so I want everyone with their full fire kit on. We're going to need to wear gloves as the beaters will get us very close to the fire. Visibility is going to be hard so we need to communicate well. I don't want anyone going off on their own and I don't want anyone falling behind. You work on my instructions and you follow them without question. Is that clear?'

'Clear, sir!'

'Then get the beaters.'

The two crews rolled up the side lockers of each truck. The beaters were primitive but effective. They were basically three-foot wooden broom handles with another three foot of roughly cut, flattened-out hose bolted on to the end. You used them like you'd use an axe to cut wood. We'd slam the perimeter of each patch of fire with them, beating it, flattening it and, with luck, extinguishing it. Then we'd move on to the next front. Wasn't it an impossible task? I asked myself as we waited for John's instruction to move. One big fire, to be tackled by just a small handful of men? It was ridiculous to think we could control it. But it was our job to try.

On John's command we headed out away from the road and towards the hillside, the other crew hot on our heels. A rough and ready path led us through a dank little wood and round some half-dry stream beds. The heath lay ahead of us when we climbed over the final stile and left the wood. From then on the gradients were tough and the terrain was tougher. The entire hill was covered in heather, bracken and gorse. There were a few tracks made by the sheep, but as they tended to go round the hill rather than up or down it they were less than useless. I slung my beater back over my shoulder and began kicking through all the undergrowth like the others. Every few paces a root or a particularly tough piece of gorse would hold me back. And every few paces the smoke got thicker.

'Use your neckerchief, Castle,' Woody called out to me when we were in a particularly bad patch of smoke. We always tucked the official neckerchiefs under the necks of the tunics to stop them chaffing when we worked. That night the others had pulled them up and tied them over their mouths and noses like cowboys. 'It's better than nothing,' Woody yelled as I followed suit. To my left I saw that Matt had done the same. Perhaps five minutes later we reached the fire and the two squads separated to fight it on two different fronts.

The stretch of hillside that John took us to looked like something out of a Vietnam War movie. It was as if fire had fallen from the sky. Patches of flames were burning in dozens of spots up ahead of us – dozens of spots covering a huge, horrible area of the hill. Could we possibly tackle this on our own? Could we even know where to start? I gazed ahead. Before and beyond each burning bush were piles of smouldering ash. They glowed malevolently under clouds of evil black smoke. More worrying still were the sparks, currently flying out in every burst of air.

Looking at them chilled the heart even more. They were the true tools of destruction. They could make this already vast fire cover even more ground. They could fly over our heads on a thermal breeze and trap us from behind. And thermal winds can blow even when every other breeze is still. You can get them all the time and in all conditions. Patches of darker coloured ground heat up quicker than surrounding areas of lighter ground. When the air above the dark earth heats up it gets ready to rise. When it does so it draws in cooler air from nearby to replace it – those are the thermal gusts. When the air is steady and the winds are low, fires can be docile. That's when we try to beat the heck out of them. When the thermals come, the fires whip up and they blaze for glory. That's when they can travel fast. You need to be on your toes – and you always want to be upwind of the fire you're fighting. If the thermals or the wind directions change then all bets are off. If fire gets behind or around you, it can be game over. A few weeks before John had joked that we could lose a fireman in a country fire or, worse, lose a fire engine. It wasn't quite so funny any more.

'Start here! Push it back! Foot by foot. Let's create that fire-break,' John yelled. We got to it. We swung those beaters like axes. We hit out at the fire with everything we had. And we didn't stop. The sparks flew like terrifying, living things with every swing of the beaters. The beater handles were so short that we ended up crouched low and dangerously close to the fire at all times. The flames were eating up all the oxygen. The heat enveloped us. I could feel it burning away at my gloves. It was all around and came from every side. Every few moments I wanted to stand tall and feel cooler air on my face. But I had to stoop back down and throw everything at my next patch of beating. We all did. After less than half an hour I was sweating more than I could remember. We moved, foot by foot along and into the fire. We stayed close. We followed John's instructions, building each firebreak, hoping it would hold, then moving on to fight another front up or down or around the vast burning hill.

When the gradients were sharpest and the smoke was heaviest it was as if we were lost in another world. 'I can't tell if I'm standing up or lying down,' Caddie yelled out at one point when he was on a particularly steep slope and the disorientation became intense. It was like that. At times it was impossible to know where you were or what was ahead of you. Except that it was always more smoke, more fire, more beating.

At one point I had to take a break. I'd lashed out at another ten yards of fire. I'd forced the flames into retreat and left black, dying ashes in their wake. So I stood tall, gasping for cleaner, cooler air. As I tried to find my bearings I could see why we'd had to tackle this by hand rather than fighting it with water. We'd never have got the engine close enough, for a start. Even if we had the water would have been, well, a drop in the ocean compared to what we'd need. The engine carries around two tonnes of water in its tank. It sounds a lot but it's not. Two tonnes of water can be used up in a matter of minutes. Having two engines helps – you can get the old relay going and refill one while you're using the other. But if the nearest water source is some way away you'll still be chasing your tail. That's why we were trying to put this fire out by hand.

I took one last breath through my neckerchief. I checked the thermals, crossed my fingers and hoped that the wind stayed low and went for it again. Sweat was running off my back. It was practically filling my boots. An hour, maybe two, had passed. It was impossible to tell. Every now and then the smoke might clear or the wind would change and we would see or hear the other squad. But mostly we were in our own hot world. And the challenges kept changing.

Our latest front was smouldering, flaring up and sparking amidst a sea of gorse bushes. The pods were popping like hand grenades. The whole hill seemed alive there. It was cracking and crackling, the sounds repeating endlessly and in all directions as the heat grew ever more intense.

'Squad, step back!' After about half an hour of savagery we'd done huge damage to the gorse fire. We'd beaten it by beating it. We'd smashed down yards and yards of broken bushes at its edges. We'd hammered out the flames and built a safe area around it. So where would we go now?

All eight of us were crouching down, leaning on our knees in exhaustion as John took stock. Matt and I were the youngest and I liked to think I was just a bit fitter than him. I was always ready to push my body to its limit. But I was gasping for air just like everyone else that night. When my lungs allowed it I stood back up. We needed to be in a helicopter to see the whole scope of the hill. It would only be from the air that we'd know if we were truly in control. But we did seem to be on the winning side. The hill no longer looked like a scene from a war film. It had long since got dark but the night was no longer pierced by an endless set of flames. If you manage the edges properly then heath fires can burn themselves out. The ash is probably quite good for the soil, like nature's own fertiliser.

'What's so funny, jockey?' Woody asked. I must have laughed out loud.

'This whole thing. All this work, all this damage. And in a week or maybe less it'll be as if we never did a thing. The fire will be out and the bushes and the bracken will all be growing up again. I can't get my head around it.'

'Well, it'd have been a lot worse if we hadn't been here. This fire would have travelled. There's farmhouses just over the lee. There'll be kids in them. Think about that.'

I did. So I was happy to keep on patrolling the area and beating down our firebreaks for as long as it took for John to stand us down. The hours had long since started to blur like the darkening blues, purples and blacks of the sky. Was it ten o'clock, eleven, midnight, later? We were on a long watching brief up there. We had gone from the drama of the fire to the calm of a long, clear autumn night. John had us separate a bit more so we could cover more ground and look for any dormant danger areas. The smoke had almost entirely gone. We could breathe more easily, our filthy neckerchiefs no longer over our mouths and noses. And we could see, as well. The view from the Stiperstones, even at night, was stunning. Tiny specks of lights showed up the occasional house. Little groups of lights told us where the nearest hamlets and villages were. Every now and then a white slash of light from a car moved across some part of the landscape like a tiny shooting star. I saw something else as I stood on the crest of one little hill. Somewhere in the far distance someone must have been having a party. Fireworks shot up into the air, little bursts of red, green and white that seemed so tiny from so far away. It was odd to think that all that way away people were celebrating a wedding, or a birthday or whatever it was. And we were up here, far from contact, exhausted but exhilarated. I bashed out at another patch of smouldering bracken. Orange sparks shot up and died. I moved on to another, then another. None of it was glowing enough to be a threat. We'd won the war.

23

Autumn Fires

It took us a good three-quarters of an hour to stumble back down the hillside towards the car park of the Stiperstones Inn. The other squad had been just ahead of us. We all cleaned up the kit best we could – as usual it had to be in good condition in case we had another emergency shout on the way back to the station. Then we stowed it all back into the appliances and stood looking longingly at the pub door. John took pity on us. 'If it's not locked up then I think we all deserve a drink,' he declared.

The pub was open, even though last orders should have been called hours ago.

'I thought it best to wait for you. A few of the regulars decided to keep me company for as long as it took,' the landlord said in a slow, soft voice. 'Drinks are on the house. What would you gentlemen like?'

We each had a pint, then another. Then we agreed it would be rude to leave so soon, so perhaps we'd have the one more. The landlord refused our money all night, though his face did get a bit more strained as the empty glasses stacked up. I suppose he'd expected us to have a quick one before heading back to town. I've no idea how many pints we sank in the end. But heath fires are thirsty work and we'd been out there for a heck of a long time.

Everything was pleasantly hazy and dreamlike as Charlie swept us down the country lanes and back towards base. I was so relaxed I didn't even think of feeling travel sick. Instead I perched on my helmet and tunic as usual and put my feet up on the seat in front of me. We were all a bit mellow and no one talked much for a while. I just gazed out of the window towards the horizon. It was that perfect time when night hints at day. The sky wasn't just getting lighter – it was as if someone was colouring it in. Pale purple and violet streaks were being painted across the clouds. Tiny areas of blue were opening up above them. The sky seemed even bigger now. The world was changing all around us. It was waking up.

'Hey, boss, do you want us to let you out so you can try and find your girlfriend?' Arfer snapped me out of my trance. He was shouting at John as we passed the farm gate where our elderly motorist had finally let us past.

'Well, I gave her your number and you'd better get in training because she's got an older sister and they like to do everything together,' he called back.

The jokes got even worse as we all stretched out in the back of the engine. We were well on our way towards the end of our shift. With a bit of luck we'd be back at the station in time for a full English, then we'd be on parade and on our way home.

Last word of the night went to Matt who had been travelling on the other engine with George, Paddy and Pete. 'Look at my effing neck!' he yelled as we got out of our smoky, dirty kit back in the station. We all looked across at him. 'It's one of the metal buttons. It must have been the heat from the fire. It's only gone and branded me,' he said leaning his head back and showing us a red, angry-looking scald mark just above his right collarbone. Closer inspection revealed that it was no ordinary scald. Our tunic buttons were embossed with the Shropshire Fire Service insignia. Matt had an exact, inside-out copy of it imprinted on to his neck.

Louise said all the right things and seemed suitably impressed when I recounted the story of the fire on our next date. I was glad that I hadn't had to embellish it for once. It really had been as exciting and as exhausting as I'd hoped. All-night jobs like that were what I'd joined the Fire Brigade for in the first place. She laughed away at Matt's latest misadventures as well – though not too much to worry me that she might prefer his company to mine. And as the weeks went by I was increasingly aware just how lucky I'd been to spot her and then to wave at her that day.

'The only things missing from this picture are a big, fat cigar and a glass of Southern Comfort,' I'd said one night when we were curled up watching telly over at her place. The next time we stayed in to watch a film on telly she disappeared into the kitchen – and reappeared carrying a tray containing a King Edward cigar and a bottle of Southern Comfort. What a wonderful girlfriend she was turning out to be! We'd tried to keep our dates a secret from the rest of the watch for a while – I'm not sure why – but it seemed important at the time. But Shrewsbury is a small town and a hard place to have a secret. One night we were cuddled up having a few drinks in the Old Post Office pub – the Ol' PO as everyone called it – when one of the men from Green Watch wandered past. By 9 a.m. the next day it seemed that everyone on Red Watch had heard about us. It did me some good, to be honest. Everyone on the watch was still making fools of themselves waving at the pretty blonde in the office window. I scored a lot of bonus points for having won her while all their backs were turned.

The weather was changing fast as summer turned into a distant memory. The leaves had gone yellow and were well on their way to becoming fully brown when I drove in to work. By early October there was a real nip in the air on the night shift. Apparently this meant we were going to be busy.

'What are we expecting a lot of over the next few months? Chimney fires, that's what,' John said. He had come down to the locker room to give Matt and me another pep talk. We'd got the gloss paint out and had been busily repainting our helmets and drinking in the fumes. 'Chimneys always go up the first time people light their fires after the summer. No one has them swept the way they should do any more. Sparks fly up and what do they land on? Big, bone-dry patches of coal soot. Mixed up with some wood tar, no doubt. Maybe even some twigs and a bird's nest. Once that stuff has caught alight the whole chimney goes. If we don't get there in time it can spread across the beams and take the rest of the house with it. Trust me. Chimney fires. We'll be doing nothing else for weeks.'

He was right, of course. Most of the call-outs went well, though it was a bit of a challenge working round one very grumpy elderly man who refused to leave his fireside armchair and was furious at his daughter for calling us out in the first place. Then there was the man from Meole.

It was grey and windy but we still had a pretty scenic drive out to him. The leaves were falling fast from a series of ancient, overhanging trees and lots of the buildings in the village were covered in thick, yellowing ivy. Our destination was a two-storey cottage surrounded by well-tended rose bushes that looked to be dealing with the change of the seasons pretty well. The owner was a tall, thin man with sharp eyes and a deeply weather-beaten face. He had a bit of a military look about him. In fact he looked a little like my old headmaster, I thought, as he introduced himself out in the front garden. He looked a bit embarrassed, the way people of his generation usually did when they called us out for this kind of job. 'I'm cross about this. But only with myself,' I overheard him tell Joe, who was in charge that day. I had a feeling that, like a lot of practical men of his age, he hated being beaten by anything. I stepped a little closer so that I could hear the rest of his conversation.

'I tried to put the fire out from the bottom but it made no difference. There's not been anything burning in the grate for quarter of an hour now. But it's still raging away inside the chimney. You can hear it, I'm afraid,' he said apologetically.

You could pretty much see it as well. I was sent on a quick recce upstairs to check for hot spots. They weren't hard to find. The chimney ran up behind the back wall of the spare bedroom. Whole strips of floral wallpaper had already peeled off the wall after the paste with which it had been applied had melted. I pulled the bed away from the wall and let the last bits of paper slip to the floor before pulling them away as well. Chimney fires can reach incredibly high temperatures and can trigger problems if the heat radiates along chimney breasts, beams or other parts of a property's structure. They can also crack the chimney lining, chimney pots and other nearby bits of masonry – though that tended to be a problem the owners had to face up to long after we had gone. Our job, as always, was to put the fire out as quickly and as safely as possible.

I went downstairs and told Joe what I'd found.

He told the homeowner, a Mr Dowling, that we'd have the problem sorted in no time. Then he turned to us. 'What are you all waiting for? Christmas? This is a chimney fire! Get the stirrup pump, get the rest of the kit and let's get going,' he barked. We got going. Our first job was to spread out a load of fire blankets and sheets down to protect the old man's carpets. He told us not to worry and that he'd clean up any mess for himself afterwards. That was never going to happen. We prided ourselves on our ability to get in and out of properties without leaving as much as a boot mark. A while ago the lads had been talking about a woman in High Hatton with pristine cream carpets that they swear were even cleaner when they left than when they'd arrived. For all our jokes we liked going over and above the call of duty like this. And this old guy deserved the attention. 'I'll just move these out of the way for you,' he said, coming forward and picking up a couple of framed photographs from near the hearth. The photos were all over the room. They were all in plain silver frames and they were all of the same woman. She was young and beautiful in the black and white pictures. She was a little older but no less striking in the colour ones. I took a quick look around as the others finished up with the fire blankets. I couldn't see any of her beyond middle age. Had she died? What was her story – and what was his?

Mr Dowling offered us tea as we got the rest of our equipment in place. 'When the job's done we might just take you up on that offer,' Joe told him. 'But first let's put out your fire.'

We tackled chimney fires with some basic but effective kit. First of all we attached a 360° nozzle to the end of a hose. That in turn was attached to a structure with a little wheel that we could push slowly up the chimney using chimney rods. While a couple of us attached the rods and got the hose moving upwards, someone else used the stirrup pump, an old-fashioned, manual, pump-in-a-bucket arrangement. When the whole thing was going water sprayed out in all directions and should cover every inch of the chimney, from bottom to top and back again. I tended to work the pump on those jobs and I was in position and ready for Joe's signal at Mr Dowling's house. 'Off you go, lads,' Joe said. I got the water flowing while Matt and Woody did their thing with the rods.

One sign of how hot and dangerous chimney fires can be is that very little of the first few bucket loads of water drips back down the chimney. At first most of it just evaporates and billows out of the top of the chimney as steam. If you're outside, this can make it look as if things are getting worse. The trick is to watch what happens to these white clouds. If they dissipate fast then they're steam and things are getting better. If the clouds hang around they're smoke and something's still burning. That day Joe came back in from the garden to tell us things were looking good.

'What we like to see is a lot of steam outside and very little water dripping down in here,' he told Mr Dowling who was clearly fascinated by the whole process. 'After a while the chimney should cool, the fires should all be out and as there will be less evaporation we'll see a lot more water escaping down into your grate. That's why my colleague here has some buckets to hand,' he said, indicating a smiling Matt in the fireplace. 'What I'll also do when the water starts to drip down is to check its temperature.' At that point a few trickles of water did indeed begin to drip into Matt's bucket. 'How does that feel?' Charlie asked him.

'It's still pretty hot, boss,' Matt replied.

'Then we've got a long way to go.'

I kept pumping the water, Matt and Woody kept adding and then taking away the chimney rods and Charlie joined us to help keep the water from spilling out on to the old man's carpet. Looking back, we should have paid more attention to the fact that they couldn't get the rods out of the chimney pot so couldn't be certain they'd got them to the very top of the chimney. But as the water temperature kept falling that didn't seem to matter.

'It's cold now, boss,' Matt said after another five or ten minutes of work. Joe reached in to the chimney to confirm it. 'Rest for now,' he said, telling me to stop pumping the water. He got the others to bring the nozzle back down to earth, then he turned back to me. 'Clean your hands, jockey, and go up and check the walls.' I went upstairs and felt the chimney breast all the way up the house. There was a faint roaring noise up there – a bit like a child blowing over the top of a pop bottle. But I put that down to the sound of the wind outside. And the hot spots had certainly gone, even in the attic. I headed downstairs with the good news, though I didn't have the heart to tell the poor old guy about his wallpaper.

'I'll make that pot of tea now, shall I?' Mr Dowling said when Joe gave him a progress report.

'That would be most welcome,' Joe told him. 'We're going to stick around for a while just to make certain that the fire doesn't catch again. It looks bad for us if we get called back to a property. And I can't imagine you'll want us tramping through here a second time once you've got your house back to normal.'

We repacked the pump, the chimney rods and all the fire blankets while Mr Dowling brought around the teas – plus a few sneaky cans of lager. 'Take them for the journey,' he said. 'It's the least I can do.' Joe went upstairs with the homeowner to do one more check for hot spots. 'Happen that's nature's way of telling me I need to redecorate' was Mr Dowling's verdict on the wallpaper.

'Well, if you want a hand I know someone who can help you out,' Charlie began, before Joe stilled him with a glance. Having a spiv number was one thing. Touting for business after a shout was another – though I wouldn't have put it past Charlie to sneak back with a flyer on his next day off.

Everyone was in a good mood when we finally left the man's house with our emergency lagers.

'I can't thank you enough. God bless you. I drink at the Brooklands Hotel and I'll buy all of you a pint if you're ever in the neighbourhood,' he told Joe as he stood at his garden gate. We were all in our usual 'just part of the job' poses, lapping it up and hoping he told all the ladies in the pub how great we were.

That's when it happened.

A final flame must have been lurking somewhere in the three-foot-high chimney pot. Woody hadn't got the nozzle all the way up there. But by moving the nozzle and the rods up and down the rest of the chimney several times he had scraped all the old soot and clinker out of the chimney flue. Now vast quantities of lovely fresh air was able to rush unimpeded up the clean chimney towards that last little bit of fire. When the oxygen got there the flame turned into a sort of giant blowtorch. We were standing in the street outside Mr Dowling's house when a shot of pure white flame powered at least ten feet out of the unsuspecting man's chimney pot and into the evening sky.

Joe reached out to grip our still satisfied customer by both shoulders – desperate to stop him from turning around until the worst was over. 'It's no problem at all, Mr Dowling, we're just glad we could help,' he said, a horrible, strained expression on his face. 'Let me show you some of the newest equipment we've got on the other side of the engine' were the last words I heard Joe say as I grabbed the stirrup pump and a couple of buckets and joined the rest of the gang trying to get back into the house as quickly and unobtrusively as possible.

It took us a good half-hour to be certain we'd got every last spark of the fire out that time. Mr Dowling took it very well, all things considered. But Joe didn't. We all got a heck of a bollocking back at base. Fair play, I suppose. It had been wrong to assume the fire was out just because cold water was coming down the chimney – and we really should have got the nozzle right out of the top of the chimney pot. 'Don't you remember your training?' Joe had yelled at the end of one particularly long rant about our general incompetence.

'They can't train you for everything,' Woody had grumbled in the mess room afterwards. I discovered how right he was the following night. For nothing in any of our training had told us how to get a baby out of a bucket.

24

A Baby and a Bucket

There was a screaming mum. There was a screeching baby. There was a hysterical next-door neighbour shouting: 'You can't leave him there! Can't you see he's in pain! You have to do something!' We'd been called to a brand new house on an estate on the outskirts of Shrewsbury. It was one of those jobs you don't expect and can't forget. It was a classic example of that old rule that when all else fails people call the Fire Brigade.

'Tell us again how this happened?' John asked when the mum drew breath and stopped screaming for a second. The rest of us were shuffling around the landing, trying to keep out of the neighbour's reach and work out a plan. Unfortunately the more the mum tried to explain the more complicated it all sounded. The upshot, though, was that the galvanised metal mop bucket had got jammed underneath the bath and the baby had crawled up to it for a bit of an adventure. The funnel-shaped strainer on the bucket had holes punched into it and the baby had decided to push his fingers through them. That's how things started to go wrong. The outside of the strainer was smooth. The inside of each punched hole was as rough and raw as heck. If the little lad pulled too hard to get his finger out it would get ripped to shreds on the metal edges. And even then the odds were that it wouldn't come free. His finger had already started to swell up like a balloon. By the time we arrived things had reached crisis point. Neither bath, nor bucket, nor baby was going anywhere, any time soon.

'If we can get the bucket free we can take the whole thing to Casualty,' Charlie had said early on. But could we get the bucket free? Not a chance. The bathroom was tiny. We were taking it in turns to look inside the room and try to help. At one point or another all five of us tried to wrench the bucket out from under the bath. 'It's like it's been backin' welded there' was Arfer's whispered conclusion, though we never did find out how it got there or why.

'What do you think we're going to do? Take out the bath or cut through the bucket?' I asked Arfer as the mum began to wail yet again. John was inside the bathroom now trying to calm her down as he tackled the bucket one last time. At one point I heard him try to say her screams were upsetting the child. That only made matters worse.

'I reckon the boss will have us cut through the bucket,' Arfer said. 'He'll either get us to cut out a whole panel so we can at least take the baby to Casualty and let them finish the job. Or he'll get us to cut right through to his finger so we can free him ourselves.'

'And when you say "us", who do you mean?' I asked nervously. I knew that tough jobs were always given to me. I liked it. I'd been happy up that ladder in the bank. I'd been OK swimming across the River Severn in my underwear. I'd not been remotely bothered by grappling the plastic owl on top of one of the busiest pubs in town. But using a metal saw right up to a baby's tiny little hand? I wasn't sure if I was quite ready for that.

'I think the boss will do it himself,' Arfer said. He was right. We took turns to look in from the landing as John got ready. Well, as he tried to get ready.

'You're joking. You're not serious. You're not using that on a little baby! Who are you? You're out of your mind!' The next-door neighbour decided to intervene when Charlie brought the Cengar saw up the stairs and passed it over to the boss. It was about a foot and a half long and had a six-inch blade. I knew from my endless exam revision that it weighed exactly 3.8 kilograms and was made in Swansea!

'It's a very accurate saw and I'll be taking the best possible care,' John began.

'I don't care. You can't put that next to a baby. And, like I say, who are you?' she turned to the baby's mum. 'Michelle, this isn't the Fire Brigade's job. They put out fires. They don't do things like this. We want the police here. Or a doctor. I don't know why these people are here in the first place.'

John tried to intervene. 'Madam, this is exactly what we do in the Fire Brigade. We help people in all sorts of situations. We're trained to do it. If the police were here then they would call us. A doctor would call the Fire Brigade as well. We're the right people to get this baby free. But we need to do it now. The poor mite is distressed enough as it is.'

The woman flailed around trying to find something else to say. Meanwhile the baby's mother said nothing. She was sitting on the bathroom floor crying. At that exact moment neither of them seemed to be paying much attention to the little kid. I squeezed past them, crouched down and started to pull some faces at him to try and take his mind off all the drama. I was pretending to roar like a lion when John had his breakthrough.

'Well done, jockey. I can take over now,' he said quietly. He squatted down on the carpeted floor. He gave the bucket one last tug, just in case. Then he got the saw in position. He pulled the trigger and got the blade moving. Bit by bit, inch by inch he edged the blade closer to the baby's hand. When he got within a whisker of it he stopped and began cutting again from a slightly different start point. When both routes had been cut he began to fold the small triangle of metal back on itself. He started to wiggle it gently. He put a bit more muscle into it. But it kept on hanging together as if it was on a thread. It was like pulling a tooth out when you're a child – but at least ten times more gruesome.

'OK, I'm going to cut just a little bit more with these tin snips,' he said softly. The baby was still crying but everyone else was quiet, even the neighbour. And five, maybe ten minutes after the first cut the slice of metal broke loose and the baby was free. The little lad's finger did not look good. It was red raw and had swollen so much it looked like a finger that had taken a battering in a Tom & Jerry cartoon. Part of me thought it looked like a hammer, part that it looked as if it had been whacked by one. But the boy was back safe in his mum's arms. And not a drop of blood had been spilled.

No one offered us tea or sneaked us a few cans of lager after that shout. The mum barely said thank you while the neighbour could hardly bring herself to look at us. And, funnily enough, that was how it went for quite a few of our next few jobs. November the fifth was just around the corner. It didn't pan out quite the way I'd expected either.

'So when do you think we'll get the most call-outs in November?' John had asked Matt and me back at the station one evening. For once I was so sure I knew the answer that I interrupted before he could give it himself. 'Bonfire Night,' I said confidently.

John looked triumphant. 'Wrong!' he said. 'We'll get most of our calls almost exactly a week beforehand. Want to know why?'

I did.

'Because every village in Shropshire wants to have the best display on the night. They'll be building their bonfires already. And a week or so before 5 November they'll go out on the prowl. They'll torch as many other bonfires as they can so theirs is the last one standing. Mark my words: it will be the weekend before that we'll be busy.'

He was right, the way he always was. We raced across the county from village to village in the run-up to Guy Fawkes Day. And no one ever gave us a particularly warm welcome.

'Put it out! We can't let it burn!' one set of villagers would yell when we thundered up.

'But don't use water! Don't get it all wet!' another set would shout.

While we got the blaze under control they would then have a bit of a row about how to salvage as much of the wood as possible. The row would normally be continuing when we got back in the truck and drove away. A lot of the time I swear they barely noticed us go.

It was the middle of November, Mr Thom had just been around with one of his food deliveries and I was tucking into an out-of-date steak and ale pie when it suddenly hit me. The exams were exactly one month away. 'What's the matter, Castle? Got a mouthful of gristle? You don't want to think too much about what might really be in these backin' pies. I saw a documentary once about a man in Italy who made them out of dead bodies he stole from the local mortuary,' began Arfer opposite me. His story went on, the way they always did. It got ever more over the top and gruesome, as they usually did as well. But I was barely listening. This time next month! In thirty days I'd know if I'd still be part of Red Watch in the New Year or if it was all over. And what would I do if I failed? I looked across the table at Charlie. Could I get a job with his painting and decorating business? I dismissed the idea straight away. It would kill me every time he told a story about a shout. Should I just try for something at Rolls-Royce or some other factory? But the thought of doing the same job nine to six every day killed me as well. I'll try the RAF again, I decided. I'll go back to school and get some A levels if I have to. At least with the air force I'll be sent away. I won't have to bump into Woody or Arfer or Caddie or any of the others down the pub.

'And he only got caught when a nun discovered two human eyeballs on a pizza. And they weren't even from the same body,'

Arfer was saying when he got to the big finish of his story. 'It's the backin' truth. Every word.'

I washed up my plate and headed down to the room that Matt and I had commandeered as a place to study. He still had a few more months to go till his exams, but he was almost as nervous as I was. 'Do you think we're going to be ready?' he asked. We'd spent half an hour throwing different scenarios at each other for the oral exams. 'OK, you're at the station and you need to get to Cross Houses. Give me directions,' he would instruct me. 'Where are the nearest hydrants to the primary school on Featherbed Lane and what are the hazards and key details we should know about the OAP home alongside the Sawbury Road in Astley?' I'd fire back when I'd finished my answer.

Back upstairs Matt and I sat in on the latest discussions of next month's Christmas party. The plan was to drag all the beds to one side and open up the folding doors so the mess room and the dorm made one big room. Half the watch wanted a tropical theme, half wanted to wear ordinary clothes and go for a traditional Christmas bash. Half the watch wanted to invite wives and girlfriends while the other half were happy to invite Betty, Mabel, Babs and Bev but wanted to stop at that. I knew that Louise was planning on wangling an invitation somehow. She said that as she'd been waved at and leered at from the drill ground every day for six months she was practically part of the furniture already. She even wanted to buy something new to wear. I couldn't bring myself to join any side of any of the arguments. Tropical or Christmas? New dress or no new dress? None of it mattered because the party was on the second Saturday of December. That was three days after my exam. Forget the wives and girlfriends: I didn't know if I'd be going myself.

'You want me to tell you a secret? Back in the day none of us studied as hard as you have, lad,' Caddie said later that afternoon when I was back at my books. 'Even Paddy agrees you're good at all the drills and he hasn't paid anyone a compliment in about thirty years. You're gonna be fine. But if you're not so sure then I've got half an hour spare right now. Get me a chair. Let's talk through the ways we use the turntable ladder one last time.'

Half an hour with Caddie normally turned into an hour. He wasn't the only one to offer me extra help. Arfer didn't go so far as to follow me into the toilets with questions again, but he did fire questions at me everywhere else. Charlie and Woody did the same at meal times. Louise got in on the act and spent her evenings picking different points on the map and asking me the quickest routes between them. To keep me on my toes, even my mum and dad started to ask where all the local fire hydrants were. I couldn't quite believe it when I added up how many supporters I had. So many people were rooting for me that year. So many people were putting themselves out to help me. Everyone was being incredibly kind. It didn't half add to the pressure.

The first heavy frosts of the year came in early December when ice-cold winds blew in from the east and sliced out towards Oswestry and the Welsh hills. The temperature drop certainly made the whole county look magical. Out in the countryside the winter sun bounced off a sharp, clean carpet of white on the fields in the mornings. It shone through a sparkling coat of white diamonds on the empty branches of the trees while ice clutched the edges of the stones in all the streams and brooks. Back in town the castle somehow looked like a real fortress now the earth around it was hard and white. Halfway down the hill from it the newly white roofs of the half-timbered, medieval buildings were like an early Christmas card. Everywhere seemed more peaceful. Everything looked so good.

'Beautiful, isn't it?' I said to George one morning when we were driving the fire engine back from our weekly shop at the Co-op.

'Beautiful but treacherous,' he replied, his glass half empty as usual. And for a moment, that morning, it looked as if he was going to be proved right.

We had barely carried the shopping bags out of the fire engine when the emergency call came through. We were told that a road traffic accident on the far side of town had left a driver trapped in his car. Every time we had an RTA call my mind flew back to the first one I'd faced in the early summer. I could always see those two dead drivers on that beautiful country road. The one in the Vauxhall Cavalier with that horrific injury. The poor passenger forced to sit facing him until we could free him. I'd never forget that and I relived it almost weekly. That December day I prepared myself for something similar. We hit a lot of traffic on the way through Shrewsbury so the journey took a few minutes more than expected. I used every extra second to steel myself for what we might find when we arrived.

'OK, what are we dealing with here?' John had jumped out of the engine first and was striding towards a policeman. I looked around us. The scene was far less dramatic than I'd feared. There was no major pile-up, no sign of some terrible collision. The street was narrow and steep and the car that the police officer was pointing to was parked relatively well, halfway up it. Its driver, a smart, middle-aged man in a long black coat and a woolly hat with a jaunty bobble on top, was sitting on the edge of the driver's seat with one leg out in the gutter. I took a few steps up towards him to see if he knew what was happening. He beckoned me to come closer. I knew I should have waited for John's instruction before wandering up there but as it all seemed so normal I decided to do some investigations of my own.

'Everything all right?' I asked from the other side of the car.

'Are you mad? Does everything look all right?' he said, clearly appalled.

I looked around. What was I missing? 'It doesn't look too bad,' I ventured. 'Where's the accident? What is it we're here to do?'

The man's eyes bulged out of his head as he stared at me.

I noticed how pale he was. Tear tracks ran down his face. He was clearly distressed so I guessed it had to be him we were there to help. But I still couldn't see why.

'This is the accident! I'm trapped here. Trapped I tell you!' he said, half shouting, half croaking. Then he began to explain. 'I parked my car here like I always do. I always get it close to the kerb so it's safe. I put the handbrake on. I turned off the engine, I got my things together and I climbed out. That's when the handbrake failed. The bleeding handbrake failed! The only thing stopping this car rolling down the street is the fact that my effing leg is stopping the door from closing. I've never been in so much pain in my whole life.'

I'd stepped around the front of the car so I could finally see what was going on. The man was right. The car looked to have shifted forward. His leg really was the only thing stopping it rolling down the hill like a mobile wrecking ball. Fresh tears were running down the man's face now. His breathing was fast and shallow and he was obviously in shock.

'Don't worry. Stay right where you are,' I heard myself say as I headed back to join the others. Those simple words certainly snapped him out of his shock.

'Stay right where I am? Where do you think I'm going to, you blithering idiot? You think I wouldn't have moved if I could? You think I'm going to run a bleeding marathon? I wanted the Fire Brigade not a bloody comedian,' he yelled down at me. I winced as I walked away. Fair play to the man. It had been a stupid thing to say. I consoled myself that I'd at least taken his mind off the pain for a few moments – and that John had been too far away to hear what I'd said.

My cover was blown the moment we approached the man with the first of our tool kit. 'Do you know what this joker said to me? Do you? He said: "Stay right where you are." Stay right where you are! You give clowns a uniform nowadays, do you? "Stay right where you are. Stay right where you bleeding are!"'

John looked at me. I'd always admired him for keeping a straight face in front of the public. For the first time he looked as if he was going to crack.

'Oh, jockey,' he said, finally. 'I think that one's going to follow you around for the rest of your life.' Then he turned back to our unhappy friend. He got back to business.

We used our tirfor winch. We attached it to the rear tow bar so that we could drag the car back inch by inch. It was enough. After an agonising half-hour we got the driver free. Amazingly he didn't even need a whole lot of roadside first aid. He'd broken a bit of skin, but all his bones were intact. 'He's not going to be doing the hokey-cokey any time soon but it could have been a hell of a lot worse,' the ambulance man told us drily when he'd checked the patient out. The man wasn't safe to drive, but he was able to walk away to his friend's house. He also insisted on buying us all drinks at the weekend when we were off shift. It's funny, but unless we were on spiv jobs together we very rarely met up away from the station. Maybe it was the Christmas spirit but most of us did go out that particular Saturday night though. Our motorist stood us all several rounds of drinks. 'To the best Fire Brigade in the county,' he said when he got the whole pub to toast our health. Then he pointed at me and aimed his comments at all the other people in the pub. At least a dozen complete strangers sat up and paid attention. I slumped as low in my chair as I could get. I knew what was coming. 'Let me tell you what this joker said to me when the Fire Brigade first arrived,' he began. I felt the colour rise in my cheeks. 'Stay right where you are! That's what he said. Stay right where you are!' The whole watch fell about laughing – as did the rest of the pub. I stood up and did a bit of a bow to show I was taking it in good heart. And I was. I didn't care. They could laugh as much as they wanted. I'd put up with this forever, just as long as I still had a job at the end of it. That was what hung in the balance. My exams were just eleven days away.

25

Exams...

'**W**hat do you mean Matt's gone?' I said in shock.

It was Monday morning. John had called me into the watch room just before our shift had begun. I'd been revising at home all Sunday and my mind was so steeped in my books that it took a while to focus on what he had said.

'We don't know all the facts yet, son, so it wouldn't be fair of me to say too much. But Matty got into a bit of difficulty with the law on Saturday afternoon. And because of that the Fire Brigade has suspended him.'

'I don't understand.'

'It's the rules. If you break the law then you can't work here.'

I brushed that aside. 'I know the rules. I don't understand what it is he's supposed to have done.'

'It's not been proved either way just yet.'

'Well, what is it that they say he's done?' I banged my hands on the desk and practically shouted the question at John. I'd never even dreamed of speaking to him like this before. But I was so gobsmacked by the news that I forgot my manners and my position. And if I'd been shocked to hear that Matt had gone, I was flabbergasted when John finally told me why. A fight, I could have understood. Speeding wouldn't have been a total surprise. Even drunk and disorderly wouldn't have knocked me for six. But it was none of these. Matt had been caught shoplifting on the high street. He'd swiped a book from a local bookshop.

And when he left the shop he'd walked straight into the path of a copper.

No one talked about anything else for the rest of the shift. Grown men gathered like little crowds of washerwomen to rake over everything they thought they knew about Matt to look for signs of what had just happened. I stood apart because the only person I wanted to speak to was Matt himself. I didn't want to use the station phone to ring him because I knew everyone would be listening in. I'd have given anything to get down to the phone box by Thoms' frozen food store. But as we weren't allowed to go that far from the engines at any time I had to stick around for the whole fifteen-hour night shift and just wonder how he was getting on. Every time I went to the mess room there was some outlandish new theory about what had happened. I had the worst night shift since I'd joined, wandering around trying to work it all out. It would have been the perfect night for a big shout. A house fire would have given us something else to think of. But as it turned out the phone stayed silent. The hours dragged. For the first time I struggled to sleep when I finally headed to the dorm.

Things were still pretty grim the following week when we began our next set of day shifts. I was asked to clean out Matt's locker. He'd returned his uniform and taken all his personal kit away the previous night, when he'd known White Watch were on shift. No surprise that he'd not wanted to face any of us. I'd called at his house a couple of times but his mum always said he was out. I kept thinking about the Shropshire Fire Service emblem that had burned into his neck on the heath fire. It probably hadn't faded yet. He'd still see it in the mirror every morning, the poor sod.

'Jockey, we need more booze for the party. You're going down the Co-op with John, me, Pete and Woody. And cheer up, mate, it might never happen,' Paddy said, poking his head round the locker-room door.

'It might,' I wanted to tell him. 'If I fail the exams one of you might be cleaning out my locker this time next week.' Instead I pulled myself up into my usual seat on the fire engine. George was driving, John was up front and Pete and Woody were trying to make me laugh at the back. 'You know the best story of all is the one about you and that woman in the car accident,' Woody said to Pete at one point.

'There's no way you're telling that story again.'

Woody laughed and turned to me. 'We all know you make an idiot of yourself on shouts, jockey. But it's nothing to what old Pete did when he first started.'

'This is the oldest story in the station.'

'So the jockey needs to hear it. It was way back when, jockey. Pete had only been on the watch for about a month, so I'm told.' Woody was about to go on but Pete sighed and interrupted him. It seemed that if a story was to be told at his expense he wanted to tell it himself. I was fascinated. Pete was the quietest man on the watch. Most nights he just sat on his stool by the bar and did puzzles in magazines. I was intrigued to hear him talk.

'I was no more than your age, son,' he began. 'I was the jockey and it was my first bad car crash.'

'Car crash? It was nothing more than a scratch,' Woody interrupted.

'It was a bad one and Woody wasn't there so he doesn't know,' Pete said firmly. 'The car had hit a tree after swerving to avoid a dog. The driver hadn't been wearing a seat belt and he was in a bad way. There was blood all over. More blood than I'd ever seen in me life.'

'And his dad worked in an abattoir,' Woody barracked.

Pete ignored him. 'I'll be honest with you, jockey, the blood knocked me for six. I wasn't best ready for all of that. So I stepped back and I let the old-timers do the leg work. They could cut the guy out and lift him on to a stretcher. What I decided to do was to look after the lady in the passenger seat. The Officer in Charge had spoken to her. She'd cut her face and bled a bit but apart from that she was basically fine. All she needed was a bit of reassurance till we got her out of there. Well, that's what I was told.' He was really smiling now, warming to his tale. 'I spoke to her from the car window. She was shaky and a bit wheezy and she'd been pushed right up forward against the dashboard, but apart from that she said she was just fine. I tried the passenger door and it opened. I managed to release the seat lock so I could ease it backwards and give her a bit more space. That's when I saw it.'

'Saw what?'

'Her intestines. They were right there. The seat belt must have cut her open, right across her abdomen. Everything that should have been inside was outside. It was all covered in blood. It was the most disgusting thing I'd ever seen. That woman could have died, and she didn't even know she was in danger. Meanwhile, everyone else had been too busy looking after the driver to spot what was going on.'

'So what happened?'

Pete was really starting to smile now, despite himself. Woody and the two others up front, who must have heard the story dozens of times, were getting ready for the punchline as well. 'I called over the Officer in Charge. I said we needed another medic, fast. A few minutes later he came over and took a look. He examined her properly and found out the truth. The only thing she'd cut was her forehead. That wasn't her insides on her lap at all. She'd just bled into her bag of blinkin' chips.'

The trip to the supermarket got me right back on track. I'd laughed so much on the way out there that I even joined in with all the usual flirting with the fellow shoppers and checkout girls. We did a couple of drills in the icy cold air when we got back to the station and had packed all the booze away. John shouted out a bit of a lecture about frozen hoses and line rescues on icy ponds. We headed to the hospital to answer a call that turned out to be yet another false alarm and we rushed back so that we wouldn't keep Mabel and Betty waiting at lunchtime.

'It's fish pie. Brain food for your exam,' Betty pronounced kindly when I grabbed my plate.

'How can you feed something that's not there? Jockey's not got two brain cells to rub together. Otherwise he'd have a better backin' job than this,' Arfer told her.

'Language!' said Mabel from the other side of the serving hatch.

The last couple of days passed in a bit of a blur. The weather was getting worse and after we were called to pull a fallen tree off a parked car out in Uffington, I allowed myself to hope that if rain didn't stop play then a howling gale might at least stop the exams. It didn't. I got up ridiculously early, shaved, had a shower, tried to eat some breakfast then drove over to head-quarters where the exams were taking place. There were just half a dozen of us being assessed in my group, six nervous, rookie firemen who couldn't really meet each other's eyes. We were all in our best dress uniform and I remember thinking that everyone looked really pale. Then I saw my reflection in a glass door. I looked like a blinkin' ghost.

'The time is nine o'clock exactly. You may turn your papers over now, gentlemen.' The first of the morning's written papers had begun. We were lined up at desks in a small, draughty lecture room. Pens scratched all around me. It felt like school. But it was a thousand times more important. My eyes moved con-stantly from the questions to my answers and then to the clock. Sometimes the second hand seemed barely to have moved. Sometimes whole chunks of time seemed to have shot by without me realising. Would I finish at this rate? Was I doing OK?

'Pens down, gentlemen. Pass your answer papers down to the front of the room for collection. You are dismissed.'

We hung around in the corridor while we waited for our next

written exam. Afterwards a few of the bolder candidates tried to talk about how many fires they'd tackled and how many beautiful blonde women they'd already saved. I could barely speak. When lunchtime came I could hardly eat either. There was a rumour that our exams were being marked straight away. Someone said we'd be given the results after the drills and oral exams in the afternoon. A big part of me wanted to run away at that point. But at two o'clock I was out there with everyone else. We were standing in squad lines for the first of the drills, watched constantly by fierce, unsmiling officers. It was funny but all the things that had started to come naturally to me at the station felt forced and tricky when an assessor's beady eyes were on me. I felt as if I fumbled or hesitated too often. I wanted to tell them I was better than this. I wanted to know what they thought.

Everyone was sweating by the time we came in from the drill yard. It was a wild and windy December day. But we'd all given it everything we had. We'd lifted the ladders, carried the hoses and tackled every scenario they had thrown at us. Now we had to sit down in the Fire Brigade version of the *Mastermind* chair and take questions. If I thought the last few days had gone by in a blur it was nothing compared to the oral exam itself. It was a bit like an out-of-body experience. I think I answered everything. I think I knew what to say most of the time. But I was hardly aware of doing it. When I left the room I had no clue how I'd done.

'They have marked our papers already. We've been told to wait. The Divisional Officer will call us in one at a time when they've double-checked it all. We find out straight away if we've passed or failed. They write a letter to our stations to confirm it today and it should be there tomorrow afternoon at the latest.' A pale-faced and breathless figure I vaguely remembered from training had caught up with me in the corridor and rushed to give me the latest intelligence. I joined the others in the waiting area. A tense, sweaty hour went by. My stomach was rumbling and I was gasping for a drink when the first of the names was called. I got ready. Everything in the Fire Brigade was done alphabetically. My surname meant I was almost certain to be next.

'Castle. Malcolm. Go through there, please,' a woman with a clipboard said sharply. I walked into the DO's office, feeling four foot six rather than six feet four.

'Sit!' he said fiercely. He looked long and hard at me and time seemed to stand still. My mind was racing, going over every answer I'd given in the exams, every moment I'd spent on the drill yard that afternoon. The DO looked down at a sheet of paper on his desk. He looked back at me. Then very quietly and clearly he told me that . . . I'd passed!

26

Staying?

For some reason I didn't want to tell the others until I'd seen the official letter. I wanted to see the result in black and white before I truly believed it. So I tried to stall them. 'I think I did OK but I don't know for sure. They've written to us. I'll find out in the afternoon post. I don't want to think about it any more. If you don't mind I don't want to talk about it.'

They did mind, as it happened. But I was saved by the bell. We had an emergency call and it sounded serious. A boy was trapped in a bog out on the top of Long Mynd. I shivered just thinking about how exposed it must be up there. I wondered how long the kid had been trapped. Even if he'd been with his parents they'd have had a long hike to find a phone and call us. If he'd been on his own for some reason then he might have been there hours before a farmer or a hardy hiker stumbled upon him.

'How old do they think he is?' I asked Arfer as we pulled out of the station. He looked a bit bemused.

'Why?' he asked.

'Well, it's a worry, isn't it,' I said.

Arfer shrugged. 'Why's it a worry? Who the hell cares? I just want to get the job done and get back to the station in time for a nice bit of lunch. It's liver and bacon,' he said.

Over to my left Woody looked equally disinterested. 'Betty's making one of her rice puddings as well. I don't want to miss that,' he said.

I shuffled around on my helmet and tried to get comfortable. I gazed out of the window feeling deflated, confused and a little bit upset. For all our jokes and silly banter we did all genuinely care about the people we helped. It was a bitterly cold morning and some kid was in trouble out on the moors. It was totally out of character for Arfer and Woody to be so cavalier about a shout. I suddenly wondered if there was some connection between this and me passing my exam. Had everything up till now been fake? Had everyone just been pretending to care because of me? Was this the true flavour of the job?

We made relatively slow progress and my mood, and the weather, got blacker all the time. We were heading towards the hills up by Church Stretton, a beautiful Alpine-looking village and the heart of Shropshire's Little Switzerland. December was the right time to be there. I'd never been to Switzerland but I couldn't believe it was much colder. The drive was about as hairy as any you'd find on any Swiss mountain as well. The road, the Burway, clung to the side of the hill and I for one was keeping my fingers crossed that it didn't let go. The lads had told me several tall tales of cars that had come off it in the past. There were blind corners galore and it was a heck of a long way down to the valley floor below.

I looked at my watch for perhaps the millionth time.

'Windsor's got ants in his pants today. Maybe he's got a date lined up back at the station. Some other bird from the offices at the back has caught his eye now he's a fully fledged fireman,' said Arfer.

I turned on him. 'You don't know I'm a fully fledged fireman. The letter won't be here till this afternoon. I'm not going to cheat on Louise. And I can't believe that none of you give a damn that somewhere out there some poor boy is trapped in a bog.'

I don't think I've ever heard people laugh so loud. Everyone in the truck was laughing. None of them were able to speak for ages.

'Windsor, it's not a boy in a bog. It's a bull in a bog,' Arfer said when he'd finally got his breath back. 'I thought you were taking it a bit too seriously. You want to get your ears cleaned out if you're sticking on this watch.'

They were still sniggering when we saw the farmer's tractor and parked the fire truck as close to it as possible. The winds were so strong we had to shout to be heard. He led us over the crest of the next hill towards a wide, shallow dip of land. There, slap bang in the middle of it, was the bull. He was a big, black and very angry beast. He was lying at a crazy angle, buried halfway up his flanks in rich, peaty mud. He was thrashing his head from side to side, letting out violent little roars and exhaling huge clouds of white steam. 'There's your poor little boy, Windsor,' said Arfer. 'Still feel sorry for him? Still give a damn how old he is?'

'He's been tryin' to get hisself out of there on his own all morning. All he does is bury himself even deeper, stupid oaf,' the farmer shouted at us.

'And you're sure you want him pulling out?' Arfer yelled, trying to make a joke.

The farmer didn't have the greatest sense of humour. 'I want him pulling out and I want it done quick. I've got a roast waiting for me back at home this lunchtime. It's been bad enough having to wait for you half the morning.'

We didn't really speak to him very much after that. He glowered a little and sighed a lot, but at least he stuck with us rather than retreating to the warmth of his tractor cab. It was obvious from the start that we had a tough task on our hands. Bogs aren't the easiest terrain to work on at the best of times. As it had been raining for days and had just started to do so again, this one was particularly tricky. We needed solid ground to use as an anchor if we tried to pull or lift the bull free. He was at least ten yards from any of it. We stood around, added our usual 'couple of coats of looking at' to the situation, then John came up with a plan. It involved two long ladders, an animal rescue sling and, of course, me.

'It'll be easy, Windsor,' I was told. 'We'll lie a ladder down on each side of the beast. You'll climb along them. You'll be able to reach over the animal's belly, just behind its front legs. Get the sling around it, climb back and pull it tight from the other ladder on the other side. Then we'll pull him out with the tractor. If you get your skates on we'll be back in time for Mabel's liver and bacon.'

We might be needing skates in a minute, I was thinking, while John briefed the farmer and the others got all the kit we needed off the engines and tramped with it up and over the hill towards us. The rain had turned to sleet and was beginning to lie on the thin films of ice on the more stagnant, smellier pockets of water on the bog. The wind was picking up as well. Soft, mushy ice bombs were being blown almost sideways now. I felt a rush of cold run up my arm as a particularly big gust got into the gap between my gloves and my jacket. The cold was also starting to seep through the plastic gloves themselves. I stomped from foot to foot, splashing in the mud, willing us to get on with it.

Woody and Arfer got the two ladders laid down on the mud, one on each side of the bull. John handed me the animal sling. 'So, you think I should start from the front?' I asked, looking warily at it. I doubted that he could pick a leg out of the marshy earth and kick me in the head with it. But I wouldn't have ruled it out.

'Yes, jockey, go from the front,' John said.

Then Arfer suddenly cracked. 'And don't look so hard done by. I'm coming with you for once,' he said. He followed me on my unsteady way down to the middle of the ladder. We wrestled with the sling, with the bull and with the elements. It was a nightmare. If the bull had been angry before, he was blinkin' furious now. He could barely move, so we were relatively safe.

But he could threaten all sorts. The noises he made and the way he strained the muscles in his body were right out of science fiction. I dug away into the tough, fibre-filled bog trying to get the sling where we needed it. Arfer pushed away at me and at the bull in turn. For ages we got nowhere. Lots of times we slumped back in the wet water, almost losing the sling as well as the will to live. But I have to say that we laughed like drains as well. The wetter, muddier and colder we got the funnier it all seemed.

'Any time today would be nice, guys,' Charlie yelled out from the safety of solid ground at one point.

'You try it! I did not sign up to this!' I yelled back.

'You got the horse out of the hole at that farm up in West Felton. That was your first day on the watch, wasn't it? You can't say you weren't warned what the job would be like.'

'That was in June! It was sunny! It was a horse!'

Arfer and I carried on fighting away in the black mud. We carried on laughing at the madness of it. I got my trousers ripped on a rock in the marsh then managed to lose a glove. But somehow, in the end, we had both metal rings from each end of the sling held together round the bull's back. We got on the other ladder. We tied the rings together and doubled up the line before the farmer moved in with the tractor. He got it as close to the quagmire as he dared. It was just about close enough. We fixed the sling to the draw bar, he went into gear and drove away. Slowly, agonisingly and with the kind of long, low squelch you'd hear in a cartoon, the bull was finally pulled free. Arfer and I sat back on the muddy ground. We were long past caring about the cold, the wet or anything at all.

'Well, I'm not sure if I can allow you two in my nice clean fire engine in that kind of condition,' John tried to say when the bull had thundered off over the hillside, the farmer had headed off for his lunchtime roast and we had cleaned up and restowed the ladders.

'Nice backin' try, boss. I'm not staying out here freezing my nuts off for a second longer,' Arfer said, climbing aboard.

'Me, too, boss,' I said.

We laughed almost all the way back across Long Mynd, down through Little Switzerland and onwards to Shrewsbury. Mabel and Betty were both standing in the mess room window when we arrived back at the station, long after lunch. But this time they didn't look annoyed. Arfer and I were in the mess room trying to clean ourselves up a bit when John came in.

'Apparently we've had a letter,' he said, handing me a white, official-looking envelope.

I shut my eyes for a fraction of a second then reached out and grabbed it. The Divisional Officer had said to my face that I'd passed. Could they have changed their minds? Or was this the official proof I needed? There was only one way to find out. I ripped it open.

'I passed,' I said. Just two words.

'Well done, Castle,' said John. 'Mabel and Betty will be very pleased. They're waiting upstairs to congratulate you.'

'I expect you'll want to thank me. After all, I taught you everything you know. You were worse than backin' useless when you first started,' said Arfer. For the first time I reached out and smacked him on the back of the head.

One more thing happened that afternoon. Apart, that is, from being given a monumentally large plate of liver and bacon, a vast bowl of rice pudding and getting an unexpected kiss on the cheek from Betty that left me covered in her lipstick. When I was back in the locker room I decided that my ripped trousers were beyond repair. I also needed a new pair of gloves. John let me into the watch room so that I could ring the stores department.

'And your name, please?' the man asked at the other end of the line. He sounded about a hundred years old.

'Castle. Malcolm Castle.'

A very long pause ensued. When I listened very carefully I could hear a slow, methodical sound on the other end of the line. I guessed that the man was turning through a long pile of papers. Time passed. But in the end his filing system came good.

'Castle. Malcolm. Found you at last. You're new, aren't you, son?'

'I started this year.'

'So I see. And you want replacement trousers and gloves?'

'Yes, please.'

There was a scratching sound as he wrote it all down. 'Just taken your first set of exams, have you, son?' he asked after a while. His filing system really was good.

'Yes, I have.'

'And you passed?'

'Yes, I did.'

'So you're staying with us, are you, son?'

I looked around the watch room and smiled. I thought about all the others joking around upstairs. I thought about the jobs we'd done – and all the beautiful women I still firmly believed I would one day carry out of burning buildings. 'Yes, I'm staying,' I told the man in the store room. 'I'm not going anywhere.'